Advance praise for
Sweatshop Warriors

Miriam Ching Louie's *Sweatshop Warriors* introduces us to women who refuse to accept their assigned place at the bottom of the sweatshop pyramid. The Chinese, Korean and Mexican immigrant women, whose testimonies are included in this work, have courageously challenged restaurant owners, contractors, corporations, governments and transnational anti-labor treaties. Here is inspiration and leadership for the labor movement and for all of us who seek creative ways of mounting resistance to global capitalism.

—Angela Y. Davis, author of *Women, Race and Class*

All the good-hearted liberals who see themselves as saviors of downtrodden sweatshop workers must read this book. As Miriam Louie powerfully demonstrates, immigrant women themselves have been organizing and fighting back on the front lines of the class war against global capital, making political connections that many of today's traveling demonstrators are just starting to think about. We need to listen to these women. This is such a beautiful, moving book; the guiding light for the new labor movement.

—Robin D. G. Kelley, author of *Yo' Mama's DisFunktional!:*
Fighting the Culture Wars in Urban America

There's no one blueprint for organizing women workers in today's garment industry, but this book puts polyvocal voices and plans on the table. Organizers and academics interested in the power of labor organizing across relations of race, class, nation, and generation will find inspiration and keen insights in this book. Miriam Ching Yoon Louie connects the threads and weaves brilliant pathways to social justice.

—Pierrette Hondagneu-Sotelo, author of *Domestica:*
Immigrant Workers Cleaning And Caring In The Shadows Of Affluence

According to a popular political saying, "wherever there is oppression, there is resistance." In today's corporate-driven global economy where sweatshops have become the norm rather than the exception, it is easy to focus only on the oppression. Long-time activist Miriam Ching Louie's important book tells the stories of the frontline warriors of resistance in the U.S. — the immigrant women sweatshop laborers who are tenaciously and creatively battling for justice and dignity. Through the organizing vehicles of community-based workers' centers, these Chinese, Korean and Latina immigrants are challenging not only the lynchpins of the corporate economy but also the traditional model of union organizing — as well as gender relations in their families and class dynamics in their ethnic communities. This book is essential reading for community organizers, for labor activists, and for others involved in grassroots campaigns taking on corporate globalization.

—Glenn Omatsu, Associate Editor, *Amerasia Journal*

A key weapon of the oppressor is to control the message — cover up the abuses, silence the sorrows and struggles of the oppressed. Luckily we have Miriam Ching Yoon Louie to listen and share the incredible stories of these sweatshop warriors — a women's movement the mainstream media has too long ignored. In the process, Miriam magnifies the women's voices and shines a bright light on the exploitation they challenge and the lessons they have to teach us all.

—Ellen Bravo, Co-Director, 9to5,
National Association of Working Women

Sweatshop Warriors

Immigrant Women Workers Take On the Global Factory

Miriam Ching Yoon Louie

South End Press
Cambridge, Massachusetts

Cover art: "El Lugar de la mujer: Una guerrillera en la lucha para la solidaridad internacional/A Woman's Place: A Warrior in the Struggle for International Solidarity," detail of mural by Juana Alicia. ©2000. Created for United Electrical, Radio and Machine Workers, Local 506, Erie, PA. Photo by Ed Bernik.
Cover design by Ellen Shapiro.
Text design and production by the South End Press collective.
Printed in Canada.

Library of Congress Cataloging-in-Publication Data
  Louie, Miriam Ching Yoon.
  Sweatshop Warriors : immigrant women workers take on the global factory / by Miriam Ching Yoon Louie.
   p. cm.
  Includes bibliographical references and index.
  ISBN 0896086380 (pbk: alk. paper) -- 0896086399 (cloth: alk. paper)
  Women alien labor--United States--Interviews. Sweatshops--United States. Foreign trade and employment--United States. International division of labor. Globalization--Economic aspects.
  HD6057.5.U5 L68 2001
  331.4/086/24—dc 21

00-051577

South End Press, 7 Brookline Street, #1, Cambridge, MA 02139-4146
www.southendpress.org
06 05 04 03 02   3 4 5 6

Contents

Dedication

Fondly remembering
my immigrant grandmothers Ching Bok See and Agnes Oh Yoon
and mother Minnie "Min-Hee" Marguerite Yoon Ching

Cheers to my garment worker and organizer aunties
King Ching and Virginia Ching Tong

Dedicated to feisty women worker warriors everywhere

Acknowledgments

This book is like a community-sized quilt whose designs drew inspiration from several teams of sewers—although I bear blame for any errors and blemishes that appear in the final product.

Thanks a million! to the immigrant women worker organizers who paused from their work to share kernels of their life experiences: Elena Alvarez, Refugio "Cuca" Arieta, Bo Yee, Viola Casares, Chan Wai Fun, Jenny Chen, Rojana "Na" Cheunchujit, Choi Kee Young, Chu Mi Hee, María del Carmen Domínguez, María Antonia Flores, Remedios García, Carmen Ibarra López, Celeste Jiménez, Kim Chong Ok, Kim Seung Min, Oi Kwan "Annie" Lai, "Lisa," Lin Cai Fen, Lee Jung Hee, Lee Kyu Hee, Lee Yin Wah, Marta Martínez, Petra Mata, Ernestina V. Mendoza, Irma Montoya Barajas, Paek Young Hee, Kyung Park, Obdulia M. Segura, Lucrecia Tamayo, Helen Wong, Wu Wan Mei, Amy Xie, and Yu Sau Kwan. Special thanks also to "Smita" and "Renuka" from Workers Awazz, a domestic workers organization for South Asian immigrant women in New York City, who also shared their stories, which need to be documented in a future piece, as does the work of the Border Agricultural Workers Union that organizes farm workers in the chili industry. You all are the salt of the earth and the spice of our lives. Please know that so many people hold you in the highest respect and trust your intuition, analysis, faith, strength, labor, and laughter to lead us forward.

Mil gracias! to the women's co-organizers who let me question them, too. Many also did double duty as translators during interviews with the women, or housed and fed me when I was far from home: Geri Almanza, Cindy Arnold, Chuan Chen, Vivian Chang, Pamela Chiang, Guillermo Domínguez Glenn, Trinh Duong, Yrene Espinoza, Ken Fong, Roy Hong, Kwong Hui, Helen Kim, Jennifer Jihye Chun, Stacy Kono, Wing Lam, Paul Lee, JoAnn Lum, Chanchanit "Chancee" Martorell, Brenda Mata, Jungsuk Oh, Gin Pang, Danny Park, K.S. Park, Suyapa Portillo, Cecilia Rodríguez, Suk Hee Ryu, Young Shin, Julia Song, Liz Sunwoo, Robert Thiem, Tommy Yee, and Young Im Yoo. Special thanks to Asian Immigrant Women Advocates and Fuerza Unida for the privilege of letting me experience women workers organizing from the inside, including those intimate moments before we put on our makeup, patted down our cowlicks, shed our slippers, and went out to face the public. I learned so much from all of my sisters and brothers in the workers centers.

Doh jie! to organizers and activist scholars that shared views while hunkered down in other movement trenches: Shahbano Aliani, Madeline Janis-Aparicio, Nikki Fortunato Bas, Edna Bonacich, Carol de Leon, John Delloro, Bea Tam and Harvey Dong, Bob Fitch, Lora Jo Foo, Pam Galpern, Peter Kwong, Chavel López, Alicia and Carlos Marentes, Elizabeth "Betita" Martínez, Jay Mendoza, Susan Mika, Marta Ojeda, Peter Olney, Edward Park, Maggie Poe, Ai-jen Poo, Cristina Riegos, Saskia Sassen, Ruben Sólis, Sandra Spector, Cathi Tactaquin, Pam Tau Lee, Mary Tong, Steve Williams, and Bob Wing in the U.S. Thanks also to the cross-border, transpacific sister and brother organizers: Elizabeth "Beti" Robles Ortega, Reyna Montero, Carmen Valadez, Beatriz Alfaro, Beatriz Lujan Uranga, Mathilde Arteaga, Alberta "Beti" Cariño Trujillo, Omar Esparza Zarate, Martín Barrios Hernández, Concepción Hernández Mendez, Father Anastacio "Tacho" Hidalgo Miramón, Jesús Granada, Hortensia Hernández Mendoza, Artemio Osuna Osuna, Lai Tong Chi, Linda To, Maria Rhee, Choi Myung Hee, Jin Kyong Park, Yoon Hae Ryun, Cho Ailee, Masami Azu, May-an Villalba, Misun Kim, Rex Varona, Apo Leong, Fely Villasin, and Cenen Bagon. Thanks for all your razor sharp insights and fantastic work. You do the global conspiracy of troublemakers proud.

¡Kamsa hamnida! to the grrrlfriends who kept me going: to the

cast of the *Jamae Sori*/Sister Sound Korean women's drumming crew—Ann Chun, Mimi Kim, Helen Kim, Jennifer Jihye Chun, Sun Hyung Lee, Betty Song, Jung Hee Choi, Ju Hui Han, Sujin Lee, and Hyun Lee—who fed the spirit and kept the beat jammin'. To Juana Alicia, *milago* muralist and cover artist for your beautiful work and saucy strength. To my old Third World Women's Alliance alums, Linda Burnham of the Women of Color Resource Center, Myesha Jenkins stationed Jo'Berg side, and Letisha Wadsworth holding down child-care services in Bed-Stuy in Brooklyn for your colored-girls-go-international Triple-Jeopardy-eyed-view of race, class, and gender and for making me laugh by loud talking stuff about the world as it turns. Thanks Letisha, for housing and feeding me during interviews with New York Chinatown workers; Myesha, for intervening during moments of confusion; and especially Linda, for picking up all the slack and fighting those exhausting battles so I could take off time to write.

All power! to my editors, both in the formal and informal sectors of the economy. *¡Salud!* to the tag team at South End Press who patched me through: Lynn Lu for your gentle support, Sonia Shah for getting the ball rolling, Jill Petty for tracking those devilish details, and especially Loie Hayes for jumping in and skillfully steering this process through to completion. *Ganbei/Bottoms Up!* to my informal collective, my dear friends who multi-task as writers, editors, organizers, translators, and information junkies: Luz Guerra, Max Elbaum, Antonio Díaz, Arnoldo García, Margo Okazawa-Rey, and Glenn Omatsu, for your Buddha-like patience reading through all those bumpy lumpy e-mailed manuscript drafts and returning with crystal clear comments on how to better interpret and strengthen our movements.

Finally, *love you/sarang hae/ho sek neidei!* to my family, AKA the Book Police, AKA hubby Lanyuen Belvin, daughter Nguyen Thi Dinh, and son Lung San Louie, as well as my sister Beth Ching and her honey Antonio Díaz. Thanks for your unconditional love and faith that I would get this book done—if I would just stop getting distracted by other campaigns and projects. Big bear hugs to Belvin, Nguyen, and Lung San for reading, editing, giving honest liposuction radical surgery feedback, or granting permission to chill when I got too weary to proceed. For taking care of technical difficulties and logistical nightmares. For reminding me to always return to the basic beat, the *kibon*—the women's stories. For helping us Chings make it through the passing of our dear mom. For never being too tired to walk picket lines, fax blast media releases, e-mail photo scans, fix graphics, download web fact checks, video demos, brainstorm and debrief actions, rant and rave about the rich, hang with the folks, and just take care of business.

Listening to the Women

The Real Experts

Outtake #1: What *60 Minutes* Cut

In December 1994, 12 Chinese seamstresses sit perched on the edge of their seats in the workers' center that has become their second home: Asian Immigrant Women Advocates' in Oakland's Chinatown. Together with an estimated viewing audience of between 23 and 36 million people, these women are about to watch a *60 Minutes* segment on the garment industry's labor practices that will include footage of correspondent Morley Safer interviewing them.

For over two years, the women have been fighting a bitter battle with San Francisco garment manufacturer Jessica McClintock to recoup unpaid wages and demand corporate responsibility. When *60 Minutes* producers approached them for interviews, they had agonized about whether to go on camera without the protection of masks or blurred images. Being seen means running the risk of getting fired and blacklisted. The producers argued that the women could tell their story most effectively if they showed their faces and spoke directly to the American public. After much discussion, the garment workers had finally agreed.

The seamstresses watch as the camera zooms in. They see themselves beginning to describe in their native tongues how the sweatshop boss threatened them and posted signs ordering, "No loud talking" and "Do not go to the bathroom without permission." Of course the women understand what they are shown saying, but they realize the sounds mean nothing to millions of North American viewers. Their words go untranslated as Morley Safer's voice-over drowns out the women's declarations. *60 Minutes* has exposed their faces and silenced them.

The show cuts to the white male sportswear manufacturer charged for his subcontractor's failure to pay back wages. He tells viewers that fashion designer Jessica McClintock—focus of the seamstresses' campaign for corporate responsibility—"is a hero to every small businessman."[1] The program's "objective reporting" divides blame equally among manufacturers, workers, and bargain shoppers.

After watching the program, the women struggle to overcome their sense of betrayal.

Outtake #2: Fighting for a Place at the Table

On July 20, 1998, at corporate headquarters in San Francisco, company executives from Levi Strauss and Co., comfortably attired in casual wear, sit at a corporate conference table across from representatives of labor and human rights organizations. The advocates argue that Levi's should set a positive example by pledging to pay living wages to the workers who sew its products at home and abroad. Despite sharp differences, everyone appears to be on their best behavior.

Then a former Levi's seamstress enters the dialogue. Petra Mata starts to explain how Levi's employees are paid below minimum wage, showing copies of recent pay stubs to make her point. A white company man interrupts Mata, questioning the veracity of the check stubs and dismissing her comments as irrelevant to the meeting's agenda. His mocking comments and body language convey the message that her English is not good enough and that she couldn't possibly know what she is talking about. None of the other groups at the table, including those with histories of sharp disagreements with the company, are subjected to such shoddy treatment.

"They treat us like we're stupid, like the only thing we're good enough to do is to sew for them," Viola Casares later declared. Casares is co-coordinator with Mata of Fuerza Unida, a fightback organization launched by laid-off Levi's workers in 1990 when the company closed down its San Antonio plant and moved to Costa Rica.[2]

Path Breakers and Tree Shakers

This book is dedicated to the immigrant women workers who are barred from board rooms where deals get cut; whose stories end up on cutting room floors; who get punished for telling the truth; who are asked to speak only as victims, not as the trail blazers they truly are. These women warriors have trekked across mountains, rivers, oceans, and borders, cutting deep paths through the heart of this nation's industries and inner cities. Tucked inside their weathered work jeans, double-knit pants, cleaning uniforms, cooking aprons, and serving caps are continents and worlds of experience. These are the women who sew our clothes; grow, cook, and serve our food; make our fancy little gadgets; care for us when we get sick; and clean up our messes. For those of us who come from communities of color and working-class families, these are the women without whose labor, love, sweat, and tears we would not even exist on this planet.

Yet the powerful and the privileged often stifle these women's voices. Luckily for us, these workers are chiseling through thick walls of censorship to make themselves heard. They are organizing themselves in workers' centers, creating their own groups when the labor or community organizations that already exist fail to meet their needs. Contrary to conventional wisdom that leans heavily on white and/or male academics, these women are the *real* experts about the inner workings of the global economy, labor markets, and immigrant communities—speaking to us from the bottom of the sweatshop industry pyramid. They stand steadfast as the first line of whistle-blowers and flak-catchers against corporate greed, government negligence, and racial wrongs. They serve as the tree shakers who knock down the fruit, the piñata busters who break open the goodies—of economic democracy, gender justice, and human rights—for all of us. They are neither victims nor superwomen.

These sweatshop warriors are simply everyday women in our communities who have much to tell and teach.

Sweatshop Pyramid of Exploitation

The term "sweatshop" was initially coined during the industrial revolution in the 1880s and 1890s to describe the subcontracting system of labor. The sweatshops that served larger companies were run by middlemen who expanded or contracted their labor forces depending on the success or failure of different clothing fashions. The middlemen's profits were tied to the amount of labor they could "sweat" out of their workers—most often women and children—through low wages, excessive hours, and unsanitary conditions. This system led to such industrial accidents as the 1911 Triangle Shirtwaist Factory Fire that claimed the lives of nearly 150 young women.[3]

The US Government Accounting Office defines poor working conditions as the hallmark of a sweatshop, specifically "an employer that violates more than one federal or state labor, industrial homework, occupational safety and health, workers' compensation, or industry registration law."[4] According to the US Department of Labor, *more than half* of the estimated 22,000 garment shops in the United States—where many immigrant women find their first US jobs—violate multiple wage, hour, and safety laws.[5]

Sweatshop workers toil at the bottom of a pyramid of labor exploitation and profit generation. Workers' immediate bosses are subcontractors, often men of their own ethnicity. Manufacturers and retailers sit at the top of the pyramid over the subcontractors who act as buffers, shock absorbers, and shields. The subcontractors compete with each other to win bids from manufacturers and are generally not paid until the work they have been contracted for is completed and accepted. Like the 19th-century sweatshop middlemen, many of today's subcontractors survive the competition by "sweating" their workers out of wage, hour, benefits, and safety rights. Sitting at the top of the industry pyramid, large manufacturing corporations design products and services, set retail prices, and find buyers and retailers to distribute their products.[6] Retailers, like

Wal-Mart, Federated Department Stores, Inc., May Department Stores, Dayton-Hudson, K-Mart, and Nordstrom buy goods from manufacturers and other wholesalers and sell them to customers at double or more what they paid. Many retailers have merged into giant conglomerates that increasingly participate in the industry both horizontally and vertically, thus determining wages and working conditions of workers at the bottom of the pyramid.[7]

The subcontracting system allows manufacturers and retailers to slash the cost of labor and facilities, and—since subcontractors, not manufacturers, are legally responsible for any labor law violations in their shops—leave subcontractors with the burden of ensuring decent working conditions. Manufacturers and retailers reap huge benefits from the sweatshop system. Garment workers in Los Angeles, for example, each produce about $100,000 worth of goods a year, but are paid less than 2 percent of the total value. For a dress that retails for $100, $1.72 goes to the sewer, $15 to the contractor, and $50 goes to the manufacturer.[8]

Subcontracting Becomes the Standard

While particularly glaring in the garment industry, sweating workers through subcontracting has emerged as standard operating procedure in industries across the board resulting in massive wage and benefit cuts on one end and unparalleled accumulation of profits at the other. Employers utilize these methods of control not only in globalized industries, like garment, electronics, toy, shoe, plastics, and auto parts, but also in the non-globalized locally-based sectors like the healthcare, food processing, restaurant, hotel, custodial, construction, landscaping, information processing, clerical, customer service, and other industries.[9] For example, universities formerly employed their own cooks, janitors, and gardeners. Now many schools subcontract these services. The workers do the same work, or more, but for lower pay and fewer benefits, while the university gets to redirect their spending, in some cases, toward higher salaries for chief administrators. According to the Institute for Policy Studies and United for a Fair Economy, CEO pay across industry and service sectors jumped 535 percent in the 1990s, far outstripping growth in the stock market (297 percent), and dwarfing the 32 percent growth in worker pay, which barely outpaced inflation (27.5 percent). In 1960 CEOs made 41 times their average employee's wage; in 1990, 85 times; but in 1999, the gap skyrocketed to 475 times.[10]

Not surprisingly, the reemergence of the sweatshop pyramid of exploitation that the US first witnessed during its industrial revolution and rise as a global power also coincides with a massive restructuring of the US economy in its domestic and overseas operations. The sweatshop pyramid has been exported internationally and resuscitated domestically, globalizing the bottom strata of workers, the buffer level of subcontractors, and the elite core of G-7-based transnational corporations.[11]

Globalization of sweatshop production is but one aspect within a broader program of global economic restructuring. The goal of this effort is to open new markets and whole new economies to the world market and corporate investors. This usually involves IMF/World Bank mandates for cutting government spending on health, housing, education, and nutrition programs; freezing and slashing wages, and suppressing workers' rights to organize; selling publicly owned property and assets to private interests; giving tax incentives and other forms of government "welfare" to corporations and the wealthy; removing government regulations and restrictions on corporations; devaluing currency so that local people could buy less and foreign interests with stronger currencies would be attracted to invest more; and promotion of neoconservative politics that funnel anger at those in the most marginalized sectors of the population and away from the elite.[12] The domestic face of globalization has become increasingly obvious since the Reagan administration began by busting the air traffic controllers union, trashing the poor, and once again making the United States safe for the Robber Barons.

The global sweatshop pyramid of exploitation comes clothed in the specific gender, race, class, and national garments of its workers, subcontractors, and elite.[13] As sociologist María Patricia Fernández-Kelly has astutely observed:

Capitalism benefits from the exceptional. As long as women's role as wage-earners may be viewed as the exception rather than the rule (even in situations where large numbers of women work outside of the home) women will continue to be liable to sexist and discriminatory policies in wages.[14] [emphasis added]

The sweatshop system takes advantage of the "exceptional," the "different," to relegate certain strata of the population into super-exploited positions and others to more privileged buffer positions—all to the benefit of the super-privileged minority sitting at the top of the power pyramid. Asian and Latina immigrant women workers' life stories map the exploitation of these differences within the global sweatshop economy.

Methodology: Calling on Family and Community Networks

This book shines a spotlight on grassroots immigrant women as agents of change, and argues that they are, indeed, the very heartbeat of the labor and anti-sweatshop movements. By highlighting the experiences of women on whose backs sweatshop industries have been erected, these stories can narrow the divide between grassroots activists on the one hand and scholars on the other. Readers who confront similar dilemmas in other racial and ethnic communities may find helpful problem-solving approaches. Finally, I hope that by documenting this slice of Asian and Latina/o movement history, our young bloods can claim this bit of their activist heritage and use it to advance these and kindred movements.

The primary source material for this book is interviews of Chinese, Korean, and Mexicana immigrant women leaders active in five independent community-based workers' centers—Chinese Staff and Workers Association in New York City; La Mujer Obrera in El Paso, Texas; Asian Immigrant Women Advocates in Oakland, California; Fuerza Unida in San Antonio, Texas; and Korean Immigrant Workers Advocates in Los Angeles, California. I chose to focus on Chinese and Korean women because of my own ethnic background, which gives me a bit of familiarity and connection with the women in these communities. I also included the stories of Mexican women because they often constitute the majority of immigrant women working in sweatshop industries in California, where I live, and throughout the Southwest, and Mexican women have launched sister organizations to the Chinese and Korean women's organizations. While I only had the resources to focus on these three ethnic groups in a few cities, these women and their organizations are part of a larger movement that includes immigrant women workers of many different ethnicities, located in many different parts of the US, and the world. I strongly urge organizers, writers, videographers, and artists in all mediums to take the time to encourage worker and grassroots women in the many emerging communities to share and document their stories and movement histories, too.

Over hearty helpings of home made *guisado* [stew], green tacos, *sopa de pollo* [chicken soup], *hamhung naeng myun* [cold spicy noodles], deep fried flounders, *chiles en mole* [chilies in sauce], steamed salted fish, *kimchee* [hot vegetable pickle], *tong choy* [hollow-stemmed greens], steaming bowls of rice and baskets of tortillas, I listened to the words of wonderful women whom I and many people in this world dearly love and admire. The interviews were principally conducted between 1997 and 2000, camped out at movement offices, sandwiched between pickets and workshops, while driving across the state to demonstrations, leafleting at factory gates, and fighting with government officials.

In addition to those women who had immigrated as adults, I also spoke with Asian and Latina women who had immigrated as children with their families (what the Korean-American community refers to as "1.5 generation" immigrants), with US-born organizers who represented the "second" and "third" generations of immigrant families, as well as with members of similar organizations including the Thai Community Development Center, Pilipino Workers Center, and the Domestic Workers Project of the Coalition for Humane Immigrant Rights of Los Angeles, California; the Latino Workers Center and Workers Awaaz in New York City; the Southwest Public Workers Union in San Antonio, Texas; and the Border Agricultural Workers Union in El Paso, Texas. Organizers referred me to other movement activists, writers, and scholars they knew and respected for more information. The material in this book is just the tip of the iceberg—the organizing in communities of color today could fill many bookshelves. This book also draws on analyses of migrant and women workers' centers in the women's home countries. Immigrant women workers in this country depend upon these cousin (if not sister) movements for analyses of conditions on the ground back home. I met a number of these organizers at the 1995 United Nations 4th World Conference on Women held in Beijing, China; at a 1996 conference of migrant worker organizations held in Seoul, Korea; and at a 1998 meeting of workers' center affiliates of the Southwest Network for Environmental and Economic Justice held in Tijuana, Mexico. At these and other gatherings, I interviewed members of the Korean Women Workers Associations United (Seoul, Korea), Hong Kong Women Workers Association (Hong Kong), Asian Migrant Centre (Hong Kong), Casa de la Mujer Factor X (Tijuana, Mexico), Servicio, Desarrollo y Paz/SEDEPAC (Coahuila, Mexico), Frente Auténtico del Trabajo (Juárez and Mexico City, Mexico), and Comisión de las Mujeres of the Comité de Apoyo Fronterizo Obrero Regional (Maclovio Rojas, Mexico).

I got away with pestering members of busy organizations because I have also clocked time in this movement. For over three decades I worked in various Asian community, student, labor, women of color, and Third World solidarity organizations. I began a 12-year stint at Asian Immigrant Women Advocates when the organization first opened its doors on November 1, 1983. Along with many other Latina/o and Asian community activists in the late 1990s, I joined in supporting the San Antonio, Texas, fightback organization Fuerza Unida in its campaign against Levi's dumping of workers, spending a year and a half assisting the women with media work.

Like so many other Asian and Latina/o labor and community activists, my vantage point stems from the fact that members of my family earned their livings in garment, restaurant, agricultural, and other low-wage jobs. My Chinese immigrant paternal Grandma Ching Bok See peeled onions and shelled shrimp for restaurants and one of her daughters sewed square-dance outfits up until her mid-70s for a San Francisco South of Market company owned by a

Lebanese immigrant family. My Auntie King understands some Spanish words—such as the order to speed up, *"¡Andale! ¡Andale!"*—since the majority of women in the shop where she sewed were Chinese and Latinas. (She used to make our cousins, my sister, and me petticoats with leftover lace from work.) My Auntie Virginia did a stint as a Chinese language interpreter and assistant to a Jewish male organizer for the International Ladies Garment Workers Union and later as a bilingual elementary school teacher's assistant. My Korean immigrant maternal grandmother Agnes Oh Yoon raised 11 children and worked alongside my grandfather who served as a minister, farmer, and member of the Korean exile independence movement against Japanese colonialism.

Before getting married, my mother worked at a variety of sales jobs and as a coat-checker at Forbidden City, the Chinese-owned nightclub in San Francisco. Dad worked as a kitchen helper. After marrying, Mom raised us five kids while Dad worked a triple-shift (at a naval shipyard, as a cashier at a Chinese liquor store, and as an attendant at a Chinese gas station) so we could move out of the projects. Years later, my children's elementary school friends sported the eclectic, bright patterned pants that their mothers and aunts sewed for them with fabrics left over from their jobs in the garment industry.

Book Organization

Chapter One examines the experiences of Chinese immigrant women garment and restaurant workers in New York and Oakland, followed by in-depth testimony from leaders of the Garment Workers Justice Campaign of Asian Immigrant Women Advocates and the "Ain't I A Woman?!" Campaign of Chinese Staff and Workers Association. Chapter Two focuses on the stories of Mexicana immigrant seamstresses in El Paso, San Antonio, and Los Angeles. It is followed by testimony from leaders of La Mujer Obrera's struggle against NAFTA-induced layoffs and Fuerza Unida's fight for corporate accountability from Levi's. Chapter Three examines the experiences of Korean immigrant women restaurant workers in Los Angeles' Koreatown, followed by testimony from leaders of Korean Immigrant Workers Advocates' Workers Organizing Project for industry-wide change within the ethnic enclave.

Chapter Four describes the relationship between immigrant women workers and their "extended family" of 1.5, second, and third generation activists who have been attracted to their struggles and the fusion process between these two different sets of people in building the movement. It also introduces the five workers' centers and some of their main accomplishments. Chapter Five focuses on the development of the women's organizations. It examines how vibrant independent workers' centers and movements emerged in response to the global sweatshop pyramid. It profiles several examples of the innovative organizing methodologies and campaigns of the workers' centers.

Chapter Six analyzes the role of the women's organizations as innovators within the broader labor and anti-sweatshop movements, followed by an interview with a leader of the joint Thai Community Development Center, Asian Pacific American Legal Center, and Korean Immigrant Workers Advocates campaign in defense of incarcerated Thai garment workers in El Monte. Finally, a brief conclusion summarizes the lessons to be learned from these women and their organizing.

Connecting Threads

Five main themes surfaced in the women's stories. First, the women worked in their homelands, within economies that have been increasingly integrated into the global sweatshop. As teenagers many of the women served as the Asian and Latin American counterparts of the 19th-century factory girls who spun the industrial revolutions inside the former colonial powers. Before them, their mothers and grandmothers labored as the counterparts of the Native American women before they were brutally driven from their lands and the enslaved African and indentured Latina and Asian immigrant women workers on plantations and farms, and as domestic workers. Though barred from factory jobs, these slaves, coolies, *campesinas/os,* [farmworkers] and *braceros* [laborers] grew the cash crops and birthed generations of workers whose labors financed the industrial revolutions. Working in the global sweatshop and plantation, and in odd jobs in the informal economy, these golden skinned daughters of former colonial subjects described how they came to serve as the foot soldiers on the march to national economic development, industrialization, and globalization. In the new era of globalization, Third World feminist scholars dubbed the disproportionately high numbers of women working in the global sweatshop since the 1960s, "feminization of labor."[15]

Second, the women migrated to urban centers inside their rapidly industrializing countries, and to the US, the country whose dominance has so deeply influenced the destinies of their homelands. As the anti-racist immigrant rights movement in England puts it, "We are here because you were there."[16] The women all came from regions that have long been the target of US capital export and labor import, and whose economies are more and more tightly woven together through global sweatshop production, distribution, and labor markets. While they face racist and nativist backlash as new immigrants, the women often traced their roots back to family members who had migrated to the US *during* and *before* the great waves of immigration from Europe beckoned by post-Civil War industrialization and expansionism. The women talked about their decisions to migrate as part of family strategies to improve economic and educational options. In other cases the women reported coming without family approval, and in times of crisis, without connections and ties to ease their journeys. They in turn have become the nuclei of new migration chains of workers. International feminist activists have dubbed this rise in women's labor migration from the global South, "feminization of migration."[17]

Third, the women worked in the sweatshop segments of the US labor market. Entering and transforming the historically segregated US workforce, the women generated new capital for corporations, developers, and ethnic entrepreneurs, revitalized inner city economies, and sustained immigrant communities during a period of economic instability. They talked about how networks of family, friends, and community contacts helped them set foot on now well-worn paths to sweatshop jobs, how they "learned the ropes," and struggled to adjust to their new lives and work environments. They also noted shifts in the origins and immigration patterns of their co-workers. They detailed how working conditions had deteriorated over the last decade, with falling wages, loss of health benefits, longer work weeks, speedups, and massive layoffs. Many expressed great fear about the future fate of their families and communities given industry changes coupled with growing hostility, hatred, and backlash against them as immigrants and people of color. The women had a lot to say about what goes on "behind the label," in the "back of the house," at the bottom of the "high fashion," "high tech" economy. Labor, feminist, race, and immigration scholars call the stratified job market within which the women work, the "segmented labor market."[18]

Fourth, the women chronicled the painful yet liberating process through which they changed from being sweatshop industry *workers* to sweatshop *warriors*. They transformed from women exploited by the subcontractors and elites to women who clearly understood where they fit into the "big picture." They started painting themselves, their co-workers, and *comadres* [women friends] into that big picture as they began to dream and talk to each other about the way that they themselves wanted to be seen, heard, understood, respected, and, yes, *paid* for all the sweat, blood, and tears they had shed while squeezed down at the bottom of the pyramid. And in standing up for their most basic human rights, the women confronted entrenched relations of class, gender, race, and national privilege not only within their industries, but also within their families and communities, including within what sociologists have called "ethnic enclaves."[19]

By the very act of speaking their minds, these women workers have challenged multiple layers of oppression stretching all the way from corporate boardrooms to labor union halls, media outlets, churches, community gatherings, and the cramped living spaces of their homes inside inner-city barrios and ghettos. Like the skilled sample makers who figure out how to design, cut, and sew the pieces of a garment, then teach this process to their fellow seamstresses, these sweatshop warriors are helping their co-workers, extended families, and communities see where they, too, fit into the big picture, and how they can work together to liberate themselves as well. Feminist organizers in the South and in the South within the North call this women's "triple shift" of labor in the workplace, family, and community to challenge "multiple oppressions" and serve as "bridge people" within and between grassroots movements for justice.[20]

Fifth, the women helped build workers' centers that enabled them to both resist the oppressions they face and begin to fashion new ways to work, live, think, and create. The workers' centers featured in this book are independent groups where workers gather and organize themselves to carry out their fights and meet their needs. Continuous industry restructuring requires the workers movement to develop strategies, tactics, methodologies, and organizational forms appropriate to specific niches of workers in the new economy. The groups emerged because the existing labor movement was not addressing the needs of these workers. The workers' centers served as vehicles through which the women could fight for their rights from the bottom of the sweatshop pyramid. The women talked about how they either went to existing workers' centers or formed them with their bare hands to fortify themselves in their fights for justice. Particularly as immigrant women, they talked about how useful these organizations were in helping them translate what was being said to them and what they wanted to say within the primarily English-speaking, US institutional, and cultural environment.

These women eventually went on to serve as the leadership core of industry-wide campaigns that reached out to their peers working in other sweatshops. They spoke of the mutual relationship between their own individual risk-taking and the forward motion of organizations that backed them. The organizations themselves were transformed through the women's participation and leadership. Many women also spoke of how the centers reached out to them to fill other unmet needs in their lives—to learn English, to become enfranchised citizens, to break their isolation, to get out from under the thumb of domineering partners, to give themselves space outside the sweatshop grind, and to taste the freedom of remaking themselves as fuller human beings.

Fusion and Innovation in Workers' Centers

These workers' centers featured in this book represent a fusion between first generation low-waged immigrant women workers and organizers who are often their children, grandchildren and extended family members. The immigrants' co-organizers came from both working and middle class backgrounds and joined the immigrant workers in building movements that fought for the rights of those on the bottom of overlapping pyramids of oppression.

The older organizers were often radicalized during an earlier stage of the global economic restructuring, which precipitated the birth of the Asian and Latina/o radical movements of the 1960s and 1970s, linked to and cross fertilized by the civil rights, Black power, Native American sovereignty, labor, women's, lesbian and gay, anti-war, and other movements of the period. The organizations have been joined by new generations of labor and student radicals. From the 1980s to the present the workers' centers have pioneered creative organizing campaigns and scored precedent setting victories during a period of ferocious attack. The workers' centers have often played the role of small innovators within the broader labor and anti-sweatshop movements.

As immigrant women workers on the bottom of the industry pyramid have begun to organize themselves, and create their own workers' centers, they have shaken up the whole structure above them. The Chinese immigrant garment workers that appeared on *60 Minutes* were shocked, then angered to find that the style of dress they would have collectively been paid $5 for—retailed for $175 each. The Mexicana and Chicana workers that made their way into Levi's corporate headquarters had first been devastated when Levi's laid them off, then enraged when they found out that the company took their jobs to Costa Rica and paid workers there for a full day's work what the San Antonio workers had made in half an hour—facilitated by a free trade initiative funded by US taxpayers. When these immigrant women workers were confronted with the big picture of sweatshop exploitation, to paraphrase labor agitator Mother Jones, they didn't just get mad—they got organized.

As you read these women's words, please remember that they are maddeningly modest about the myriad contributions and sacrifices they've made to build this movement. They are more willing to build up their *comadres* and organizations than claim bragging rights for themselves. They tend to focus on what they've gotten from the movement more than what they've given. And once again, they've put themselves on the line, this time by telling their stories in public. Thus, in some cases I have used pseudonyms and omitted certain pieces of identifying personal information. I deeply thank these wonderful women for sharing their wisdom.

While immigrant women workers and their organizations inspired this book, in no way does it represent the official positions or histories of the organizations it chronicles. This book represents just one colored girl's hit on happenings in this sector of the movement. In fact, I find myself chuckling now in anticipation of the criticisms certain *compas/ tong zhir/ dong ji/* homies are sure to make about what was said or not said in this book. But this is all part of the process of discussion and debate that comes with development and growth. As my daughter Nguyen says, "It's all good."

1   *60 Minutes,* 1994.

2   Kever, 1990.

3   Sweatshop Watch, 1997; and US Government Accounting Office, 1988:11.

4   US Government Accounting Office, 1988:17.

5   Yeh and McMurry, 1996:1/Z5.

6   Chin, 1989:A10; and Bonacich and Appelbaum, 2000.

7   See Bonacich and Appelbaum, 2000:80-103 for an analysis of the restructuring of the retail industry.

8   Wypijewski, 1994:471-472.

9   Landler, 2001.

10   Anderson, et al., 2000:3-4. Figures are not adjusted for inflation. "Stock market" refers to Standard and Poor 500.

11   G-7 stands for Group of Seven countries—the United Kingdom, Canada, United States, Germany, France, Italy, and Japan.

12   Louie and Burnham, 2000:48; Martínez and García, 1997:4; Sparr, 1994; Vickers, 1991; and Suárez Aguilar, 1996.

13   Back in the late 1960s, the Third World Women's Alliance, a US-based internationalist women of color organization, began to describe the intersection of race, sex, and class, as "triple jeopardy" (Beal, 1970). Veteran of the Combahee River Collective, a counterpart Black lesbian feminist group, and social welfare professor Margo Okazawa-Rey calls gender, race, nation, class—as well as sexuality, dis/ability, ethnicity, language, age, religion, etc.—the "matrix of oppression and resistance" (Combahee River Collective, 1983; Okazawa-Rey, August 2000). See forthcoming alternative report on the status of US women of color to the 2001 UN World Conference Against Racism edited by the Women of Color Resource Center.

14   Fernández-Kelly, 1983:90.

15   Committee for Asian Women, 1995a; Fernández-Kelly, 1983; Vickers, 1991; Lourdes Arizipe, 1981:453-473; Lim, 1983:76-79; and Benería, 1994:49-76. For more on women's labor in free trade zones and the global sweatshop industries, see Asia Monitor Resource Center, 1998; Fuentes and Ehrenreich, 1984; Southeast Asia Chronicle and Pacific Studies Center, 1978 and 1979); Nash and Fernández-Kelly, 1983; Nash and Safa, 1985; Boserup, 1970; De la O and González, 1994; Enloe, 1989:151-176; and Mitter, 1986.

16   This slogan appeared on a picket sign at an immigrant rights rally of South Asian and Caribbean protesters during the 1980s.

17   See for example Villalba, 1996; Hondagneu-Sotelo, 1994; Kyeyoung Park, 1997; Sharon M. Lee, 1996:1-22; Grace Chang, 2000:129; Conover, 1997:124-132; Stalker, 1994; Asian Migrant Centre, 1996b and 1998; Daniel Lee, 1991; Sturdevant and Stoltzfus, 1992; China Labour Education and Information Centre, 1995; and Huang, 1997.

18   For more on the impact of gender and race on labor market segmentation, see Amott and Matthaei, 1996:317-354. Additionally, a significant portion of African-American, Chicana, Puerto Rican, and Native American women did

not make the move "up the ladder" into better jobs, but were instead squeezed out altogether by deindustrialization and cuts in social welfare programs. During the 1980s for the first time in US history, the labor force participation rates of African-American and white women began to merge. The closing of the gap between Black and white women's labor force participation rates indicates not only that growing sections of white women are working outside the home; it also means that Black working class women are falling through the cracks. See Burnham, 1989. The Clinton administration's 1996 welfare "reform" legislation and other state programs are pushing African-American, Latina, Asian, and white women to take workfare jobs as non-unionized minimum and sub-minimum wage workers with little in the way of childcare, nutrition, housing, or health assistance to support this move. See Burnham and Gustafson, 2000.

19   Light and Bonacich, 1988; Kwong, Peter, 1987 and 1997; Mar, 1991.

20   Latin American feminists discussed the *"triple jornada,"* or triple shift, of women's work during the 1980s when international financial institutions imposed structural adjustment programs on Third World nations besieged by rising debts to First World nations. The unpaid work of poor women increased as they were forced to shoulder the costs of cuts in wages and social subsidies. Thanks to Luz Guerra for bringing this term to my attention. For examples of organizing around issues of multiple oppression, see for example issues of the Third World Women's Alliance newspaper, *Triple Jeopardy*. See also Moraga and Anzaldua, 1981.

Chapter One

Holding Up Half the Sky

Chinese Immigrant Women Workers

Sandwiched between produce shops overflowing with honey tangerines, fuzzy melons, string beans, ginger, and tong choy in New York City's Chinatown, a small grubby sign reads "Chinese Staff and Workers Association" (CSWA). Inside are stacks of newspapers, leaflets, and picket signs; overflowing file cabinets; ever-ringing telephones; the staccato of Cantonese conversation; the smell of take-out food; and constantly replenished cups of steaming *hong cha* [red/black tea]. This storefront could just as well be in San Francisco, Penang, Singapore, Saigon, or anywhere that Chinese workers gather to talk, eat, and organize for their rights.

A woman drops by to volunteer. She insists on using a one-name pseudonym, "Lisa," laughing when teasingly compared to Cher or Madonna for her choice. She's taking no chances since she and co-workers were blacklisted for demanding overtime pay and shorter hours. Although in 1995 the Department of Labor penalized Streetbeat Sportswear, a subcontractor for Sears, Roebuck and Co., for nonpayment of wages and violations of minimum wage and overtime laws, their workers continued to toil for over one hundred hours a week, for less than $2 an hour. Lisa and her co-workers suffered various injuries and constant fatigue. "I got x-rays taken and it shows that the [back] bone is kind of bent. If I sit or work too long, my back just can't take it anymore. That's why I need to rest a little," Lisa explains, shifting in discomfort.

Lisa and her co-workers joined with CSWA and the worker-student-youth alliance National Mobilization Against Sweatshops (NMASS) in August 1997 to kick off a campaign to hold manufactures and retailers such as Sears accountable for workers' injuries. In May 1998, sweatshop owner Jian Wen Liang and his foreman stormed CSWA's office with thugs, threatening to kill organizers. The garment workers and their allies held their ground for another 14 months, and finally forced Streetbeat Sportswear and its contractors to pay almost $300,000 in overtime and damages owed.[1]

Chinese women's labor has been pivotal in the rebirth of garment, restaurant, and other low-wage industries in the United States' inner cities. Their work has also been critical to the industrialization of southern China, to Hong Kong's integration into the global economy, and to the development of special economic zones along China's coast catering to multinational corporations.[2] While Chinese men in the railroad, laundry, fishing, and restaurant industries trail-blazed the Chinese labor movement in this country, since the 1970s Chinese women have increasingly taken the lead.[3] Women have transformed Chinatowns in the United States from bachelor sojourner societies into diverse, vibrant family-oriented communities.

In this chapter, immigrant women leaders take us behind gated windows and blocked exits to what they call the "back of the house" of the garment and service industries. They compare their prior work in China and Hong Kong to their experiences in sweatshops "made in the USA." While ethnic Chinese factory owners sweat their women workers at the bottom of the industry pyramid, famous-name white-owned companies perched at the top call the shots in this racialized and gendered hierarchy. Women speak bitterly about how working conditions have declined to 19th-century levels because of corporate greed, globalization, and industrial restructuring, and how immigrant bashing has hidden their exploitation. They talk about how dominant ideologies in China and the United States collude with employer threats and union apathy—and a pool of hungry workers ready to slave at even lower wages—to silence women. Finally, they reflect on the injustices that drove them to the breaking point and on their experiences of joining and leading movements of Chinese rebel women.

"You know how China is — they love boys and hate girls"

Retired garment worker and activist Wu Wan Mei serves as the spirited mistress of ceremonies at CSWA's annual Lunar New Year celebration. At the event, the frenetic drumbeat of dragon dancers incited peals of laughter from workers' children. With her short salt-and-pepper permed hair Wu has the look of a lively grandma—which she is. She was born in pre-Revolutionary China in Toisan, Guangdong, a *da jie* [big sister] to six siblings. Her father was a "very, very, very small businessman," who sold *cha siu* [barbecue pork] while her mother took care of the children.

> I went to school in China for eleven years to become a teacher. At that time the government mandated that we had to do so because teachers were badly needed. I started teaching in 1953. At Liberation in 1949 I had just graduated from junior high school and was about thirteen or fourteen years old. It was very difficult for women to go to school at that time. You know how China is—they love boys and hate girls! My dad was very traditional. He would not let me go to school [with the boys].[4]

The 1949 Chinese Revolution marked a sea change in the lives of women like Wu. Before then, Confucian ideology dictated women's subordination first to their fathers, then husbands, and finally sons. As in other socialist countries, women were seen as a vital resource for economic development. The Communist Party promoted women's integration into the paid labor force, instituting daycare and sewing centers to facilitate women's participation. In opposition to women's Confucian-mandated subservience to father, husband, and son, the party resurrected the proverb that "women hold up half the sky." Marriage laws enacted in 1950 and 1980 guaranteed women's rights to divorce and to choose their mates freely. Sexist feudalistic practices such as concubines, bride-prices, arranged marriages, and the purchase of child brides were outlawed, while widows' rights to remarry and women's rights to property were guaranteed.[5]

Still, the "love for boys" and "hate for girls" that Wu describes lingers in China. By the late 1980s, women continued to earn about 30 percent less than men for the same work.[6] Seventy percent of all workers dismissed from their jobs are women.[7] By the late 1980s, only about 45 percent of all girls were enrolled in school.[8] Under China's "one family, one child" population control policy, girl babies are disproportionately abandoned.[9]

Second Stage Labor Migration

Most of China's women migrants to the United States hail from the country's southeastern region, which has historically had higher rates of global trade, commerce, industrialization, female labor force participation, and emigration of its workers.[10] In particular, the Guangdong and Fujian provinces in southeastern China, located near large navigable rivers and seaports and sharing a history of early western colonization, have been at the forefront of China's globalization process. Guangdong province serves as a thoroughfare between Hong Kong—the port of entry connecting China with the West—and the rest of China.

Hong Kong was one of the first sites of the global assembly line that sprang up during the 1960s, as transnational corporations sought low-waged, non-unionized, largely female workers to manufacture garments, electronics, toys, and plastics. Hong Kong is completely dependent on the capitalist world market, with a stunning 90 percent of its manufactured goods exported overseas. In the 1960s and 1970s, women constituted 70 percent of Hong Kong's factory workforce.[11]

Since its annexation by the British in 1842, Hong Kong served as China's permeable membrane for the flow of capital, goods, and people. Before normalization of the West's relations with China in the 1970s and the decolonization of Hong Kong in 1997, Chinese immigrants had to pass through Hong Kong to process their applications for immigration. For many women and their families, migration to Hong Kong was the first step in a multi-stage migration process, from rural to urban areas, then on to inner-city jobs in the United States.

Wu worked as a teacher in mainland China before immigrating to the United States and jobs in New York's Chinatown garment shops. She says,

> My mother- and father-in-law were very young when they immigrated to the US. I don't remember exactly when they came, but first they were in Hong Kong.... My mother-in-law sponsored us to come since my father-in-law had already passed away.... Hong Kong was part of the passage to America; you had to go there first to get a visa. We lived in Hong Kong for about half a year in a place we rented temporarily. If you got someone to sponsor you to immigrate to the US and you were just going to Hong Kong to get your visa signed and processed, they let you do it. In China there was no American consulate.[12]

Helen Wong was also born in Guangdong province. Her parents later moved to Hong Kong to make a better living. In Hong Kong, she worked in the garment industry until she had to stay home to care for her children. Similar to many Mexican immigrant women workers who belong to extended family chain migration networks, Wong had family members who worked and lived intermittently on both sides of the border between China and Hong Kong. Extended family members on both sides pooled income and juggled childcare arrangements. In 1988, Wong immigrated to Oakland with her family through her father-in law's sponsorship.

> My parents were born in Guangdong. I have two older brothers and a younger one. One older brother is in mainland China and the others are in Hong Kong. My brother was born [on the mainland] but my parents were so poor they had to leave their kids behind when they went to Hong Kong to try to make some money. They left the kids with my grandmother on my mother's side. After 1950 it got really crazy in China. My brother stopped writing and we couldn't send money or letters back to him. For several years we lost touch. But whenever they could get letters through, my parents sent money to help him survive, for food, clothing, and necessities. He's a farmer. After he got older, we sent money back when he got married, had children, and so on.[13]

Oi Kwan "Annie" Lai, a garment worker in New York, is an energetic woman with thick jet black hair. Her parents are from Guangdong province and moved to Hong Kong before she was born. Her father worked as a chauffeur while her mother worked in a factory making packaging for radio batteries. Lai's eyes fill with tears as she remembers the poverty she grew up in. Like many girls across Asia, she quit school and started working in a toy factory at the age of twelve because her parents could not afford her public-school fees. She was one of the young women who helped create Hong Kong's economic miracle, eventually sewing garments for export to Western countries for some two decades in Hong Kong factories.

Lisa, born in Toisan in Guangdong province on the Chinese mainland in 1957, is a first-generation immigrant to the United States, but a second-generation garment worker. Both she and her mother worked in garment shops in Hong Kong.

> My dad worked in a metal factory. After they got married, my mom went to Hong Kong in 1979 and worked as a garment worker. Just my mom and my younger brother went at first. My father's mother was over there in Hong Kong, so my mother went there to take care of her. I have three brothers. I'm the second oldest. I went to school in China for eight years. I also worked in *yi chang* [a garment factory] in Toisan. It was a medium sized factory. We sewed suits and women's apparel for distribution inside China. I started working when I was around 17 or 18. I gave most of my wages to my parents, and just kept a little bit for myself. That was how it was in China.[14]

According to Bo Yee, an Oakland garment worker with 27 years of experience in the Hong Kong garment industry, conditions in Hong Kong's garment shops were fairer than in the United States.

> In Hong Kong workers get 17 paid holidays each year, paid sick leave, and bonuses. Seamstresses seldom work more than eight hours a day. If you do have to work overtime for a special order, you also get overtime pay and the company provides your dinner. If you get laid off, at least the company pays you severance pay. Sewing is not such a bad job in Hong Kong; at least you can make

a decent living above the minimum wage sewing by piece rate.... In Hong Kong, workers have more bargaining power with employers. For example, when sewing a new style, workers try the work out first to see if the proposed wages are fair. If not, workers will come together for a brief work stoppage until they can get a fair wage for the new style. But usually they can work out a fair compromise with the supervisor.[15]

The Globalization Nightmare: Second Stage Capital Flight

Relations between the United States and China were normalized after President Richard Nixon's 1972 visit. Shortly after the death of Mao Zedong in 1976 and the routing of the Gang of Four, Prime Minister Deng Xiaoping's government pushed to reintegrate China into the capitalist world market under a program of "four modernizations" (in industry, agriculture, science and technology, and national defense) and building a Chinese-style socialist market economy.[16] As a result of these changes, by 1990 nearly all of Hong Kong's labor-intensive toy, electronics, and mass-produced garment factories had shifted to China. Women workers in Hong Kong who lost their factory jobs were forced to choose between pushing dim sum carts, laboring in fast food outlets, or working part-time as maids and homecare attendants.[17] At the same time, Hong Kong was drawing increasing numbers of migrant women workers from the Philippines, South Asia, and mainland China to fill jobs described by Asian migrant rights activists as "3D" or "dirty, dangerous, and dull."[18]

"In the early 80s, the nightmare started," says former factory worker Lai Tong Chi, who works with the grassroots Hong Kong-based Women Workers Association. "During that time I wasn't as aware as I am now, but the factories already started closing down and moving to other parts of Asia," she says. Lai followed the jobs to China, training mainland workers in production techniques until they learned and she was laid off. When she returned to Hong Kong she could no longer find garment work and was turned away from hotel room cleaner, sales, public transit, and home helper jobs.

I get angry as I think back to when I was young and the employer beat me and they pushed me to work faster, exploiting me. And now they say, "you are too old." In the 70s when I was working in the factory, older women at the age of 60 or 70 were being employed. Employers needed them, so they had to work. Now the government is totally irresponsible because there is no insurance and job security for us. We workers devoted a lot to the development and affluence of Hong Kong. And now we are being kicked out as worthless. A lot of the employers are using age restrictions, and women over the age of 35 find it difficult to get jobs. But the government refuses to have any legislation safeguarding the right to work.[19]

From the corporate perspective, the labor force on the two sides of the border are complementary, reflecting the integration of the two economies.[20] One writer compared high-priced Hong Kong with New York's Manhattan where only the rich can afford to live. South China increasingly houses poor people who commute long distances to work.[21] The Asian financial crisis of the late 1990s and Hong Kong's transition from British Commonwealth status to the 1997 "one country, two systems," integration with China only served to speed income polarization.

On the China side of the border, hundreds of thousands of young women workers have migrated in search of jobs to the special economic zones on China's south coast.[22] The dangerous conditions in these zones became apparent in a November 1993 factory fire that killed 87 workers and injured 46.[23] Export processing centers employ over 20 million Chinese workers, with some 6.5 million migrant workers in Guangdong province.[24] According to the China Labour Education and Information Center,

> Most of the women working in these enterprises [special economic zones] are from the villages. They are driven by poverty at home and are compelled to live away from their families. Popular among these peasant workers is the saying, "Wanna make money? Go to Guangdong!" So the saying goes and regions with rapid economic development headed by Guangdong Province have become the gold-digging dreamland of the Chinese peasantry. However many of these young women encounter forced

overtime, lack of union protection, unsafe working conditions, poor housing and living conditions, physical and sexual abuse, and denial of their basic right to organize.[25]

Peoples' organizations affiliated with the Chinese Communist Party, such as the All China Federation of Trade Unions and the All China Women's Federation, have devolved into toothless social groups at best and instruments of coercion at worst. According to Chan Wai Fun, a seamstress in Oakland's Chinatown who worked as an office manager at the port of Guangzhou in Guangdong province,

> The union really didn't stand up for the workers or criticize the administrators. One good thing about union membership was that sometimes they gave you discounts on events, like free tickets to go see the circus. I don't really remember much about the women's association. It just meant that on International Women's Day, they would give us a flower.[26]

According to Lee Yin Wah, today's Communist Party in China adopts a kind of "don't ask, don't tell" stance towards workers' rights:

> There's no real organizing work going on. They really could care less about what you think.... Didn't you go to the international women's conference in Beijing? From that you can see what kind of organizing method is used in China. They can circumscribe whatever you do. Everyone from all over the world was there, but the government circumscribed you so you couldn't see what was really going on. But at the same time, when you look at China you see how big a country it is. Controlling and running such a big society is not such an easy task.
>
> When you're in China the party never tells you what your rights are. As far as they're concerned you've already got all the privileges you need if you work eight hours a day, get paid a salary, and can make a living.... The propaganda says, "This is the home of the workers. You are in control." But the workers do not feel in control. The party is very well organized in the institutional sense. Every factory, no matter how big or small, has committees. Au-

tonomous organizations unconnected to the party are not allowed.[27]

Today, workers who dare to organize for their rights face stiff
competition from the 150 million or more unemployed or laid-off
workers from rural China.[28]

Women Come to Gold Mountain

Before 1875, Chinese women had trickled into the United States
as slaves, forced prostitutes, or merchants' wives. Between 1875 and
1945, Chinese women were systematically barred from immigrating
to the United States.[29] The 1945 War Brides Act allowed Chinese-American soldiers fighting on the Pacific front to marry hometown girls and bring them back to the United States. Between 1946
and 1952, women constituted almost 90 percent of Chinese immigrants to the United States. More Chinese women than men continue to immigrate, furthering the feminization of migration.[30]

The Chinese community in the United States was radically
transformed by the Immigration and Naturalization Act of 1965
that removed racist quota restrictions, allowed family reunification,
and set preferences for the recruitment of professionals, techni-
cians, and other wealthy immigrants. Chinese, Filipinos, Koreans,
Indians, and other Asians migrated in massive numbers under the
new law.[31] Labor historian Peter Kwong dubbed the new Chinese
immigrants from higher professional and social strata backgrounds
"uptown Chinese" in contrast to the "downtown" working-class
immigrants who preceded them.[32]

Many new immigrants sought US citizenship so they in turn
could sponsor more family members. Since 1965, some 40,000 Chinese per year have migrated to the United States from China, Taiwan, and Hong Kong. By 1980, the Chinese-American population
was once again mostly foreign-born. By 1985, 81 percent of Chinese
immigrants entered under family preference categories and only
about 16 percent as professionals.[33] Helen Wong immigrated with
her husband and five kids to Oakland from Hong Kong in 1988 at
the urging of her father-in-law. Her extended family developed a
very conscious strategy to bring its members to the United States.

We are Guangdong people but both my husband and his father were born in Hong Kong. After my mother-in-law got her citizenship, she sponsored the rest of the family. Then after that they sponsored one family after another to come over. My father-in-law's family were all adults by the time he came to the US [in 1977]. He had to sponsor them one by one after he lived here awhile and got his citizenship.[34]

Wu Wan Mei immigrated to New York's Chinatown through the sponsorship of her mother-in-law, who worked in a laundry uptown and had lived in the United States for many years. Like many newcomers, it took Wu and her family some time to adjust to life in the States.

In the beginning it was very hard to adapt and I wasn't at peace with the decision to come here. Our sons had wanted to come. (laughs) But after they came here they decided that they didn't like it after all. Then they said, "Let's go back to Hong Kong!"[35]

Jenny Chen, who was born in Toisan, went straight to work in a garment sweatshop after marrying a "gold mountain man" and following him back to New York. She found adjusting to US life very stressful.

Aiyah! I regret coming here. When I was in China, after graduating from high school I worked in restaurants. I learned a lot of different things about how to run a restaurant. It was better work, more interesting. Now I'm behind a machine all day, sewing away. Sometimes when they pay you, they hold back a portion of your pay. For the younger women like me, we often wish that we could just go to school and get some different kind of work. Lots of times you're not even getting paid, but you have to go in to work on Sundays. Then you've got to look at the boss's face. Yuhhh! (laughs) You just wish you could be doing something else. And you don't have any time to spend with your kids. I heard from my friends in San Francisco that the price is not as good as here. You go to work earlier and get out earlier, right? Here work varies a lot and you still see lights on in the shops at night. My daughter's friend's mother works in the day, comes home to feed her kids, then goes back to work at night. She's always tired.[36]

After immigrating to Oakland with her husband and son at the invitation of in-laws, Lin Cai Fen followed the trail of women seeking work in garment factories, including her mother-in-law.

> Not speaking English, the only job I could get was sewing in a sweatshop. All the Chinese immigrant women seemed to work in garments. I sewed at piece rates and could only make one dollar per hour. The job was terrible and the pay was too little for me to support my family. For new immigrants who know very little English, men work in restaurants and women in the garment industry. This is the reality that new immigrants face.[37]

New Migrant Streams:
Refugees and Ransomed Workers

Along with the growing legal immigration of Chinese are newer streams of undocumented immigrants from China, refugees and immigrants from Vietnam and elsewhere. For example, the Sino-Vietnamese War of 1979 and earlier Vietnamese measures to break the control of ethnic Chinese entrepreneurs over trade and retail businesses created a large wave of Chinese-Vietnamese refugees to the United States. Eighty-five percent of the "boat people" who fled Vietnam for the United States in 1978 were ethnic Chinese.[38] Many of these families had lived in Vietnam for several generations. A large proportion trace their ancestral roots back to villages in Guangdong and speak both Cantonese and Vietnamese.

Since the late 1980s, undocumented workers from Fujian province in China have immigrated to the United States. Fujian province has long been the source of Chinese immigration to Indonesia, Malaysia, Singapore, Thailand, the Philippines, and Taiwan. In 1993, the flow of undocumented immigrants from Fujian briefly became a big US news story when the *Golden Venture,* a steamer carrying 286 undocumented Fujian immigrants ran aground a few hundred yards from Rockaway Beach in Queens, New York. The workers had promised to pay $30,000 to their smugglers, called *luo ti* [snake heads], if they successfully reached the United States.[39] Headlines were made again in January 2000, when 15 Chinese men from Hong Kong stumbled out of cargo containers carried aboard the giant freighter *Cape May,* which had docked in Seattle, Washington. They had agreed to pay their smugglers tens of thousands of dollars in future wages. Inside were the bodies of three of their comrades who had died during the crossing.[40] This credit-ticket labor trafficking is the current version of the 19th-century system that brought Chinese migrant male workers from Pearl River delta villages to Hawaiian plantations, Californian fields, and transcontinental railroads.

Other immigrants overstay tourist visas or cross the border from Mexico. In the late 1960s, my second-generation, Chinese-American husband Belvin was asked to go meet some "cousins" from the home village to help them cross the Mexican border into the United States. Eventually, they entered the United States without him having to make the run to the border. Arranged marriages of convenience are another way to facilitate legal immigrant status.

Sweatshop and factory employers frequently pit undocumented workers against those with documents. Both ethnic subcontractors and Euro-American businesses profit from undocumented workers' labor, according to Peter Kwong's excellent book *Forbidden Workers: Illegal Chinese Immigrants and American Labor.* Government agencies are often unable, and organized labor unwilling, to defend these workers' rights.[41] Kwong describes how organized crime, corrupt government officials, travel agencies in China, and US employers have developed a lucrative underground smuggling industry that taps into family groups in search of work.

"In this case ethnic solidarity brings about its opposite," Kwong says. "The people who know you the best also know the best ways to rip you off."[42] The enclave community entraps workers and justifies their exploitation under the ideology of "ethnic solidarity," by which employers claim they provide jobs for poor people no one else wants to hire and that "outsiders don't understand us and how we do things."[43]

Jenny Chen describes how garment sweatshop bosses pit workers from Guangdong and Hong Kong against undocumented workers from Fujian province.

A lot of the shops are run by Cantonese, Taishanese, or Hong Kong people. They close a little earlier than the shops on East Broadway where there are a lot of Fukinese. They work long hours. They don't even eat that much. No time to even *sik faan* [eat rice], no time to *sik jook* [eat rice porridge]. When I came in 1990 and I was pregnant, the boss was nice about it. The boss would carry the clothes over for me to sew so I wouldn't have to get up and lift the heavy stuff. But now the boss says, "That's your problem."

A lot of time before we even go to work the Fukinese are already there. And when we leave at eight at night, they're still there. We already work long hours, but the Fukinese work even longer. Sometimes I sew 14 hours a day. In the past people would discriminate against those without legal status. But what's going on now is that a lot of the bosses will actually discriminate against those with legal status, because they tend to be less willing to put in that many hours. So the Fukinese are being used, and we're being compared against them. If you don't feel like working as many hours, you get a lot of pressure.

Near the Triple A Restaurant down at the end of the block on East Broadway, right under the Manhattan Bridge you see a lot of Fukinese waiting around for work, mostly men [day laborers]. The women usually go to work in the factories. A lot of times the Fukinese will go around selling *mantou* [steamed buns]. They're doing everything.[44]

Made in the USA

In New York City, Chinese and other Asian and Latina immigrant women comprise the majority of the garment industry's workforce, replacing the earlier pool of European and Puerto Rican immigrants and retired African Americans. Over 60 percent of New York's 7,000 to 7,500 garment factories are sweatshops.[45] In 1960, there were eight garment sweatshops in New York City's Chinatown. By 1984, there were 500. Between 1969 and 1982, the number of Chinese women workers in Chinatown garment sweatshops jumped from 8,000 to 20,000.[46] Today, there are an estimated 93,000 workers in garment manufacturing in New York City.[47] The labor of Chinese garment workers produces an effect that ripples beyond the garment industry. Entrepreneurs who began as sewing subcontractors frequently reinvest profits into bigger businesses and real estate. Women working ten to twelve hours a day, six to seven days a week, buy prepared food and other convenience items, boosting local restaurant and grocery businesses.

Los Angeles is now the nation's garment manufacturing center with the greatest number of employees: 120,000 people, of whom 14 percent are Asian, including 7 percent Chinese, 4 percent Korean, and 3 percent are other Asians. Among Latinos, Mexicans accounted for 47 percent, Central Americans, 14 percent, and other Latinos 6 percent. Of the remainder, European Americans were 8 percent, African Americans 2 percent, and the remaining 9 percent unidentified.[48] There are about 400 garment manufacturers, about 20 to 25 major labels producing for the mass market, and 5,000 subcontractors including a relatively large number operating underground. Many workers take work home. Chinese women workers average $5,464 annually, other Asian women $7,500, and Mexican women $6,500—a far cry from fat cats such as Georges Marciano, an owner of Guess?, who pocketed a cool $8.7 million in salary, bonuses, and perks in 1992.[49]

In the San Francisco Bay Area, there are an estimated 20,000 garment workers, 85 percent of whom are Asian immigrant women. In 1960, there was only one garment subcontractor listed in the Oakland phone directory. By 1990, 150 East Bay garment factories were registered with the Department of Industrial Relations' Division of Labor Standards Enforcement, with 478 more shops in San Francisco. The actual number of shops is probably higher because some owners do not register. The industry generates about $5 billion in annual sales and accounts for more than one-third of San Francisco's manufacturing jobs. San Francisco's three big garment manufacturers, Levi Strauss, Gap, and Esprit, have outsourced the bulk of their manufacturing overseas, so smaller manufacturers predominate in the local industry.[50]

Nationwide, home workers earn as little as $2 an hour, often toiling 60 to 70 hours a week without overtime pay. Regulators report that the practice of home sewing is most widespread in New

York, California, and the Dallas-Fort Worth area, where the home-sewing population ranges from 20,000 to 80,000.[51] Many labor organizers and advocates say that home sewing workshops illegally use child labor.[52]

Until the 1950s almost all of the clothing sold in the United States was accurately labeled "Made in the USA." Today, 60 percent of the clothing sold in the United States is imported.[53] Quicker turn-around time, lower shipping costs, and sweatshop wages paid to immigrant women workers anchors some production within US borders. Global trade agreements such as NAFTA, APEC (Asian Pacific Economic Cooperation), GATT (General Agreement on Trade and Tariffs), and the proposed MAI (Multilateral Agreement on Investments) and FTAA (Free Trade Area of the Americas) pit global assembly line workers against each other in what activists have dubbed "the race to the bottom"—a global effort to slash environmental and labor standards to attract employers.

"When GATT goes into full effect in 2005," says Lora Jo Foo, an Asian Law Caucus attorney and founding member of the Sweatshop Watch coalition, "all the jobs are going to run away to China. I know this is controversial, but I think we need to start talking about keeping a certain number of jobs in this country for immigrant women in our communities."[54]

Sweatshops Go from Bad to Worse

The global factory has trapped women across China's vast diaspora in a roller-coaster ride of rushes and dead seasons, expansions and expulsions, lurches and backfires. Despite corporate assertions to the contrary, the reversion to 19th-century sweatshop conditions is part and parcel of the globalized expansion of the bottom of the industry pyramid. Immigrant women workers with years of experience working on both sides of the Pacific complained bitterly about the deterioration in working conditions over the past decade. They described plummeting pay and benefits, ever-longer hours, production speedups, increased injuries, and harsher treatment from bosses.

One problem is the piece rate system, in which workers are paid according to each procedure they finish. They are paid a certain amount to sew a collar, attach a zipper, or hem a skirt. Piece rates are determined by what the manufacturer pays the subcontractor—not by the wages workers need to live above the poverty line. This widespread system of underpayment encourages subcontractors to abuse workers, and intensifies the self-exploitation and competition between workers.[55]

"The pay rate is just the same on Sunday. There is no such thing as overtime. You can take a break if you want to. But sewing by the piece means you don't get paid for it, " says former garment worker Helen Wong.[56] "I almost broke down in tears when I first started," says Jenny Chen.

> When I was in China I never touched a sewing machine because I didn't have to. So it was very tough. Really the boss is the one who taught me how to do it. Eventually I learned I could handle it. I started working at nine and usually finished by eight at the earliest.
>
> Wages vary depending on piece rates, but if you get some good work, you can sew faster. I'm young and us younger ones can do more and move quickly when we get *see you guy* work. *See you guy* [soy sauce chicken] is a nickname for sewing that's easy to do. It's not like *ji tau gwat* [pig head and neck bones] that looks like a good piece of meat, but turns into a bunch of bones that are hard to swallow at soon as you put it in your mouth. (laughs)
>
> Like sometimes you work seven long days but you can only get $300. When you get *see you guy* you can make about $70 to $80 a day if you work really fast. But that's pretty rare. A lot of times you can't concentrate, you're in a bad mood, you're sick, you just can't do it. I sew the seams and sometimes the seams have a lot of other little pieces that must go inside and you can make more money. But sometimes it's really hard to do. If you average out what you make over the long term, it doesn't really add up to all that much money. During Chinese New Year you're very, very busy. You don't even have time to visit friends, clean your house, and cook like you're supposed to. But during the last couple of months [April and May], the work has been very slow.
>
> Most people can't make $10,000 a year. Forget about $10,000; if you make $7,000 a year to qualify for union medical benefits,

you're lucky. A lot of times for different reasons, many people are not able to make that amount. In fact many bosses don't want them to. Even if you make the money, but you don't get paid, or the boss pays you in cash and you have no proof, you can't get health coverage. You've got to do whatever you can to get on the books. Sometimes people have to buy their paychecks. Can you believe it? Say you were able to work at the beginning of the year, but you couldn't make enough by the end of the year. So you have to pay $10 or $20 to buy your paycheck.[57]

"In the beginning when I first started working," says Wu Wan Mei, "the hours were better. The union also seemed to be a little bit better."

Now it's totally different. For example, now the union demands that you make at least $7,000 in order to get medical benefits. Before you were only required to make $3,000, then $5,000. Now it's up to $7,000 and a lot of people don't make that much. Of course, now we're working longer hours but with no overtime pay.[58]

Working in New York's Chinatown, says Annie Lai, "really kills you!" Bosses pit older seamstresses who work a "mere" 10-hour day against undocumented seamstresses from Fujian who literally work day and night. According to Lai, jobs in the mid-town Manhattan garment district used to be a little better than those in Chinatown, but now bosses can pressure workers to come in six days a week.[59]

Lisa quit Streetbeat Sportswear in New York City when her hours exceeded 100 hours a week. "We told the boss, 'We just can't keep working like this. We're getting destroyed. We need to have a day off.' And the boss said, 'No you can't have a day off.' So we just left. We couldn't take it anymore. There were about 60 to 70 people in that shop."[60]

"Many of my friends develop pain and illnesses related to their work," says former garment worker Helen Wong.

They have to move their hands in the same motion over and over again so that some women have very sore hands and shoulders and back pains. They have to sit for a long time and many develop bad circulation or hemorrhoids. The dust in some of the factories is so thick you can see it in the air and you develop allergies. So sometimes we work with masks made by ourselves. Otherwise, we'd be sneezing all the time. When I went home from work sometimes, when I would blow my nose, the colors of the fabrics I worked with that day would appear on my Kleenex. I've heard of some women who have had lung and breathing problems because of having worked in garment manufacturing for so long.

I now work in the hotels and many women who leave the garment industry also do the work that I do, which is to clean hotel rooms. I have 18 rooms to clean in eight hours. We push heavy carts and move around very quickly. We often get bruises and bumps from banging into the furniture. Also, our fingers become irritated and cracked from the cleaning liquids we use. My thumb also gets very sore from pulling sheets all day. It is very stressful and we come home very tired.[61]

Sweatshops in Other Industries

Garment workers are not the only sweatshop workers subjected to long hours, low wages, and occupational health hazards. Immigrant women working in restaurants, convalescent homes, hotels, electronics, and other secondary sector jobs also endure sweatshop-like conditions.

Amy Xie is originally from Guangzhou, the capitol of Guangdong Province in China and lives in the Bronx. She used to work as a hostess at Silver Palace Restaurant for 12 to 14 hours a day, six days a week. The restaurant had promised her a monthly salary of $1,600, but ended up only paying her $800 with no overtime, sick or vacation leave, or health care benefits. Sometimes she worked straight through her lunch hour.

Xie lifts her long skirt to reveal startling dark purple bruises all over her legs, caused by standing all day at work. She has a hard time running to keep up with her young son.

> They would yell at you from the back room when there were too many people, especially on weekends when everyone comes in to eat dim sum. The bosses would curse and swear at you over the walkie talkie. Everyone could hear them. It was so humiliating! Now I walk so slow after working there. I never got any workers compensation from them.

One time I fell down when it was snowing in the front of the restaurant. The boss makes so much money, but they are so cheap. They wouldn't even let me go to the hospital to see a doctor of my choosing. They said I had to go to their company doctor, who told me I didn't have any problem. If I hadn't gone back to work that day, I wouldn't have been paid. They don't give you anything. They didn't tell me about workers comp. That's what happens. You know Chinatown.[62]

Lew Ying Choi, a Chinese home care worker, worked 72-hour weeks for the Evergreen Residential Care Home in the Bay Area with only one day off a week and no overtime pay. She suspected that her boss was cheating her out of her pay when she received five payroll deduction stubs but no paychecks. The owner yelled at Lew when she asked about what happened to her paychecks and Lew quit.

Disempowering Messages

"We must organize for our rights," says former restaurant worker Lee Yin Wah. "We can't just worry about our families. We have to come together to protect our interests." Today, Lee is the sympathetic and skilled organizer workers first meet at CSWA, the woman moving stealth-like behind the scenes at every successful event, the clear voice behind the bull-horn at many a Chinatown picket line.

A lot of new immigrants from China get trapped inside a very closed community. Many are not highly educated. They accept what the restaurant and garment bosses' associations tell them. Because they don't speak the language and know what is going on, they put up with the bosses' controlling them. They are just happy to get a job. They compare the $20 they get paid a day to wages back in China. That's more than they would have made working a whole month in China. But living expenses here are a lot higher, too.

When I first came here my relatives told me, "As long as you've got a job and aren't starving don't pay attention to anything else. If someone tries to hand you a leaflet on the street, don't take it. Just take care of yourself." They told me that I had to be more selfish and that all the stuff the communist party told me back home about helping other people wouldn't work here, that was just a bunch of crap. People here also tell you if you work hard, you can start a business, make a lot of money, go back to China to buy a house, and make more money. All of the immigrants, documented or undocumented, who came by boat or by plane, this is their plan. People just go along with this way of thinking. But in reality for most people the chances are nil that they'll be able to get rich through hard work. In China they say you don't need rights, you're already provided for. Here they say, don't even think about it, you'll never get your rights, so why bother?[63]

"Even if workers want to join picket lines, many are afraid to come out in front," says Amy Xie. "The first time I went to the picket, I was scared, too. You know the bosses have all of these Mafia-type gangster guys in the back to support them so the workers are afraid to come out in front."[64]

Problems Can't Be Solved Alone

In describing how they got involved in the movement, women often spoke about the dynamic relationship between their own actions and those of the broader struggles they joined. Community-based labor organizations provided the women with infrastructures of solidarity, resources, training, accumulated experiences, ties with other struggles and sectors, and strategic vision. Of course, each woman faced her moment of reckoning, when she decided to stand up for her rights whatever the risk. As the conflicts escalated, so did the demands on each woman's commitment and leadership. Throughout the process, the women brought their own life experiences, skills, and networks into the movement, shaping its reach and direction. Lee Yin Wah explains that CSWA's Women's Committee helps women break their isolation. "Quite a few of the women workers are very strong," says Lee.

They get a lot of pressure from the bosses, from their families to back down. But many stick to the fight anyway. It's not easy for women workers to fight for justice. They have to deal with survival, how to take care of their kids, and what to do with their husbands. Through our activities we try to stay in touch. We stress that problems can't just be solved alone by oneself.[65]

According to Lee, most of the women workers who visit CSWA complain about back wages they are owed. Although workers often resign themselves to violations of their rights, their bosses' failure to pay them for work they've already performed is often the straw that breaks the camel's back.

In 1992, CSWA started a back wage campaign. Some employers were arrested and convicted for their failure to pay back wages. "Most employers see owing back wages as just part of the business," says Lee.

> Almost all factories owe at least one month of wages. Some owe workers for nine weeks, or longer. Sometimes the bosses owe them for half a year. Maybe the boss gives a little money to string them along. The boss keeps saying, "Oh, I don't have the money now, but when I do, I'll give it to you."[66]

Unfortunately, labor unions are not always willing to help these workers. Jenny Chen and her 19 co-workers at Empress Fashion in New York City first approached their union, ILGWU/UNITE, when their employer failed to pay them $60,000 in back wages.

> On April 17, 1993, the federal authorities came and closed the shop. The owner reopened it in November, then closed it down again and ran off. We went to the union first, but the union didn't do a thing.... I had stayed at the shop because it was union and I needed medical benefits when I was pregnant. But the union doesn't really help you. The union runs ads and press releases in the newspaper that they have a hotline, and if you are owed your hard-earned pay, come in. But a lot of times when you go there, they just yell at you. Like in our case, they treated us very badly. They scolded us, "Why did you take so long to come here? Look, this is basically a done deal." They say they're going to help you, but things drag out and you never hear from them again. *Ho ma phan* [It's a hassle].
>
> I heard from some friends that the boss was out of jail. He told them, "These workers don't speak a word of English. What

do you think they're going to do? Do you think they can put me back in jail? Even if I go to jail I'm not giving them a penny back!" I'm still very angry at this boss. He took our sweat and blood money.[67]

In the Streetbeat Sportswear case, workers who were also rebuffed by UNITE took their claims to CSWA. According to Lisa,

First the pressers came to CSWA. After that they talked to people and got in touch with me and other seamstresses and told us to come here and talk, too. We came, so now here we are. We felt like what the boss did to us was not fair…. We were very active and united in fighting for our rights. We went to every rally, every demonstration, at the manufacturers and Sears. Streetbeat contractors paid some workers $25 to come to their counter demonstration. Because we were picketing and giving them all kinds of pressure they were afraid that their business would go down. They were looking for ways to sue us.

A lot of young people came out to support our campaign because they saw how our boss was treating us unfairly. We were under a lot of pressure. A lot of the garment bosses were all talking about how we were troublemakers…. The bosses put our names on a blacklist [of the Kings' County Apparel Association].[68]

In June 1998, sweatshop owner Jian Wen Liang was arrested and arraigned for 31 counts of criminal labor violations. In October 1999 the Manhattan Supreme Court dismissed Streetbeat's $75 million "SLAPP" (Strategic Lawsuit Against Public Participation) suit against workers, Chinese Staff and Workers Association, National Mobilization Against Sweatshops, and Asian American Legal Defense and Education Fund.

Victories Against McClintock and Gifford

One of the most visible and effective actions by garment workers began at a sweatshop in Oakland. In 1992 the Lucky Sewing Company, a subcontractor to fashion designer Jessica McClintock, laid off Bo Yee, Fu Lee, and their co-workers without paying back wages owed. The women were shocked when they discovered that dresses for which they were to have been paid $5 retailed for $175 each. Similar to a number of emergent leaders in other campaigns, Bo Yee had experience in workplace actions before immigrating to the United States. She had also attended leadership training sessions organized by Asian Immigrant Women Advocates (AIWA) before the layoffs hit.

The Lucky Sewing Company garment workers joined with AIWA to launch a campaign against Jessica McClintock in September 1992. At the first demonstration at corporate headquarters, the women were so afraid of being blacklisted that they wore Halloween masks. Soon, they stopped wearing the masks.

Besieged by protests, on December 17, 1994, Jessica McClintock offered a "charitable donation" through the Northern California Chinese Garment Contractors Association—on the condition that workers would sign a contract releasing McClintock from responsibility for their back wages. Then on January 8, 1994, the contractors published the names of workers who refused to sign in the *Sing Tao* newspaper, an act tantamount to blacklisting them. The tactic backfired. The women only grew more angry and determined. In March 1996, the two sides finally reached a settlement that included an undisclosed payment of back wages, an education fund for garment workers, a scholarship fund for garment workers and their children, and a bilingual hotline for workers to report any violations of their rights in shops contracted with McClintock.

Former home healthcare worker Lew Ying Choi also went to AIWA for support in winning back wages. AIWA introduced Lew to attorney Eugene Pak at the Employment Law Center. On October 19, 1994, the Labor Commissioner ordered Lew's former employer to pay $53,820.24 in back wages, interest, and penalties. The employer appealed the Commissioner's decision and the two parties reached a settlement for an undisclosed sum.[69]

Workers' centers have also seen successes in getting money out of runaway shops. Garment workers at the Laura & Sarah Sportswear and MSL Sportswear shops in New York City commonly toiled 12 hours a day, seven days a week, under a union contract negotiated by UNITE Local 23-25, producing garments for the Kathy Lee Gifford, Jaclyn Smith, and Tracy Evans labels. When the boss told workers not to come in over the weekend in November 1997, they got suspicious. When a worker saw the boss starting to move the machines out at night, she alerted coworkers, the union, and CSWA. CSWA organizer Lee Yin Wah recalled:

> The workers were so smart. They knew the boss was up to something. We helped the workers stake out the factory at night. It was so cold. We brought a lot of cars and people stayed in the cars all night.
>
> On the second day the union and the police came. When the workers told the police what happened, the police said they couldn't do anything, because the machines were private property, and that workers had to go to the labor department. The union said, "yeah, yeah." The workers got very quiet. They had spent the whole night staying out in the cold, and then they had to stand there and watch the machines being taken away. They said the union didn't do anything to help them. So 90 workers came over to our office. We didn't have enough chairs for people to sit! (Laughs)
>
> We told the workers that they needed to go to court to get an order to stop the boss from selling the machines. This was important because if the boss got rid of the machines, maybe there wouldn't be enough money left to pay the workers the wages they were owed, right? We helped them go to the state attorney general's office and do a big case. The garment workers network helped build a lot of support for the workers. Through their own experience they learned that they have the power if they work together to defend their rights.[70]

After a two-year battle with pickets, community education—including production of a play that was performed in the East Village—and court action, in January 2000, the workers won a settlement of $400,000.[71]

Workers' Centers Build Bridges

Annie Lai worked 60 to 70 hour weeks sewing garments for the Donna Karan label (DKNY) at a garment shop in New York City, unionized by UNITE. Despite the long hours, weekly salaries averaged $270.

It felt like being in prison. If we were two minutes late we were docked one half-hour of our pay. We had to keep our heads down all the time once we started working. No looking up. No talking to anyone. Can you imagine? A big room with rows and rows of machines and all of us looking down. Three surveillance cameras watched everything we did. They checked our purses before we left at the end of the day. No going to the bathroom—it was often padlocked. No water, with the drinking fountain broken. No making or receiving phone calls, not even for emergencies.[72]

Lai was fired for receiving a phone call from her daughter's school informing her that her daughter was ill. After Lai tried to win her job back for the second time, DKNY pulled the contract, forcing the shop to close.[73] But Lai's courage in standing up to the boss and the manufacturer emboldened her co-workers. With CSWA and NMASS's help, a campaign against DKNY calling for corporate responsibility was launched. On June 7, 2000, on behalf of Lai and workers at other DKNY subcontracted shops, the Asian American Legal Defense and Education Fund filed a class action lawsuit against DKNY for failure to pay overtime to workers forced to work 75-hour weeks, in some cases for below minimum wage.[74]

"CSWA really helps," she says. "But it really requires me going and fighting. If I don't fight, CSWA's help would be of no use."

Bilingual, bicultural workers' centers and a movement infrastructure to support them are crucial when unions fail to address workers' needs. "If a little kid goes to school and doesn't speak English and has an Asian teacher that speaks the language, it helps right?" says Jenny Chen. "It creates a bridge. Well, CSWA is like a bridge. Imagine how these workers could communicate with the outside society about their issues without CSWA."

CSWA, AIWA, and immigrant women worker organizers recognize the need for women to have family support for their activism. While some family members fear reprisals from employers and feel that women's activism detracts from precious family time and household responsibilities, others provide crucial support for women's activism.

AIWA has sought to organize the children of garment and electronics workers. AIWA's Youth Build Immigrant Power Project members have been learning the tools of community organizing, leadership training, workplace outreach to immigrant women, and fundraising. Amy Kwong organized her fellow Berkeley High School students to boycott Jessica McClintock. "I first joined AIWA because I wanted to be involved in helping to fight for garment worker issues and do something positive for the community," says Kwong.

> My mom is a garment worker and I have seen and heard about the day-to-day issues in garment shops. AIWA is important because it allows the garment workers a place to come to when they have problems in their workplace that their bosses are ignoring. AIWA makes the community aware of the unfair treatment towards garment workers.[75]

Similar to a number of other leaders, CSWA's Wu Wan Mei had prior organizing experience in her home country. She was active in revolutionary youth and educators' groups throughout China's turbulent post-Liberation years. Her CSWA friends admire her as a staunch women's liberationist who stresses the importance of organizing both men and women.

> In terms of women's position, I have to say that the situation has never changed. People always look down on women. But in the modern world we women should stand up for our rights. We are responsible for the family. We face a lot of pressures. Raising children should be seen as another job. Women have to go out there into the community to work and survive economically. Women make up half the world and hold up half the sky. We have to break down the old backward ways. We must continue to fight for women's liberation and rights.
> There are many obstacles and challenges we face in organizing women. Because of the extremely long hours women work, it is a big challenge to bring people together. Women are in a real time crunch with so much work and responsibility. Women's work is never done. But we're beginning to open up some space in that area. We also organize men. We reflect the whole community, multi-trade, multi-issue, workers in the construction, garment, and restaurant industries. It's not right to just organize

women. Men listen to women in this organization. Every time I talk, they have to listen! We encourage people to have mutual respect as workers.[76]

"We Women Must Stand Up Now!"

Lin Cai Fen immigrated to the United States in October 1987. Formerly a teacher in Guangdong province, she now works as a housekeeper in a convalescent hospital while her husband works as a butcher at a meat market. She started out in the garment industry making only $1 an hour at piece rates. Cai Fen first learned about AIWA through her mother-in-law Sun May Louie, now a retired seamstress. As a member of AIWA's Worker Membership Board, Cai Fen traveled to the 1995 United Nations World Social Summit in Copenhagen to testify about conditions in US garment sweatshops. With catchy Chinese proverbs always on the tip of her tongue, Cai Fen has written stirring appeals calling for community support for garment workers' struggles. Her mother-in-law is also active in AIWA while her husband attends AIWA gatherings, and her son helps do outreach to workers in the sweatshops.

During an animated meeting, Cai Fen listens as an AIWA board member laments that the Japanese, Koreans, Latinas, and African Americans are more united than the Chinese. Another member says that Chinese people only worry about themselves, as in the saying, "people who just whip the snow from their door steps do not mind that I've got snow on my roof." Cai Fen chided her fellow board members.

> Let's not get too disappointed with Chinese people. Look, CSWA is also a Chinese organization. We should have some confidence in the work they've done and the work we've done, too. We should be looking for better methods to organize more people. We need to wake up the masses. Three thousand Chinese workers in New York demonstrated to open up construction industry jobs to people of color in 1992. Each organization has its own strength that we can learn from. Our members need to meet people from other organizations so we can share these experiences. We all need to start somewhere.
>
> Now I'm learning English so I can be more effective in this

society. Before when people yelled at me for not understanding them, I couldn't say anything. I felt just terrible. Now at least I know enough to say, "Hey, why don't you help me learn?!"

Unless we fight for our human rights, we can never change our fate. But the most important thing is that we, as immigrant workers, should stand up for our human rights and link our arms with other workers, immigrants, women, poor people, minorities, the homeless, and everyone else that is fighting for a decent life. We women must stand up now![77]

Lin's call to action echoes far beyond the borders of Chinatown barrios. Chinese and Mexican workers almost simultaneously entered the rock bottom of the US labor market with the 1848 annexation of Mexico and the 1849 rush to Gold Mountain. A century and a half later as Chinese immigrant women fight against sweatshop slavery "from can't see in the morning to can't see at night," their Mexican sisters staunch the hemorhaging of tens of thousands jobs by NAFTA.

Chinese garment workers and AIWA activists picket Jessica McClintock, Inc. corporate headquarters in San Francisco.
Photo by Tu-Minh Trinh (1992)

Bo Yee

Seamstress, Janitor, AIWA Organizer

I was born in Guangdong province, in China. I went to Hong Kong when I was around 20 years old. I had already met my husband. (laughs) We were kind of matched up through a blind date. Then he came back to marry me in China. Actually, what happened was that I was laying in bed reading a famous novel when I heard a big crowd gathering outside. My big sister used to make all the important decisions. It turns out that she had brought a man for me to see. It was kind of like checking out the goods! Well, at that point, my sister had already decided we should get married, so I did so during my second year in middle school. First we were engaged for about a year. My husband is ten years older than me. At that time there were a lot of short women around. My husband jokes that he could have just grabbed anyone, but he decided to go for a taller woman like me.

My kids are old now. I got married when I was 17 and had my first child when I was 20. We were married for two years before moving to Hong Kong. My husband did not want to have kids too early, so we took some precautions at first. Plus I liked to enjoy myself because I was still young then. As soon as we moved to Hong Kong in 1958, I went to work. I haven't stopped working since then! I started to sew for a big place. I changed around to a lot of different shops. Two of the shops folded. The first one did not tell the labor department that they were going to close down because it happened so suddenly. The second one knew beforehand. When the boss was going to close down secretly, we found out and sent a letter to the Department of Labor. That made the boss so scared that he started to meet with the workers.

In the next incident at that same shop, we workers were not happy about the holiday pay they were giving us. Holiday pay used to be calculated in relation to our salary, divided by 21 days. But then the boss wanted to just pay us a flat HK$20 to $30. Because this was unfair we sent a group letter to the Department of Labor again. I was not a leader in this case, but I learned a lot through this experience.

Especially in my department we worked as a group and had high team spirit. If the price was not right, we would negotiate with the supervisor. If we didn't get what we wanted, we would just walk out. The boss would come running after us to get us to go back to work. This was an unusual situation in Hong Kong, even at that time.

Afterwards, with the rush of immigration of new workers from China, the bonds of solidarity were broken and undercut. Whenever you work with a lot of people from mainland China, it's hard to come together as a team. Maybe this is due to some of the political history there. People from mainland China are practical. They look for shortcuts to get what they want rather than working together over the long term to make change.

Since I've come to the US, I've found that people can't seem to work together. In my experience, seven out of ten women here are from mainland China. Maybe this is their first job sewing. They learn here. In China they were farmers plowing the land. That's why they feel like making $10 a day is a lot of money and that finding any work is precious. They don't want to jeopardize their jobs.

I've seen two kinds of psychology among people from mainland China. One is very frugal, economical, and hard working. The second doesn't work hard because they didn't have to work hard jobs in China and got off to eat snacks in the afternoon. Some people from Hong Kong also have had a more comfortable life. When they first come here it's very hard to adjust. You just look at all those hard working people and you wonder how you are going to make enough money to live and get accustomed to this way of life. My first job was at a white guy's garment shop. The older immigrants there worked with a bowl of rice in front of their machine. They'd just work and eat, work and eat. I thought it was terrible and that maybe it would be easier to go back to Hong Kong.

Now I've adjusted to the work. I've got three jobs—one sewing, one as a janitor, and one as an organizer with AIWA. And I'm not even counting the work I do at home!

I started working at a factory a month after I got here. I immigrated to the US because of my two sons. They were not going to be happy in Hong Kong after the 1997 changeover. My husband did not want to come the US but he did come in 1985.

I started working at Lucky Sewing Company in June 1986. Working there was like being a prisoner in a sealed cage. All the windows were locked. They wouldn't let you go to the bathroom. They had "No loud talking" signs posted. There were about 20 of us there working ten hours a day, seven days a week, endlessly, without rest. Most of the workers were from mainland China, although some came from Hong Kong and there were a few Latinos. The boss' wife created a tense, competitive atmosphere between the workers. She would praise some people and downgrade others. Because of my experience, I can work faster than newer workers from China who are not as skillful. They would sacrifice their lunch and break time to try to catch up. I hated the way the boss made us compete. There were three of us in one department who had to produce 200 pieces. They would push us to see who could finish first. They were getting people to exploit themselves. How disgusting! I hate this!

I couldn't communicate with the Latino workers, but you can have fun without speaking each other's language. You motion. You use body language and whatever method you can. The relations with Latinos were better. We were not forced to compete with each other.

I thought America was a very advanced country, but working in sweatshops here, I see that the garment industry is very backward compared to Hong Kong. I see workers exploited by Chinese bosses. It makes me feel very sad and unhappy. I feel like we should be standing up for our rights and doing something. We need to let people in the public know what is going on in the sweatshops.

Hong Kong is my country. There I can do what I like. I can write letters. I can speak my mind. But here I do not have the language. Now if someone can help me speak my mind, of course I'm going to do it.

The Lucky Sewing Company workers got so angry when the boss's daughter called the police on us because we wanted our back pay. They are the ones that owed us money, but they still used the police to kick us out! Can you believe it? We tried to tell the police how unfairly we had been treated so they wrote down the address of the Department of Labor and drew a kind of map for us.

First we went to Oakland Chinese Community Council [OCCC] for help. Someone at OCCC said they could help us file a complaint with the Department of Labor, but after that we came to AIWA. I was a member of AIWA and had attended the Leadership Development Program class about the garment industry. I'll never forget the workshop where we talked about the distribution of profits. That discussion gave me a very strong impression of AIWA. So it rang a bell when we ran into problems at Lucky Sewing Company.

Our case plays a very important role in the fight against sweatshops. It is setting a precedent for other workers to step forward and bring forth their grievances. It is still very difficult to get people together, especially people who do not know each other. Even people who are very good friends get scared to criticize the bosses' actions. They worry about themselves and their own families and are afraid to come out to protest. I think the campaign has already affected the contractors. They are not treating workers as harshly as before. They know they'd better behave themselves. For example, my boss tried to change the shop to paying by piece rates, but was hesitant to do so because of me, since he knows I am involved in the [Garment Workers Justice] Campaign.

I think AIWA can improve its work by organizing a wide variety of activities to bring more people in. Let the people talk about their broad experiences. Let them pinpoint where the problems are, and from there, how to organize themselves to solve these problems.

People have criticized me for sticking my neck out like this. This is the Asian mindset. But my sons and my husband believe that I am doing the right thing. They agree with me. (laughs) Perhaps my husband would even push harder because we share similar ways of thinking.

—Oakland, May 17, 1994

Oi Kwan "Annie" Lai

Garment Worker, Campaigner against DKNY

I was born in Hong Kong in 1953. My dad drove one of those passenger vans that carry six to eight people, like a small bus. My mom worked in a factory making packaging for radio batteries. I'm the oldest of five children; another came to the US in 1998.

My parents were born in Dai Luck, Pun Yu, Guangdong province. I'm not sure when they moved to Hong Kong, but they were long time residents, got married in Hong Kong, and we were all born there. We lived in Kowloon, near the airport. We always saw the airplanes flying overhead.

I went to school until fifth grade. I started working when I was 12 in toys. First I made packaging for toys and also sewed samples. I've worked in the garment industry for more than 20 years. The factories in Hong Kong mostly get business from American, Canadian, or European companies; at my factory we got work from all three. I did a lot of sample sewing. We made underwear and stuff. The label was pretty well known.

I gave all my salary to my parents because our family was very poor. At that time in Hong Kong we had to pay money to go to school. [Her eyes water.] I couldn't study long because my mom didn't have the $8 a month it cost to go to school. *Mo chin* [no money]. So that's why I left early to start working. Because I was working it was better for all my brothers and sisters, and they were able to go until middle school. After that they started working, too.

Hong Kong factories are not as bad as New York; actually pretty good. For instance, it's not as crowded as here. Also the bosses aren't putting as much pressure on the workers like here, and when they had you work overtime, they paid you.

I started sewing when I was 17 or 18, in 1969 or 1970. I worked in the garment industry in Hong Kong until I immigrated to Canada in 1979. Then I sewed for a French company in Montreal. At that time it was easy to come to the US and apply for a green card. So that's how I ended up over here.

I started working in Chinatown garment factories right away.

I've taken samples home to work on and I've sewed in factories. When I first came over to Chinatown, I really didn't like it. In Canada the boss was already giving me $7 an hour (Canadian). He paid by the piece, but if you didn't sew fast enough, he would give you $7 anyway as the minimum. But I exceeded that so I could usually make about $8 an hour. Every year in the summer we got off two weeks vacation and also two at Christmas. Canada also has a five-day workweek. After coming over here, I thought about how life had been before in Canada. Oh, I really didn't like it here!

New York's Chinatown really kills you! When I first came to New York, a friend of a friend working in a Chinatown garment factory said that there was a job so I went. But it was really hard at first. In one week I made $150 to $160, much lower than what I was making in Canada. And you would go to work at nine in the morning and not get out until seven at night. The factories are dirty, really filthy.

A friend introduced me and my husband in 1982. We kind of went out for a year or so before getting married. My husband works as a driver, delivering goods. In Brooklyn there are factories that make tofu and he delivers it to stores. Our daughter Winnie was born in 1988; Jennifer, this one, was born in 1991. The whole time I've lived in New York, I've lived in Brooklyn.

I feel like these last few years have been the worst, the hardest. Because all these undocumented Fuk Chau people are coming, and they will just work day and night because they have to pay back the money they owe for their fares. The bosses especially exploit them. When we go to work at nine and leave at seven the boss is not all that happy that we're working a short number of hours. I see so many Fuk Chau people working until nine or ten o'clock at night. They still don't want to leave. So, the boss likes those undocumented workers more and doesn't like us because he knows they're so vulnerable. They're very young—some have left their children behind in China—and now we're older. We can't work those kind of long hours. We have families here. Even getting off at seven, by the time you get home it's eight-something.

Before in Midtown hardly anyone worked on Saturdays. You'd be afraid if you had to work on Saturday that someone might take your purse or something. But now these last six or seven years, Oh! there are so many Latino and Chinese workers up there. Everybody is competing for jobs. When I first started working in Midtown, sometimes the boss would really plead with us to come to work. Now they just say, "If you don't do it, it doesn't matter, I've got a lot of other people I can hire."

My East Points [factory] boss fired me in 1997 as an example to workers not to get calls at work—even if your kids get sick. I worked there six or seven years. But sometimes my kids, especially when they were smaller, would get fevers and stuff. My husband would call and ask about what to do, but they wouldn't let me take the call. One time my husband fainted but no one was supposed to call me. When my daughter got a high fever and the school said, "We have to call your mom," my daughter said, "No! Her boss is mean and will get mad about it." They tracked me down via my social security number and called.

But I also feel the boss did a lot of other things that weren't right. For instance, she would pressure us to keep our heads down. "Don't raise your head. From when you start until you finish your work, put your head down." One woman pulled her spine because of this. They locked the bathroom, too, and wouldn't let us use it. Also, in the summertime, the water fountain broke. They didn't get someone to fix the thing for two weeks even though it was so hot. Maybe they wouldn't let us drink water so then we wouldn't have to go to the bathroom at all!

One time when they laid off a worker, the person went to the labor department, sued, and won some of their money back. After that the boss came in and pressured all of us to say that we had accepted cash and forced us all to sign these papers. Everyone was afraid that the boss would get mad if they didn't sign, but no one knew what the paper said. But when the boss ordered them, everyone quickly signed. Because I don't speak English, I didn't know what the paper said and I didn't sign it. I felt that if it's not clear, I didn't want to sign it or one day I might run into a problem. Several dozens of people signed it, everyone else. They got all these foremen and people to come to my machine to try to pressure me. I said, "No

I want to take it home and look at it more before I sign it." And they said, "No! You can't. You can't take it home. We'll just tell you what it says. If you don't sign it, then you don't have to work here." So I felt like they were always using intimidation and all kinds of tactics to pressure and control us.

When I was first reinstated to the factory in November 1998, there was nothing unusual. It was like how we were before among the workers. People were friendly and asked how I had been. But then the next day on November 10th, the change was like night and day. No one paid any attention to me. As soon as they saw me they would avoid me. Ahhh! At lunch time everyone would eat away from me. It would just be me at one table by myself. And it wasn't just the Chinese; the Latinos all avoided me too. So I got the feeling that the big boss and the foremen were controlling everything because it didn't make sense that even the Latinos would be like this toward me.

They said they were closing the factory on December 31, 1998. I found out that the factory had opened again. On February 4, 1999, I went back to the factory to get my W-2 form at lunch time and saw all the rest of the workers. Everybody was working, all those people who were there on December 31st when the factory was closing. So I went to talk to the boss. I said, "Don't play with me!" She said, "Leave!"

I don't know how long they had been open; probably always. The boss has two company names. One was Couture, and one, Choe. They closed the Choe company. Couture continued to operate, but I don't know when they actually called the workers back. I kept this newspaper ad from February 3rd that said they were hiring people. After reading the newspaper, I went back on the 4th and discovered everyone was working there.

I've given my boss a lot of opportunities but she doesn't want to meet me halfway. She keeps putting me down, shoving me down, but I have to continue fighting. Some people got mad at me because the boss told them, "Oh, wages used to be paid half cash, half check. Now it's totally paid by check because of her." The boss doesn't want me to win because if I go back there, she can't commit any more illegal actions; if I lose, she can. This abusive sweatshop system is not right.

On January 4th I had gone to the union and told them that my boss had just closed the factory. The union people said, "Oh, there's nothing we can do about it. Because you're suing the boss and the manufacturer, DKNY, the manufacturer is mad at your boss and not giving them any work. So your boss had to close." The union was blaming me for suing! So I said, "My boss didn't pay for overtime so why shouldn't I be suing them? If they are closing down like that, isn't that directed at me?" The union asked, "Did you get the rest of the money they owe you yet?" I said no. They told me I'd better get a lawyer to go after it. How come every year we pay a couple hundred dollars dues but the union doesn't even help us? It just helps the bosses.

At first I didn't know to come to CSWA because I went to the Department of Labor to complain. This Chinese person was trying to help me get my overtime pay and took my case. After finding out that I'd gone to the Department of Labor, the boss gave me a 1099 Form for $6,000. My boss was going to use this 1099 Form to get back at me for suing, saying I'd have to pay a lot of taxes. I was afraid so I called Mr. Chun at the Department of Labor asking what should I do. He said, "Don't worry Mrs. Lai. You're a union worker. You are working in a union factory. You shouldn't get a 1099 Form. Your boss is doing an illegal thing."

Mr. Chun told me to go to the UNITE office. When I went to Local 22, the business agent said, "Right, you got cash. You're supposed to get this 1099 Form. In fact, you should pay taxes." I was really angry and upset. I asked if my boss wasn't the one at fault for giving me cash. I said, "Why aren't you saying anything about my boss doing anything wrong?" The union told me they couldn't do anything because the company was controlled by an "evil force."

I got really angry. So I called Mr. Chun at the Department of Labor again. Then he told me to go to CSWA and said, "They might ask you for a little money." But by then I was furious. I told him, "If I can afford it, I will pay." But since I started coming to CSWA in March or April 1998, they've never asked me for money. If this association did not exist, things would really be bad off. With a case like mine who would help us? Look at me, just one person fighting; it's not like a lot of power. I don't speak English. When I got the letter from the boss, I could have just stayed at home crying and saying, "I don't know where I can go. I'm lost." But if we have CSWA supporting and helping us we can do a lot.

After CSWA and NMASS sent letters to Donna Karan demanding that she take responsibility for the sweatshop conditions of her subcontractor, not only did she not take responsibility, she pulled out all her garments and took them someplace else, causing the factory to close. Seventy workers had no work. This company has such a big name, how can it have this kind of sweatshop factory? They sell clothing to rich people. I mean, I can't afford any of the clothes I make on my salary. It's more than $1,000 for a garment. It's not for poor people to wear. I was making $6.50 an hour. Why do we have to accept this kind of sweatshop system? I used to sew about 80 garments a week. I was careful in my work because they sell these garments for thousands of dollars. The Koreans got paid $7 an hour and Chinese workers less. Latinos did the cleaning, pressing, and hand work, and got the lowest wages.

So in May 1999 we had a press conference in front of the Donna Karan headquarters telling everyone what happened. After that, seven of the Latinas who used to work with me came out and joined our campaign. Together we held another press conference in front of DKNY in June. Since then many other garment workers, young women, and students have also supported us, and we picketed a new DKNY store in August. Other DKNY garment workers are facing similar conditions and coming forward. Then we had a big meeting in November with women workers and students where we talked about our case and how we need to fight back. We all picketed her store again. We are saying to Donna Karan that she has to take responsibility to reinstate all of us, pay the wages and damages we're owed, that all her clothes will be made in factories obeying the law, that 75 percent of her clothes be made locally, and that she say sorry to us for the treatment we suffered making her clothes.

I feel like I'm in the US now, but why is it such a bad system? Hong Kong is such a small place that you wouldn't have this kind of treatment. But *Meiguo* is such a big country that they have this process to control and intimidate workers. It's just outrageous! I just feel so angry. This time they really pressured me, pushed me to have to fight. Because the conditions in the factory and the way the boss and DKNY has treated us were so bad, I have felt terrible pressure. I hope we win this campaign so that other women see that we can fight and win.

My husband has supported me all along the way. But my mom is yelling at me. Why? Because the boss is putting pressure on our family to get back at me. My mom lives with us in Brooklyn. I can't worry about my mom. I feel like what I'm doing is right. If I were influenced by my mom's thinking I wouldn't go anywhere. [laughs] Ehhhh! My two daughters are really mad at the boss. They say, "Don't mess with our mom!"

—New York City, March 28, 1999, and April 2, 2000

Chinese and Latina workers, CSWA, and NMASS take their protest to a DKNY subcontracted shop on 8th Ave., New York City, November 29, 2000.
Photo by CSWA

1   National Mobilization Against Sweatshops, 1999b.

2   See Salaff, 1995; Asia Monitor Resource Center, 1998a; China Labour Education and Information Centre, 1995.

3   Kwong, Peter, 1987:151-154 on the 1982 strike by 20,000 New York Chinatown garment workers; Lam, 1976; Yung, 1986:290; interview with Bea Tam Dong and Harvey Dong, May 4, 1997, on the 1974 garment workers strike against the Great Chinese American (Jung Sai) Company, owned by Esprit de Corps and the Lee Mah electronic workers strike against Farinon; interview with Lora Jo Foo, April 11, 1997 on the Jung Sai garment workers strike and 1980 San Francisco hotel workers strike.

4   Interview with Wu Wan Mei, March 26, 1999.

5   Borchard, 1995:117-122.

6   Borchard, 1995:122.

7   *Chinese Women Investigation,* cited in Borchard, 1995:121.

8   Schädler, 1995:128.

9   Hom, 1992a:173-191.

10   Salaff, 1995; Hook, 1996a; Hook, 1996b; Mei, 1984; and Solinger, 1999.

11   Interview with Linda To of Hong Kong Women Workers Association, March 15, 1996.

12   Interview with Wu Wan Mei, March 26, 1999.

13   Interview with Helen Wong, August 7, 1990.

14   Interview with "Lisa," March 30, 1999.

15   Bo Yee testimony, May 1, 1993. See AIWA, 1995a:6.

16   Kwan and Leung, 1998:191-241.

17   Salaff, 1995:xvi-xxiii.

18   Asian Migrant Centre, 1996b.

19   Committee for Asian Women, 1995b.

20   Lee, Ching Kwan, 1998; and Salaff, 1995:xvi-xxiii.

21   Tsang, 1994:125-43, cited in Salaff, 1995:xviii.

22   Solinger, 1999; and Spence, 1990:673-74.

23   Asia Monitor Resource Center, 1996.

24   Kwan and Leung, 1988:192.

25   China Labour Education & Information Centre, 1995:2-9. The Chinese government calls this labor reserve the "floating population." Kwan and Leung, 1998:203, 191-241.

26   Interview with Chan Wai Fun, June 25, 1990.

27   Interview with Lee Yin Wah, October 24, 1996.

28   Kwan and Leung, 1988:203.

29   Hing, 1993:36.

30   Hing, 1993:48. See also Yung, 1986 and 1995.

31   Compared to previous waves of Asian immigrant laborers, the higher income and educational levels of the more professional and wealthy strata of

newcomers and their children later gave rise to the "model minority" myth of pan-Asian upward mobility.

32 Kwong, Peter, 1987:5.

33 Hing, 1993:81.

34 Interview with Helen Wong, August 7, 1990.

35 Interview with Wu Wan Mei, March 26, 1999.

36 Interview with Jenny Chen, May 18, 1997.

37 Testimony of Lin Cai Fen, May 7, 1995, in Center for Women's Global Leadership, 1995.

38 Strand and Jones, 1985:28, cited in Hing, 1993:283.

39 Kwong, Peter, 1997:1-7.

40 Verhovek, 2000: A1.

41 See Kwong, Peter, 1997; also 1994a:25-29 and 1994b:422-425; Ying Chan, 1993:20; and Warren Hodge, 2000.

42 Interview with Peter Kwong, May 21, 1997.

43 For an example of the view of the Chinatown garment industry as an example of ethnic resiliency, see Zhou, 1992.

44 Interview with Jenny Chen, May 18, 1997.

45 Center for Economic and Social Rights, 1999:5.

46 Abeles, 1983:23-25; also see Kwong, Peter, 1987:30.

47 Center for Economic and Social Rights, 1999:5.

48 Bonacich and Appelbaum, 2000:171. Bonacich and Appelbaum argue that ethnic subcontractors, particularly Korean owners who employ mainly Latina/o workers, play the role of "middle minorities," buffering white and Jewish manufacturers and retailers from the Latina and Asian sweatshop workers toiling in post-Rodney King LA.

49 Bonacich and Appelbaum, 2000:181 and 218.

50 Angwin, 1996:C1.

51 Houston Chronicle Service, 1994:23A; Gerlin, 1994:B1.

52 See Bonacich and Appelbaum, 2000:184-187.

53 Sweatshop Watch, 2000:1-3.

54 Sweatshop Watch presentation at "Sweatshop Labor on the US Marianas Islands" Community Forum, February 3, 1999, UNITE office, San Francisco.

55 Bonacich and Appelbaum, 1994:177-181.

56 Interview with Helen Wong, August 7, 1990.

57 Interview with Jenny Chen, May 18, 1997.

58 Interview with Wu Wan Mei, March 26, 1999.

59 Interview with Oi Kwan "Annie" Lai, March 28, 1999.

60 Interview with "Lisa," March 30, 1999.

61 Testimony of Helen Wong at community hearings on health problems in Asian immigrant communities, April 20, 1990.

62 Interview with Amy Xie, March 29, 1999.

63 Interview with Lee Yin Wah, October 24, 1996 and March 29, 1999.

64 Interview with Amy Xie, March 29, 1999.

65 Interview with Lee Yin Wah, October 24, 1996.

66 Interview with Lee Yin Wah, March 29, 1999.

67 Interview with Jenny Chen, May 18, 1997.

68 Interview with "Lisa," March 30, 1999.

69 Asian Immigrant Women Advocates, 2000b.

70 Interview with Lee Yin Wah, March 29, 1999.

71 Chinese Staff and Workers Association, 2000.

72 National Mobilization Against Sweatshops, 1999a.

73 See the Center for Economic and Social Rights, 1999, for a detailed analysis of the specific violations of the workers' rights and the culpability of the manufacturer, subcontractor, government agencies, and UNITE.

74 Greenhouse, 2000. Asian American Legal Defense and Education Fund. 2000.

75 Amy Kwong, 1998.

76 Interview with Wu Wan Mei, March 26, 1999.

77 Interview with AIWA Workers Board members, including Lin Cai Fen, April 19, 1994.

Viola Casares and Petra Mata of Fuerza Unida and Geri Almanza of PODER demanding corporate responsibility at Levi's headquarters in San Francisco. Photo by Pamela Chiang (1998)

Chapter Two

¡La Mujer Luchando, El Mundo Transformando!

Mexican Immigrant Women Workers

At their *Día de Los Muertos* [Day of the Dead] celebration on November 1, 1994, *las mujeres* [the women] look gaunt but on a spiritual high. The women are members of Fuerza Unida, the organization they created with their own hands and hearts when Levi Strauss & Co. laid them off and ran away to Costa Rica in 1990. They have trekked all the way from San Antonio with sleeping bags to haunt Levi's plaza and corporate headquarters in San Francisco, California.

So that CEO Robert Haas will hear their cries for corporate responsibility loud and clear, the women shout at the tops of their lungs, *¡No tenemos hambre de comida; tenemos hambre de justicia!* [We're not hungry for food; we're hungry for justice!]. The women gently break their 21-day hunger strike savoring the miracle of *pan dulce* [sweet rolls] and steaming cups of coffee carted in by their many supporters. Their *comadre* [girlfriend] Puerto Rican activist Luz Guerra calls these *huelgistas de hambre* [hunger strikers] *las nuevas revolucionarias* [the new revolutionaries] who picked up where Emiliano Zapata, Pancho Villa, the *soldaderas* and *adelitas* [women soldiers and companions] of the 1910 Mexican Revolution left off.

Throwing back their heads in laughter, they clap and tap their feet as Chicano *poeta/músico/activista* Arnoldo García serenades them with his new rendition of a traditional Mexican song:

La Fuerza Unida

En los frentes de liberación
de este pueblo de trabajadores
Existen mujeres fuertes y valientes
Existen mujeres que saben luchar

En ciudades y campos se forman
dando fuerza y visión a los pueblos
Son trabajadoras radientes de luchas
Son trabajadoras de justicia y paz

Su cultura y trabajo respeten
Con la fuerza de su dignidad
Son las costureras pidiendo justicia
Son las costureras que saben luchar

Son las desplazadas de la Levis
Luchadoras del gran movimiento
Son las costureras de la Fuerza Unida
Son las costureras de liberación[1]

As Mexico's former dictator Porfirio Díaz lamented, "Poor little Mexico, so far from God, so close to the United States."[2] Mexico's fateful proximity to the developing "Colossus of the North"[3] has long shaped the destiny of its working people and the national, race, and class formation of the United States. Ever since the United States annexed half of Mexico's territory by seizing Texas in 1836 and launching the Mexican-American War (1845-1848), Mexican workers have served as a giant labor reserve and shock absorber for the bumps and potholes of US economic development.[4] Sharing a 2,000-mile border with its powerful neighbor to the north, Mexico is the homeland of an estimated 40 percent of US immigrants.[5] Migration to the United States also serves as a safety net for Mexico's economic and political system, yielding remittances of at least $6 billion a year, one of the largest sources of Mexico's foreign exchange, along with the oil, tourism, and maquiladora industries.[6]

Chicana labor historian Vicki Ruiz says that Mexicanas crossed the border as "farm worker mothers, railroad wives, and miners' daughters" to join male relatives recruited by those burgeoning industries during the spate of post-Civil War US industrial expansion.[7] Especially since the 1920s, Mexican immigrant women and US-born Chicanas have emerged as the backbone of many of the lowest-paying, most back-breaking jobs in Texas, California, New Mexico, Colorado, Arizona, and Illinois, such as the agribusiness, cannery, pecan shelling, food processing, garment, and domestic service industries. Mexicana labor migration has also increased to the US Northwest, Midwest, East, and South.[8] By the end of 1996 there were 9.6 million Latinas in the United States, including 5.7 million women of Mexican origin, 1.1 million Puerto Rican women, 485,000 Cuban women, and another 2.3 million women of Latin American descent.[9] Latinas continue to have the highest concentrations of workers in "blue collar" operative jobs and the lowest in management and professions among all races of women.[10]

The rise in export-oriented production for transnational corporations along the US-Mexico border since the 1960s and other aspects of economic restructuring have accelerated Mexicanas internal and cross-border labor migration. Many of today's *nuevas revolucionarias* started working on the global assembly line as young women in northern Mexico for foreign transnational corporations. Some women worked on the US side as "commuters" before they moved across the border with their families. Their stories reveal the length, complexity, and interpenetration of the US and Mexican economies, labor markets, histories, cultures, and race relations. The women talk about the devastating impact of globalization, including massive layoffs and the spread of sweatshops on both sides of the border. *Las mujeres* recount what drove them to join and lead movements for economic, racial, and gender justice, as well as the challenges they faced within their families and communities to assert their basic human rights. The women featured in this chapter play leadership roles in La Mujer Obrera [The Woman Worker] in El Paso, Texas, Fuerza Unida [United Force] in San Antonio, Texas, and the Thai and Latino Workers Organizing Committee of the Retailers Accountability Campaign in Los Angeles, California.

Growing up Female and Poor

Mexican women and girls were traditionally expected to do all the cooking, cleaning, and serving for their husbands, brothers, and sons. For girls from poor families, shouldering these domestic responsibilities proved doubly difficult because they also performed farm, sweatshop, or domestic service work simultaneously. Refugio "Cuca" Arrieta, the only daughter of farm worker parents in Ciudad Jiménes, Chihuahua, reluctantly left school early:

I stayed home because I had to take care of my younger brothers. I went to school and finished no more than the first, second, and third grade. At the nearby *ranchitos* [little farms] we learned how to read and write. Before starting school I had already learned how to read and write. I taught myself.[11]

Petra Mata, a former seamstress for Levi's whose mother died shortly after childbirth, recalls the heavy housework she did as the only daughter:

Aiyeee, let me tell you! It was very hard. In those times in Mexico, I was raised with the ideal that you have to learn to do everything—cook, make tortillas, wash your clothes, and clean the house—just the way they wanted you to. My grandparents were very strict. I always had to ask their permission and then let them tell me what to do. I was not a free woman. Life was hard for me. I didn't have much of a childhood; I started working when I was 12 or 13 years old.[12]

Neoliberalism and Creeping Maquiladorization

These women came of age during a period of major change in the relationship between the Mexican and US economies. Like Puerto Rico, Hong Kong, South Korea, Taiwan, Malaysia, Singapore, and the Philippines, northern Mexico served as one of the first stations of the global assembly line tapping young women's labor. In 1965 the Mexican government initiated the Border Industrialization Program (BIP) that set up export plants, called maquiladoras or maquilas, which were either the direct subsidiaries or subcontractors of transnational corporations. Mexican government incentives to US and other foreign investors included low wages and high productivity; infrastructure; proximity to US markets, facilities, and lifestyles; tariff loopholes; and pliant, pro-government unions.[13]

Many of the women worked in electronics and garment maquiladoras before crossing the border to work in US plants. María Antonia Flores describes her co-workers in the Juárez electronics plant where she worked as *puras jovenas* [all young women], while the supervisors were *puros varones* [all male]. Describing her quarter-century-long sewing career in Mexico, Celeste Jiménez ticks off the names of famous US manufacturers who hopped over the border to take advantage of cheap wages:

> I sewed for twenty-four years when I lived in Chihuahua in big name factories like Billy the Kid, Levi Strauss, and Lee maquiladoras. Everyone was down there. Here a company might sell under the brand name of Lee; there in Mexico it would be called Blanca García.[14]

Many of the women worked in the maquilas because of the unstable economic status of male family members—where men are either absent, unemployed, or earning well below the "family wage," i.e., the wage sufficient to support a family. Marta Martínez, a laid-off Levi's worker first learned to sew from her mom:

> I was born in Mexico City in 1959. My mom was a seamstress who ran a little workshop about this size. [She points to Fuerza Unida's small sewing coop production area.] Once in a while she was able to get a contract and work for a maquiladora. Dad worked as a *campesino* [farm worker]. I had four sisters and three brothers. I'm in the middle. But I was able to finish 12 years of school so I got to be a teacher…. In 1983, I worked for the Castro company on this side, making baby clothes. It wasn't hard to learn. I already knew from my mom how to use an industrial machine.[15]

Transnational exploitation of women's labor was part of a broader set of policies that critical opposition movements in the Third World have dubbed "neoliberalism," i.e., the new version of the British Liberal Party's program of laissez faire capitalism espoused by the rising European and US colonial powers during the late 18th and 19th centuries. The Western powers, Japan, and international financial institutions like the World Bank and International Monetary Fund have aggressively promoted neoliberal policies since the 1970s.[16] Mexico served as an early testing ground for such standard neoliberal policies as erection of free trade zones; commercialization of agriculture; currency devaluation; deregulation; privatization; outsourcing; cuts in wages and social programs; suppression of workers', women's, and indigenous people's rights; free trade; militarization; and promotion of neoconservative ideology.

Neoliberalism intersects with gender and national oppression. Third World women constitute the majority of migrants seeking jobs as maids, vendors, maquila operatives, and service industry workers. Women also pay the highest price for cuts in education, health and housing programs, and food and energy subsidies and increases in their unpaid labor.[17]

The human costs of Mexico's neoliberal program and extended economic crisis are evident in the 60 percent drop in real minimum wages between 1982 and 1988 and the 30 percent drop in internal consumption of basic grains during the 1980s.[18] In 1986, some 62 percent of the economically active population of Mexico earned sub-minimum wages.[19] In 1994, the World Bank estimated that 38 percent of the total population of Mexico lived in absolute poverty. Two out of five households had no water supply, three out of five had no drainage, and one in three had no electricity.[20]

The deepening of the economic crisis in Mexico, especially under the International Monetary Fund's pressure to devaluate the peso in 1976, 1982, and 1994, forced many women to work in both the formal and informal economy to survive and meet their childrearing and household responsibilities.[21] María Antonia Flores was forced to work two jobs after her husband abandoned the family, leaving her with three children to support. She had no choice but to leave her children home alone, *solitos,* to look after themselves. Refugio Arrieta straddled the formal and informal economy because her job in an auto parts assembly maquiladora failed to bring in sufficient income. To compensate for the shortfall, she worked longer hours at her maquila job and "moonlighted" elsewhere:

> We made chassis for cars and for the headlights. I worked lots! I

worked 12 hours more or less because they paid us so little that if you worked more, you got more money. I did this because the schools in Mexico don't provide everything. You have to buy the books, notebooks, *todos, todos* [everything]. And I had five kids. It's very expensive. I also worked out of my house and sold ceramics. I did many things to get more money for my kids.[22]

In the three decades following its humble beginnings in the mid-1960s, the maquila sector swelled to more than 2,000 plants employing an estimated 776,000 people, over 10 percent of Mexico's labor force.[23] In 1985, maquiladoras overtook tourism as the largest source of foreign exchange. In 1996, this sector trailed only petroleum-related industries in economic importance and accounted for over US$29 billion in export earnings annually.[24] The maquila system has also penetrated the interior of the country, as in the case of Guadalajara's electronics assembly industry and Tehuacán's jeans production zones.[25] Although the proportion of male maquila workers has increased since 1983, especially in auto-transport equipment assembly, almost 70 percent of the workers continue to be women.[26]

As part of a delegation of labor and human rights activists, this author met some of Mexico's newest proletarians—young indigenous women migrant workers from the Sierra Negra to Tehuacán, a town famous for its refreshing mineral water springs in the state of Puebla, just southeast of Mexico City. Standing packed like cattle in the back of the trucks each morning the women headed for jobs sewing for name brand manufacturers like Guess?, VF Corporation (producing Lee brand clothing), The GAP, Sun Apparel (producing brands such as Polo, Arizona, and Express), Cherokee, Ditto Apparel of California, Levi's, and others. The workers told US delegation members that their wages averaged US$30 to $50 a week for 12-hour work days, six days a week. Some workers reported having to do *veladas* [all-nighters] once or twice a week. Employees often stayed longer without pay if they did not finish high production goals.

Girls as young as 12 and 13 worked in the factories. Workers were searched when they left for lunch and again at the end of the day to check that they weren't stealing materials. Women were routinely given urine tests when hired and those found to be pregnant were promptly fired, in violation of Mexican labor law. Although the workers had organized an independent union several years earlier, Tehuacán's Human Rights Commission members told us that it had collapsed after one of its leaders was assassinated.[27]

Carmen Valadez and Reyna Montero, long-time activists in the women's and social justice movements, helped found Casa de La Mujer Factor X in 1977, a workers' center in Tijuana that organizes around women's workplace, reproductive, and health rights, and against domestic violence. Valadez and Montero say that the low wages and dangerous working conditions characteristic of the maquiladoras on the Mexico-US border are being "extended to all areas of the country and to Central America and the Caribbean. NAFTA represents nothing but the 'maquiladorization' of the region."[28]

Elizabeth "Beti" Robles Ortega, who began working in the maquilas at the age of fourteen and was blacklisted after participating in independent union organizing drives on Mexico's northern border, now works as an organizer for the Servicio, Desarrollo y Paz, AC (SEDEPAC) [Service, Development and Peace organization]. Robles described the erosion of workers rights and women's health under NAFTA:

> NAFTA has led to an increase in the workforce, as foreign industry has grown. They are reforming labor laws and our constitution to favor even more foreign investment, which is unfair against our labor rights. For example, they are now trying to take away from us free organization which was guaranteed by Mexican law. Because foreign capital is investing in Mexico and is dominating, we must have guarantees. The government is just there with its hands held out; it's always had them out but now even more shamelessly.... Ecological problems are increasing. A majority of women are coming down with cancer—skin and breast cancer, leukemia, and lung and heart problems. There are daily deaths of worker women. You can see and feel the contamination of the water and the air. As soon as you arrive and start breathing the air in Acuña and Piedras Negras [border cities between the states of

Coahuila and Texas], you sense the heavy air, making you feel like vomiting.[29]

Like Casa de La Mujer Factor X in Tijuana, and the women workers' centers and cooperatives whose work the Frente Auténtico del Trabajo (FAT) has prioritized especially since 1992, SEDEPAC also participates in national networks of Mexican women workers such as the Red de Trabajadores en Las Maquilas, which meets annually in different cities in the northern border region, as well as in binational networks like the Southwest Network for Environmental and Economic Justice.[30]

Maquiladorization Accelerates Migration

Many of the Mexicanas migrated to the United States in a two-stage migration process, similar to many of the Asian women workers. Migration to the northern border region offered women proximity to family members working on the other side, and after the initiation of the Border Industrialization Program in 1965, potential employment opportunities as well. Patricia Fernández-Kelly has suggested that by recruiting mainly young female workers, the border maquiladora program ended up drawing even more migrants to the border, yet failed to reduce male farm workers' unemployment caused by termination of the Bracero Program as the Mexican government had originally planned. Many migrants to the northern border eventually cross into the United States.[31]

For example, La Mujer Obrera organizer Irma Montoya Barajas was born in the central Mexican state of Aguascalientes. At age ten she moved with her parents to Juárez in northern Mexico, where her father found work as a carpenter while her mother took care of her nine brothers and sisters. Similarly María Antonia Flores was born in the central state of Zacatecas, but moved with her family to Juárez when she was eight years old. There her parents found odd jobs working in maquilas, restaurants, and as food vendors. Petra Mata of Fuerza Unida traces her roots to Nuevo Laredo, Tamaulipas, across from Laredo, Texas. But she and her parents were actually born in the little village of Bustamante, Nuevo León. They moved when they could no longer survive through farming, and Petra's grandfather and father, like many Mexican and Chinese immigrant men, got jobs working for the railroad. Over time Mexican migration networks have become more regionally diverse. María Antonia Flores explains that while many workers migrate from areas adjacent to the border:

> People come here from almost all of the states in the south of Mexico to find work due to the economic problems throughout the nation and precisely because of the pull of all the maquiladoras located on the border. So every day people arrive at the maquilas from the south looking for work and trying to better their struggle to survive. But they find *nada, nada* [nothing]. Around here many people come from Coahuila, Durango, Zacatecas, and Chihuahua, but over there in Tijuana, there are also people from Chiapas, Oaxaca, San Luis Potosí, that is to say almost all of the states.[32]

Alberta "Beti" Cariño Trujillo, a dedicated organizer for the human rights commission in Tehuacán, Puebla, originally comes from the southern coastal state of Oaxaca. With her mother and siblings, Cariño struggled to survive in Oaxaca while her father worked as a migrant laborer picking oranges up in California.

Cariño is anxious to make contact with US immigrant and workers' rights groups to develop an information network. She and her co-workers teach a night school for garment workers and their children in Tehuacán. The human rights workers are concentrating on the fight for better wages and working conditions locally, and against toxic-waste dumping and water contamination by the maquilas, lack of childcare and educational opportunities, domestic and street violence, unwanted pregnancies, and high stress levels, especially among single mothers. They also want to provide accurate information about what life is like for immigrant workers in the United States to dispel any illusions potential migrants might have.[33]

Indeed the information "grapevine" extends into the farthest corners of Mexico. In the *colonia* [newly built, poorly served, suburban settlement] of Nezahuacoyotl on the outskirts of Mexico City, members of a local poor women's group shared their knowledge of the United States during a visit from international participants of a

November 1989 garment workers' conference in Mexico City. Many of the women were themselves internal migrants to the world's largest city and they proudly told conference delegates of a free breakfast and milk program they developed so that poor children would not go to school on empty stomachs.

A Chicana activist's description of her work with immigrants in Los Angeles, unleashed an animated exchange with the Mexicana *colonia* organizers. "Chicago is a bad place for Mexican workers." "Don't go to Fresno, they already have too many Mexicans; you can't find a job anymore." "Orange County is very conservative and does not like Mexicans." "Go to Washington to pick apples. My cousin got a job there, and she likes it so much, she's going to send for her two daughters."[34] Perhaps some of such Mexicana organizers contributed their experience to the United Farm Workers Union efforts in the 1990s to organize Mexican immigrants in Washington's apple orchards. [35]

When the Border Was Just a Bridge between Neighborhoods

The wide variety in the immigration and citizenship status of the women and their family members reflects the permeability of a border that workers of Mexican descent have criss-crossed since US annexation in 1848. After centuries of relatively free movement within the region, only in 1924 did the US government create the Border Patrol and the notion of the "illegal alien," thus transforming Mexican workers into potential fugitives of the law unless they could secure official permits. Yet employers escaped responsibility and often used the fear of deportation to lower the wages of undocumented workers.[36]

The period from World War I until the Great Depression marked the first big wave of migration when the US government launched a contract-labor program for male migrant workers, the predecessor of the Bracero Program.[37] Mexican government recruitment efforts initially targeted men from the central western states of Michoacán, Jalísco, and Guanajuato. These workers served as the links of migration chains stretching between rural Mexican communities to specific US farms and towns.[38] Over time, tributaries from all the Mexican states contributed to the flow of Mexican workers across the border.

The elder relatives of many of the women interviewed for this book had worked in the United States, especially as farm workers, railroad workers, and miners. Some had been born in the United States or had become US citizens at other times in their lives, yet continued to migrate across the border in both directions. For example, Celeste Jiménez was born in the northern state of Chihuahua in 1939. Yet she explains:

> My father was born in Candelario, Texas, and my mom in Sierra Blanca. I'm 100 percent Mexican. My father worked raising cattle and my mom was a housewife. There were ten children, eight girls and two boys. I was born in Mexico. I'm the third oldest among the kids. My dad was a US citizen. My mom was a Mexican citizen. She was born in California but lived in Chihuahua most of her life. My mom's parents came here [to the US] in 1942. In 1964, my mom and dad came here too, but they didn't work anymore because they were getting too old. In 1982, I came here directly from Chihuahua. I'm a permanent legal resident.[39]

Similarly María del Carmen Domínguez describes the peripatetic wanderings of her farm worker father and how her mother moved closer to the border, anchoring the family:

> My father was born in California and lived and worked in Mexico many, many years. He also worked in El Paso, Texas and traveled to Los Angeles to work in the fields with machines and doing other jobs. My mother was born in Chihuahua, Mexico. She bore and raised four children. She stayed in Ciudad Juárez most of her life.[40]

Although Carmen "Chitlan" Ibarra Lopéz was born in Chihuahua where her father worked as a miner and her mother as a homemaker, she traces her cross-border roots to her grandparents' generation:

> I became a naturalized US citizen through my mother because my mother was born in the US. She was born in the US but she went

back to live in Mexico. What I heard was that during the Mexican Revolution [1910-1920] my grandparents came to live in California. They went to Wasco. They were farm workers. They picked cotton. My mother and her brothers and sisters were born in Wasco. Me and my sister lived with one of mom's sisters for a while.[41]

Following the trail of Mexican migrant chili workers, long-time Juárez residents Alicia and Carlos Marentes packed up their belongings and crossed the international bridge separating Juárez and El Paso in 1971. After serving a stint in the Texas Farm Workers Union, they helped found the Border Agricultural Workers Union in El Paso in 1984. After a decade of struggle, the union opened a beautiful center in 1995. This shelter acts as an oasis for chili workers who are hired through a humiliating human auction system to toil 12-hour days in Texas and New Mexico under a haze of toxic pesticides at temperatures that alternate between scorching and freezing. Women and undocumented workers get paid the lowest of the low, averaging a scant $5,300 a year, while even male workers with documents earn only $6,000.

Alicia coordinates classes where women learn to make handicrafts that they can sell during the dead season when they can find no work in the fields. Her friendly face clouds with sadness as she reminisces, "So many of the campesinos Carlos and I started working with back in 1980 have already passed away because of their hard lives. We have lost whole generations of farm workers." Carlos says that workers must become visible within the broader society if they are to improve their lives. Yet the anti-immigrant backlash is dehumanizing and criminalizing these workers. He shakes his head saying, "I remember when the border was nothing more than a bridge you crossed from a poor neighborhood to a richer one. That was before they started enacting all the anti-immigration legislation, rounding up immigrants, and militarizing the border."[42]

Ironically, and some insist intentionally, cross-border movement of people is increasingly restricted precisely during an unprecedented flow of capital, trade, goods, services, information, and culture, especially since the enactment of the North American Free

Trade Agreement (NAFTA) in 1994. According to immigrant rights and environmental justice activist Arnoldo García, NAFTA has proven a total disaster for Mexican workers, farmers, and small business people and spurred more migration:

> During NAFTA's first year and a half, the US trade deficit with Mexico grew by a whopping $4 billion and some 80,000 US jobs were lost. Mexican workers' wages declined 40 to 50 percent, ravaging their buying power. While the cost of living has risen by 80 percent in Mexico, salaries only increased by a mere 30 percent. Mexico's inflation rate runs over 51 percent; 2.3 million Mexican people have lost jobs and the peso has been severely devalued—from 3.1 pesos to the dollar in January 1994 to 7.6 pesos in March 1996. Over 20,000 small and medium businesses have gone belly-up in the face of increased multinational competition. And NAFTA's much touted labor and environmental side agreements have proven to be weak and ineffective.[43]

The Clinton administration doubled the budget of the INS after enacting NAFTA. The 1996 "Illegal Immigration Reform and Immigrant Responsibility Act" then mandated hiring another thousand border patrol agents. According to the Urban Institute, only four out of ten individuals who are in the US illegally crossed the southern border while the other six entered with legal visas as visitors, students, or temporary employees who failed to leave when their visas expired. These immigrants have documents and have been in contact with the INS. Only about one-third of the undocumented population is from Mexico. Yet 85 percent of all the resources of the INS, including the Border Patrol, are trained on the border with Mexico—reflecting both racist backlash against Mexican workers and the INS's evidently unquenchable thirst for money and military hardware.[44]

Mexico's extended economic crises prompted a major demographic shakeup in migration to the United States. These new stresses forced workers from large industrial urban centers without previous traditions of US migration; more people from the urban and middle classes; and more women, children, and elderly people to risk crossing the border. Political scientist and immigration expert

Wayne Cornelius dubbed this new, more heterogeneous pool of migrants *los migrantes de la crisis.*[45] Commenting on the utility of the border to politicians and employers, La Mujer Obrera organizer Carmen Ibarra Lopéz reflects:

> It's very hard for us as Mexican workers to understand the line on the border. I think that's why nobody has really, really put attention on the border's workers because it's a very different situation. It's like another world when you come through El Paso. I think the kinds of problems we are seeing workers come in with are not just because of the lack of good opportunities, but also because of a lot of discrimination. When I say discrimination, it's because we have a lot of members who under the amnesty law have a perfect right to come to the US and become citizens.[46]

Feminization of Migration

Women do not always migrate or stay home based on male family members' unchallenged decisions, but sometimes play the principal role in initiating migration. In her insightful study of the immigration of undocumented Mexican workers, sociology professor Pierrette Hondagneu-Sotelo warns that contrary to popular stereotypes, extensive research on Chicano and US-based Mexican families suggests that not all families are characterized by uniformly extreme patriarchy. Although sexism persists, she says that urbanization and women's growing role as income earners have begun to erode male dominance to varying degrees, and that traditional social relations and cultural resources neither disappear nor stay the same but are being constantly reshaped through the processes of migration and resettlement.[47]

Indeed, women made decisions to cross the border under a variety of circumstances, including invitations from their partners, other relatives, and friends. Some initiated the move themselves. For example María del Carmen Domínguez decided to move from Juárez to El Paso because she got tired of commuting to work:

> I came to El Paso in 1972 because I needed to work to support my family. At that time I had two children. Eight years later I had another child that is my baby right now who's 18 years old. I came

to work in the factories. I was 15 years old when I was pregnant
with my first boy and I got married when I was 17, almost 18 years
old. I met my husband through friends and the family. He worked
in the construction of houses and putting up fences. When I was
living in Juárez, I worked for two years in El Paso, crossing the
bridges everyday from Mexico. That was too hard so we decided
to come to live in El Paso and I stayed here. During the time I was
crossing the bridges, I was coming to work in a garment factory.[48]

Petra Mata also began working in the United States as a
cross-border commuter. She started working as a maid when she
was 12 or 13 years old after the tragic death of her mother and subsequent abandonment by her father. Although she worked hard and
scrubbed floors on her hands and knees, she only made $10 a week.
She recalls, "During the five years I worked for the same family, the
highest pay I ever got was $16 a week." Later Petra moved to the
United States permanently after she got married. She and her husband took up their friends' invitation to come, first as undocumented immigrants. Later Petra and her husband got US citizenship
to "have a voice, a right to vote."[49]

Lucrecia Tamayo, a garment worker and leader in the Thai and
Latino Workers Organizing Committee of the Retailer Accountability Campaign decided to make the big move from Acapulco,
Guerrero to Los Angeles after her marriage failed. During her "stop-
over" in Tijuana, that famous "travelers advisory and transit center,"
she secured the means to make the crossing and picked up information on possible job leads in Los Angeles, the metropolis with the
second largest Mexican population in the world, after Mexico City.
Lucrecia relied on a female relative, the well-developed migrant "underground railroad," and a waiting job market:

> I got married in Mexico, but the person I married was treating me
> bad, so I moved here 15 years ago in 1982. I came by myself.
> (laughs) I came by *el cerro* [through the mountains], with a coyote.
> Oh, it was scary! There were so many people, I was in the front
> with the driver, and over there, a mountain of people. And the
> driver was very nervous about running into immigration. I only
> had one sister who was living here.
>
> I came to the United States because after [my former hus-

band] left, I had a little girl to take care of. It wasn't my parents' obligation to raise her. So I had to find a new life. I came straight to Los Angeles. I lived with my sister for about a year. About six months after coming here, I started working in garment. When I was in Tijuana I heard about this kind of job by word of mouth. The people who came back to Mexico told us all about how life is here, about the kinds of work you can get. If you don't know about it, they teach you.[50]

Working *al Otro Lado* [on the Other Side]

Until recently women who crossed the border were frequently able to land jobs in *El Norte* [the North], often performing work similar to what they had done in Mexico. Arriving in such well-established Mexican immigrant communities as El Paso, San Antonio, and Los Angeles, the women found jobs fairly quickly, in some cases even before they settled permanently in the United States. They heard about work through family members, friends, and neighbors. Women changed jobs as they got adjusted to US working conditions and "learned the ropes."

After moving from Juárez to El Paso with her husband, Irma Montoya of La Mujer Obrera got a job working as an electronics assembler and inspector at a plant that made thermometers:

My cousin's husband told me about the job. I worked there from 1987 until they laid us off in 1995. I made good money there, $6.30 an hour and the working conditions were good, too. But in 1995 they shut us down and moved to Mexico. There were about 400 of us who lost our jobs. My husband lost his job after working for 20 years making Tony Lamas boots. Now he can only find work as a janitor.[51]

María del Carmen Domínguez heard about jobs through the grapevine. After commuting from Juárez, she changed to better jobs as she gained more experience and learned what was available:

I worked for 15 years in garment factories. The first one was Rudy's Sportswear where I worked for almost five years. I worked for one year at Emily Joe and almost nine years at CMT Industries as a seamstress.

My friends told me about the job in the first factory. I think I
got paid minimum wage there. In the last one I got paid more,
sometimes up to $5.50 or $6 an hour because it was by the quota.
At the other factories I was paid by the hour. I didn't get paid for
overtime. In the last factory, at CMT, we got some benefits, like
vacations and some holidays.

The first shop I worked at was so small. It expanded, but
then they had a problem about wages and their contracts and it
went bankrupt. The second one was a small factory, but it was too
ugly! I didn't like it, so I quit. (laughs).[52]

Tina Mendoza of Fuerza Unida started working in Mexico
when she was 16 years old as a secretary. After she came to the
United States, it took her some time to adjust and find the right job:

At first I did not like it here. I come from a family that is very close
so I felt really alone here. After I made friends I got used to the
life here. First I got a job working with chemicals that they put on
animals [insecticides] for about two years. After that I got a job
working as a cook frying chicken. Then I got a job at a
maquiladora factory. After that I started working at Levi's. I
stayed for eight years until they laid us off.[53]

Like many US-born Chicanas who work in low-waged industries alongside Mexican immigrant women,[54] Viola Casares, a
third-generation Chicana, started out doing farm work. Her father
had picked cotton in Lubbock, Texas, and worked in Arizona. Over
her husband's objections, she eventually landed a sewing job:

In a year [after getting married at 18] I got pregnant, then had my
first daughter Sandra. After six months, I went back to work in
the fields. We went to Michigan and picked strawberries and to-
matoes. When I was pregnant I used to get morning sickness at
my job packing onions.... My husband was real macho and jealous and would not let me work. I was supposed to stay home. The
kids were grown and going to school.... Because of his jealousy I
stayed home for a while. But the children really needed extra
things....

I [started] work[ing] for Farah making pants for a couple of
months. Then it was the same thing again with my husband. He
[began] harassing me until I quit. But I really needed to work. He

had started drinking. I began working at Levi's in 1980. I thought I was finally going to have a secure job. I told myself that I had to work and that I was not going to let him stop me again. With work I could make a better home and get things for the kids.... At Levi's I thought it would be okay, that I would be able to work and support us until I could retire some time. But all of a sudden we lost our jobs. I was so worried, "Wow, what are we going to do?" It's so hard being a single mother.[55]

Wages, working conditions, and benefits tended to be better at the larger factories than the smaller shops. For example, even though the Farah Manufacturing Company in El Paso was the target of a major struggle and national boycott by the Amalgamated Clothing and Textile Workers Union (1972-1974), as a large factory of some 4,000 workers, wages and working conditions were better than what women had experienced in Mexico or in smaller US shops.[56] Carmen Ibarra López learned about job openings at Farah through her younger sister.

It was good pay at the time. The minimum wage I think was $1.60 an hour. I got paid by the hour. We worked in very good conditions especially because the Farah on Gateway was in a new building.

I was there when the strike began. I just remember I didn't pay too much attention. First of all, in Mexico everything was different. I just remember one day at noon at lunch time I saw the workers walking out. And I was trying to find out about it and asked "What's going on?" But we didn't have too much information about it even though I worked inside. Probably they had a workers' or union committee to lead the strike, but I don't know. That's why it's not until now that I realized how unions work. I think it was just because the unions select a few workers, but they don't give out as much information as other organizations do, like La Mujer Obrera does. Yes, that is what you need, a lot of information.[57]

Despite low wages and less than optimal working conditions, many of the women expressed satisfaction with being able to work outside their homes and contribute to their family's well-being. They were proud of their skills and job performance and enjoyed the friendships and camaraderie they developed with their co-workers. Refugio Arrieta worked in a variety of restaurants and garment factories in El Paso:

> The garment factories were small, maybe about 100 people. It's small to me. I worked at Tex-Mex International. They made jeans. I worked as a seamstress, an operator. They paid us the minimum by the hour. Sometimes we worked overtime. There were no benefits there. Sometimes I worked 40 hours a week, sometimes 50 hours when I put in overtime. At the last one it was 20 hours because that's how it was before they closed. I worked at Tex-Mex four years. We were all friends there. (laughs) It was like we were all schoolmates.[58]

María del Carmen Domínguez's close relations with co-workers deepened as they banded together to confront the boss on failure to pay holiday leave as promised:

> The CMT factory was large and busy. I was working very well. It was comfortable for me, and I liked it a lot. When I was working there I think there were about 250 workers. Right now they have maybe 1,000 workers. They sew garments like tuxedos. It's more skilled work. Devon was one of the labels. I don't remember the others. We also sewed vests. I think you get paid more money for sewing men's clothes.... I was the organizer in my area and we had ten women and I controlled it. (laughs). Yes, *ellas* [they] would say "I love you." And I would say, "I love you, too." We were all partners. Yeah. I love to help the people. And I would fight, fight, fight in CMT, every day. (laughs) Yes, that's a long time to fight![59]

Since she's now a highly skilled and vivacious organizer, one can easily imagine Petra Mata as a highly competent and outgoing worker before she lost her job at Levi's:

> I did the hard, more difficult operations, like sewing the pockets on the sides of the coat. For three and a half years I sewed this way before they put me on utility so I could do any operation. Then they made me a trainer to teach the new people. I liked working with the girls and helping out. Finally they made me a supervisor for eight years. I was very happy with my job because I got to work closely with my co-workers.[60]

NAFTA the SHAFTA

Like the Hong Kong and Korean workers who transnational corporations dumped during the second stage of globalization, hundreds of thousands of US manufacturing workers, many of them women of color, also found themselves out on the street as their jobs ran away to Mexico, Central America, the Caribbean, and Asia. After the Border Industrialization Program had begun in 1965, the Reagan administration launched the Caribbean Basin Initiative in 1983 during the height of US military adventures in Central America. US military intervention in and capital export to the region accelerated the migration of workers, including Salvadoran, Guatemalan, Honduran, Nicaraguan, Dominican, and Haitian women who subsequently found jobs working in the garment industry in Los Angeles, New York, and Miami.

Prior to the enactment of NAFTA in 1994, US-based companies utilized Item 807 of the US Tariff Code, which specified that tariffs applied only to the value-added portion of products assembled abroad. If US apparel firms cut their garments at home and had them sewn offshore, they only had to pay tariff on the labor value added by sewing—which could be very small, given the low wages of Third World women workers. Item 807 was principally used to exploit seamstresses in Mexico, Central America, and the Caribbean because of the region's proximity and the political clout the United States has exercised in the hemisphere since the days of the Monroe Doctrine. Thus, government trade policies effectively encouraged corporations to take jobs overseas to bolster US foreign policy objectives.[61] In 1960, 2 percent of apparel was imported; in 1980, 30 percent; and in 2000, 60 percent. Conversely the number of US manufacturing jobs plummeted. While apparel employment peaked in 1970 with 1,363,800 jobs, by 1999 the figure had fallen to 696,000.[62]

In 1990, Levi's, whose brand name jeans together with Coca-Cola and McDonald's hamburgers have become practically synonymous with the "American way of life" around the world, closed its San Antonio plant and moved to Costa Rica where workers earned in *a day* what the average San Antonio seamstress had made in *half an hour.* The San Antonio factory was Levi's largest US manufacturing facility at the time. Overnight some 1,150 mainly Mexican-American women suddenly lost their jobs. Fuerza Unida, the fight back organization the laid-off San Antonio workers founded in 1990, asserts that "we were early victims of NAFTA." With direct experience in the consequences of "free trade" policies, Fuerza Unida actively organized against the passage of NAFTA, sporting "AFTA NAFTA the SHAFTA!" and "Levi's, button your fly, your greed is showing!" picket signs. Between 1981 and 1990 the company had already closed 58 plants laying off 10,400 people.[63] But the San Antonio workers were the first to organize a sustained fight back demanding corporate responsibility.

Under Republican and Democratic administrations alike, beginning with Reagan's, corporation-friendly politicians extolled the virtues of globalization and free trade policies while maintaining a conspicuous silence on the devastating impact of these policies on workers and their communities. The San Antonio workers' painful testimony gave voice to the economic and psychological trauma workers go through every single time a plant closes or a company "downsizes."[64] Denied useful retraining and other assistance, the former Levi's workers lost not only their jobs, but also their cars, homes, and peace of mind. Viola Casares says she will never forget the moment Levi's company representatives announced the plant closure:

> In less than 15 minutes, the men in suits ruined our whole lives. As long as I live, I'll never forget how the white man in the suit said they had to shut us down to stay competitive. The funny thing is that no one said anything. We stood there like mummies. I heard some people fainted. They didn't even tell us in Spanish, just in English. We didn't want to lose our jobs. Nothing can replace a job with dignity.[65]

Petra Mata says she experienced the trauma twice, first at a secret preparation session management convened for supervisors, and again on the plant floor with the rest of the workers. Staff were told to keep the company's plans secret pending a general announcement to all the workers. Petra recalls:

> At 7:30 a.m. BOOM! they called for a general meeting in the mid-

dle of the plant. A guy got up on one of the tables and announced it. *¡Hijole!* That was something that we'll never forget for the rest of our lives, like it just happened yesterday. When everybody heard the announcement we started screaming, hugging each other, crying and asking, "Why? Why? Why?" But they have never answered. They never told us why. There was no reason to shut us down really. We made good quality clothes and high quotas every week. In May 1989 we got the $200 Miracle Bonus because we made such high production levels....

A lot of people went crazy because they didn't know how they were going to live without a job. When you lose your job you feel like nothing but trash, a remnant, a machine to be thrown out. They take away your dignity. You get scared. How are you going to pay for the car, the house, the kids to eat and go to school? *¡Hijole!* After so many years of working for Levi's, overnight we had nothing.[66]

Levi's now sends work to some 700 sewing and finishing subcontractors in 50 countries. From 1997 to 1999, Levi's closed 29 of its manufacturing and finishing plants in North America, slashing some 18,500 employees—nearly half its remaining work force.[67] Levi's also sacked workers in Belgium and France. Over the protests of human rights groups the company announced plans to restart production in China.[68] CEO Robert Haas told the *San Francisco Chronicle* that most of the work from the closed plants would be moved to contractors elsewhere in the Americas, most likely to Mexico and the Caribbean.[69]

In another example of what "Made in America" now means, in March 2000, Levi's, Calvin Klein, Brooks Brothers, Abercrombie & Fitch, Talbots, and Woolrich were added to a class action lawsuit alleging violations of garment workers' rights in Saipan, the Marianna Islands, a US "trust" in the Western Pacific where over 13,000 garment workers typically work 12-hour days for $3.10 or less an hour, seven days a week, often without overtime pay. The $1 billion-a-year industry in Saipan relies on "guest workers" mostly from China and the Philippines, many of whom must pay a cash bond up to $5,000 for a one-year contract to work.[70]

El Paso has been also been devastated by plant closures. The Labor Department said some 10,000 workers in El Paso had lost their jobs because of NAFTA by 1998, the most anywhere in the United States.[71] For example, Levi's, which had been El Paso's largest private employer, closed three of its six plants, laying off some 1,400 workers in 1997.[72] On August 29, 1997, the Greater Texas Finishing Corporation, a division of Sun Apparel, Inc., closed its El Paso operations to send production to Mexico, including the Tehuacán free trade zone. At the time Sun Apparel's largest contracted label was Ralph Lauren's Polo brand. Some 200 laid-off workers included veterans who had served the company for more than 18 years. In a statement calling for support, the laid-off workers said, "Most of us were let go with little more than a good-bye and directions to the NAFTA training and unemployment offices to join the more than 7,000 other workers in El Paso who have lost their jobs to NAFTA and have been unable to get new jobs."[73]

La Mujer Obrera (LMO) is a Mexicana/Chicana women workers' organization founded by garment workers and Chicana/o movement organizers in El Paso in 1981. LMO fought hard against the passage of NAFTA, having first hand experience with maquiladorization enacted under the "twin city" arrangement between El Paso and Juárez during the Border Industrialization Program. Since NAFTA's passage LMO has organized the thousands of workers laid off by NAFTA. LMO says that of the 20,000 displaced workers in El Paso by 2000, 97 percent were Latino; two-thirds, women; one third, single mothers; 50 percent, between 30-45 years of age with the majority of the rest over 45 years old; and 4,000 were in job training programs.[74] After a running battle with state and federal agencies, NAFTA-displaced workers won a $3 million extension in government-funded training for laid-off workers in addition to the original $4.2 million allocated. But María del Carmen Domínguez says that workers in El Paso remain in a profound state of crisis:

> The economic crisis is the big, big problem right now. The women come to La Mujer Obrera because of unemployment. The factories are closing left and right now, and more of the

women are becoming single parents. Problems within the families
are rising because of this situation. It's hard when women don't
have the money to pay the utilities, the rent, or food. When they
are confronted with the denial of public services—no welfare, no
food stamps.[75]

While workers in large and medium-sized plants lost their jobs
to globalization, like their Chinese counterparts, Mexican immigrant
women working in small sweatshops also reported declining wages
and working conditions. Los Angeles, the apparel manufacturing
center of the Untied States, employed some 122,500 employees in
April 1998.[76] Lucrecia Tamayo, an undocumented worker from
Mexico, describes her experience working in Los Angeles sweatshops:

> The first day I started working I felt like I was working the whole
> 24 hours! O *sea* [that is to say], ever since I worked in this country
> I have worked over 12 hours a day, from 7 a.m. to 8 p.m. at night,
> without Sundays off, *siempre, siempre trabajando* [always, always
> working]. I earned $100 a week, working from 7 a.m. to 8 p.m. ev-
> ery day. I worked in four factories over a 15-year period. In the
> first place I worked there were about 30 people, in another about
> 60.
>   I worked six years in the El Monte shop.... There were about
> 20 Latinos working there, with Thai workers in another room....
> We were paid by the piece, so the pay varied. Sometimes I made
> about $260 a week. Oh, that owner! I used to only get off twice a
> year, like for a two-hour break if I had to take my child to the doc-
> tor. In the case of emergencies, I had to ask my sister to take my
> child or else the owner would start screaming at me.[77]

Joining the Movement

Much of the education and leadership training the women received took place "on the job." The women talked about how much
their participation in the movement had changed them. They
learned how to analyze working conditions and social problems,
who was responsible for these conditions, and what workers could
do to get justice. They learned to speak truth to power, whether this
was to government representatives, corporate management, the me-

dia, unions, or co-ethnic gatekeepers. They built relations with different kinds of sectors and groups and organized a wide variety of educational activities and actions. Their activism expanded their world view beyond that of their immediate families to seeing themselves as part of peoples' movements fighting for justice.

The women joined the movement through a variety of routes. Some women sought out workers' centers when they experienced a particular grievance at work. María del Carmen Domínguez just showed up at La Mujer Obrera with over a hundred co-workers one day. People packed into the tiny office, soon spilling out into the street. Workers complained that the boss was trying to cheat them out of holiday pay promised in the personnel policy. La Mujer Obrera provided an infrastructure of support for the workers during their wildcat strike and negotiations with management. Through this process the organization gained new leaders and members, including Domínguez. She recalls:

> We won! They had to give us back pay for our holidays and vacations, yes, for everything, for all the workers. I knew about La Mujer Obrera before the strike because their organizers used to come to the factory, outside the doors, and bring leaflets. So when we had problems (laughs and snaps her fingers), we remembered them.[78]

For a long time Domínguez felt angry that she had not known the law and about what women workers could do to defend their rights. Through her participation in the movement, she developed her skills, leadership, and awareness:

> When I stayed at work in the factory, I was only thinking of myself and how am I going to support my family—nothing more, nothing less. And I served my husband and my son, my girl. But when I started working with La Mujer Obrera I thought, "I need more respect for myself. We need more respect for ourselves." (laughs) *Pero* [but] this also meant big changes for my husband, too! (laughs). But he supported me so much through many, many years. He died three years ago.
>
> I also learned so much about how to use the computer and communicate with other people because the kind of communica-

tion you need to work in an organization is different from in a factory. I learned about the law and I learned how to organize classes with people, whether they were men or women like me. I learned how to develop curriculum and citizenship materials in Spanish. I made a book, yeah![79]

Domínguez also cherishes her friendships with women worker organizers from communities across the United States and overseas:

> I did a lot of traveling for the organization. This is very good because now I know more about where and how we are living in the United States. I got the opportunity to meet with other women, worker women, which is very important to me. Projects like the Lucy Parsons Initiative [a collaborative of Mexican, Chinese, and Dominican women leaders from workers' centers supported by the Funding Exchange] are very good. I love it! And I got to know different organizations, who is doing what kind of work, and who are the women representing these groups.
>
> I have also gone to international meetings…. I represented La Mujer Obrera in 1989, after there was the big *temblor* [earthquake] in Mexico. We participated in a giant march. It was very good with so many women in the streets. We worked with the September 19th Garment Workers Union.[80]

In other instances, women first came into contact with the workers' centers through family members, friends, and recruitment into specific programs and activities organized by the centers. Carmen Ibarra López learned about La Mujer Obrera from her aunt Esperanza Rodríguez, a veteran seamstress who labored 37 years in the garment industry and continues to work as a janitor:

> She invited me to come to the meetings so I started coming. I began doing a lot of volunteer work, and I was a member of the Board of Directors and of the *Comité de Lucha*. Finally Cecilia [the group's former director] asked me to work here…. When I started out, I just gave away flyers and La Mujer Obrera's newspaper. I participated in meetings, and when no one from La Mujer Obrera could attend a meeting I was in charge of going. And also I helped in ordinary ways, cleaning, mopping, doing the bathroom. I don't mind doing it. I still do it because I like the workers to come and see this place clean.[81]

The confidence and skills women gained while standing up for their rights at work spilled over into other jobs. Ibarra adds:

I remember, about six years ago, Larry, the boss, sent his daughter to talk to us. She said that Larry was having a lot of problems paying his IRS bills. She asked us in the name of Larry if we wanted to support him. So we asked how he wanted us to support him. And she said if we could work eight hours but he was going to just pay us for seven hours. By that time I had just become a member of La Mujer Obrera and I said, "No way! I'm not going to do it. Why?" She said, "Well, *es que* [it's that] he doesn't want to close the factory. You can keep your job." But I said, "No way!" So a few of us said no, but the rest said yes. But even with that he shut down in March 1991.[82]

Irma Montoya came to a special summer camp that La Mujer Obrera organized for NAFTA-displaced workers after the electronics plant where she worked fled to Mexico. Montoya stayed on and became an organizer. One day when she went to testify to state and federal legislators about the impact of NAFTA and workers' need for quality job training and placement, her picture appeared in the *New York Times*.[83]

Refugio Arrieta first became involved with La Mujer when she came to attend English classes:

I came to classes one or two days a week for two hours each, and I ended up staying. Some of my friends from the factory also came here to attend the classes. We worked a lot to help out. We have demonstrations, we have meetings with the politicians. I am the president of *La Mesa Directiva* [Board of Directors] here. I received the La Mujer Obrera award.[84]

In some cases the organizations conducted systematic political education to consolidate a core of women worker leaders. María Antonia Flores, María del Carmen Domínguez, and Eustolia Olivas were trained as the initial worker leadership core of La Mujer Obrera. Flores recalls:

On some occasions Cecilia gave the training, at other times Guillermo, people who came from different parts of the city, and political teachers, including from Mexico. [Cecilia Rodríguez and

Guillermo Domínguez Glenn helped launch La Mujer Obrera and the Centro Obrero in El Paso.] They gave classes in politics and everything related to study, from Paolo Freire's methods to the political economy of Mexico. Trainings lasted two or three weeks, a month, three months, or sometimes daily when the teachers were here. What we got first from study we later put into practice.[85]

If one meets Flores today, it is hard to imagine her as the person she describes before her involvement in the movement:

> I have learned so much here. I used to be shy. I hardly spoke. I was a submissive housewife. I had all the characteristics of a Mexican woman who was only made for marriage. But once we came here to this organization, we all learned something. For working class women it's harder to develop ourselves as leaders. I did not have these experiences in mind when I first came here. At least I did not know what it meant to be part of an organization. I got my liberation after being suppressed for 15 years and limited to the house and home labor. I came out in the world. Before that I did not even know that such a thing as women's oppression even existed; one just thinks its normal.
>
> When you are just sitting there listening to your husband, you think it's perfectly natural that you have no rights as a woman, as a person. Your rights are violated and you don't know it. When you go out into the outside world, you find another reality. I think that's what has made me so protective of this organization.[86]

"I don't want other people to go through what we went through"

The government raid on the El Monte sweatshop on August 2, 1995, marked a turning point in Lucrecia Tamayo's life. She transformed from being a frightened worker to the campaign nerve center who relishes speaking out and going to demonstrations against big name retailers that profited from her labor:

> The second of August woke me up. It was like I was a blind woman before that. I like going to the actions and demonstrations. Before when the owners screamed at me, I got real small. I

wondered what I had done wrong to make them so mad. Now I know we have rights.

I have had two jobs since the raids at El Monte. Because of the publicity around our case, the owner knows who I am. The owner would call at six a.m. in the morning telling you whether or not you could come in. I didn't like it. There is no written contract. Everything is just done by his word. I was only getting paid $80 a week. But since I started working there I wrote down the hours I worked and how many pieces I sewed, like I learned to do. After a year, I took my calculations to KIWA [Korean Immigrant Workers Advocates]. Paul [Lee, a KIWA organizer] went with me to talk to the owner and they paid what they owed me soon after.

I'm the information source for our group of workers. If a problem comes up, I call everyone up to let them know what's going on. Ever since the raid on the El Monte shop, I have kept track of all the paper work and keep workers informed. I no longer have any fear. My only fear is immigration. But the rest, no. I do not want other workers to suffer. I don't want other people to go through what we went through. This experience opened up my eyes. It made me conscious. It gave me the motivation to speak up and fight against the owners. My husband thinks I'm crazy. I always ask Paul "When are we going to have the next demonstration?" I like to yell and scream at the retailers in the stores that made so much money off of us.[87]

"This is the best school you could have"

Fuerza Unida allowed laid-off Levi's workers to channel their anger and sense of betrayal, while building on the friendships and ties they had relished in their jobs. A combination of curiosity and revenge first attracted Viola Casares to Fuerza Unida:

I remember when people were passing out information. I was curious and wanted to find out what they wanted to tell us. Because of my curiosity, I started going to the meetings. At first there were 25 to 30 ladies who started meeting at a small church hall. We began talking about how we have to do something. We needed to get more information about what is really going on. We needed to find out what the company was going to give us.

We needed to do something because of the awful way they shut down the plant. I got interested. I was angry about what they did to us without warning. At first I just wanted to get back at them. I started as a volunteer, then became a board member, then a co-coordinator.[88]

Casares expanded her vision and network of friends through her involvement with Fuerza Unida:

I've done a lot of traveling and met wonderful people. I've learned that I am not the only one who has had problems. This experience has opened up my mind and views. For example, because of lack of information and education and the way I was raised by my family, I used to think that being gay, being homosexual was a sin. But I don't believe that any more. We are all human beings.... I learned from my broken marriage, my job, and Fuerza Unida. I have a second chance to pass on what the movement taught me. I never thought I could have done the things that I have. Losing my job opened my eyes. I used to work and live in my own little world. We were taught to just look out for our own family and to compete with other people. Levi's taught us to compete against other workers to be part of their machine. Fuerza Unida taught us that we are part of a bigger family, that we should care about our sisters.[89]

Marta Martínez ran into problems making her way through the company rehiring and government job training programs after the layoffs but stuck with Fuerza Unida through thick and thin:

I've been with Fuerza Unida from the beginning. They offered some of us work at the other plants. I worked there for three months. I had to quit because they treated us so bad. Even the other workers there were mad at us. They said we were stealing their jobs. The supervisors accused us of being lazy, saying that's why the plant shut down and moved out. They were very rude to those of us who came in from the old plant. I went through the ESL, GED, and job training classes. The training mainly helped the people who could speak English. But they didn't really help people find jobs. With Fuerza Unida, I worked on the protests, the hunger strikes, everything.[90]

Similarly, Tina Mendoza put her energy into Fuerza Unida after the Levi's layoffs:

I've been working with Fuerza Unida for eight years. The first two years I just went to meetings, but after that I started coming to the office regularly to help out. We work on everything. We never say we can't do it. Our biggest problem is with English. We do all these things so that Fuerza Unida can live on, so our struggle can continue, so that we can serve as an example to women about what is possible. We work to build pride that we are women. I have learned a lot here. I met so many different people and learned about what they do, about different struggles. For me I feel great pride to be a part of this struggle.

At first I was afraid and ashamed to go the demonstrations. I tried my best to cover my face so that I would not be seen. Now when I go, I scream as loud as I can. I do not cover my face. Fuerza Unida injects you with a lot of energy. *Ojala* [I hope to God/Allah] that we will continue to move ahead.[91]

Fuerza Unida members later reached out to low-waged workers in other plants and industries. Obdulia "Obi" Segura first came to Fuerza Unida after hearing about the food bank available for unemployed workers and low-income families in need:

I try to help out at Fuerza Unida, doing whatever kind of work I can. I started coming here about two and a half years ago, first because I heard about the food bank. Now I help with sweeping, office work, and whatever needs to be done. Even though the women have their own families and homes to take care of, they all give a lot to the work of Fuerza Unida, to help other people in need. There are women in this world who will not do anything for anyone else, who are very egotistical. But that is not the way of Fuerza Unida. Petra and Viola do everything they can to help the people, to build cooperation. That is the character of working with Fuerza Unida. Here we are always ready to help, to love each other, to work together. This is what moves me to volunteer here in whatever way I can.[92]

Petra Mata, who had already picked up many leadership skills as a daughter, wife, mother, and seamstress, got baptized in the fire of fighting the world's largest garment manufacturer:

I learned so much at Fuerza Unida. This is the best school you could have, working with people, listening, chairing meetings —all the things you have to understand to carry out the struggle. Here we are not just individuals. We go to support and participate in all struggles in the movement. We work with Asian, Filipino, African American, Mexican, white. We are part of the same vision, the same movement. In the past when Levi's said, "blah blah blah," we said, "yes sir." Now we ask, "Why? Wait a minute. I don't like it." They should do what's right, or fair at least. Companies cannot do without workers, it should be half and half, 50-50, not just 100 percent going to one side. That's what we learned through Fuerza Unida.[93]

"Sometimes God knocks us around a little bit"

For some of the women, showing compassion, solidarity, and faith in the face of hardships is sustained by deeply held religious beliefs. Viola Casares says she tells Petra Mata, "I think sometimes God knocks us around a little bit to make us think and to remind us to be thankful for what we have." Casares reaffirmed her faith during a visit to maquiladoras in Honduras with a US delegation hosted by the Mennonite Church:

> Sometimes when I get discouraged I pray for God to give me a sign to let me know if what I am doing is right. One day we were scheduled to visit different maquilas including a place called Interfashion. No one knew what we would find there. But when we got there, the first thing we saw when we walked through the door was women sewing Levi's and Dockers label pants. God had given me a big sign to see that what we were doing was right. He showed us exactly what was going on in the factories our jobs had run away to. It was a miracle!
>
> We saw just what Levi's was doing to our sisters in Central America. We saw that their chairs and working conditions were really uncomfortable and that they got paid so much less, with no benefits. The place looked just like a prison and workers were treated like prisoners. I saw that with my own eyes. It made me really angry. That company just cares about profits.[94]

Similarly Carmen Ibarra López of La Mujer Obrera explains: "All the time I like to do my job with *fé* [faith]. Yes, I have a lot of faith in God—period. I feel very, very respectful of all the religions. I do my job because I have faith in God."[95]

Bringing Home the Fight for Women's Rights

Work, migration, and activism are all threads that run through the women's histories. But as working class women, they also endured distinct challenges as daughters, lovers, wives, mothers, sisters, and grandmothers. With their participation in movements seeking to overturn oppressive class, gender, and racial practices have come changes in their views of gender and family roles.

Viola Casares complained that her husband had run around with *sus mujeres de la cantina* [his women of the bars], while projecting his jealousy on to her. He refused to let her work outside the home despite their poverty. Casares swears that 1990 was absolutely the worst year in her life. That dark time she lost not only her job of nine years, but also her marriage. She finally separated from her husband who had become a jealous alcoholic and broken her nose during a beating. The stress from the loss of her job and marriage, combined with her declining health, put Casares in the hospital:

> I told him, "If you want to get back together it's got to be 50-50, not 90 percent going to your side." But by that time his drinking had gotten really bad. We never got a divorce although we were separated for six years. He didn't want to give me a divorce. He'd come and stay for a couple of weeks. Our oldest daughter loved him dearly. He was such a strong man with his macho image. When we were living together he would run around with other women. I was a good wife and faithful, but I told him, "One of these days, I'm going to leave." He would come back and cry. He had his regrets. I think a lot of it was because of his drinking. I've lost a lot of uncles and cousins to drinking. His father used to drink. My husband died from drinking when he was only 46 years old. I guess that's why I loved, hated, and pitied this man all at the same time. He lived in his own way. Maybe he did not know how to show love because he was not shown love since his father also drank a lot and ran around with women.[96]

Casares managed to climb out of the well of depression by channeling her energy into taking care of her children and grandchildren and building Fuerza Unida as a support center for women like herself. She explains:

> I'm glad that I became part of Fuerza Unida. It's really changed my life. What I went through with the plant closure and my marriage prepared me for the work I am doing right now, even for the death of my husband and coping with the loss of my job. I think that if I didn't have this organization, I would be completely lost now. Fuerza Unida made us strong women, strong mothers. I like to be independent. I told my husband when he tried to come back, "You have to want the new Viola, not the old Viola that only stayed home."[97]

The barriers women had to surmount because of their gender status were made doubly difficult because of economic hardships they faced as working class women. The women worry about their children, grandchildren, parents, and siblings. A number had experienced the loss of family to substance abuse and violence. The workers' centers acted as a women's support network. Remedios García tried to manage her stress and loss by staying active:

> It's been almost seven years that my oldest son was murdered. That affected me greatly. Since that time I've gone from illness to illness to illness. (starts crying) I haven't been able to recuperate. It's been seven years or more that I've stayed like this. *Aieee!* He was out with his friends. When the telephone rang that night and I thought it must be an emergency as soon as I heard it. *Aieee!* The doctor said I must not always think about this and move on to do other things. But it's my son, I told him. So a lot of problems have come from this. I started having problems with my husband, with a lot of things because it affected me personally. But, nevertheless, one has to go on living. I can't recuperate so that's why I've been like this, do you understand? I feel a lot of guilt, that I didn't spend enough time with my son. I've had one complication after another. For this it is good to have a lot of friends and continue working…. I have my mama, my children, and people who need me. And they have me.[98]

Many of the women met their partners, had children, and started working outside the home when they were teenagers. They described a range of positive and negative experiences with partners. A number of the women had separated from their first husbands. Despite her high levels of skills, Elena Alvarez is suppressed by a jealous husband who will not permit her to work for pay. She can only leave the house with his permission, even though their household is in dire financial condition. Carmen Ibarra López experienced a serious bout of depression when her first marriage did not work out, so she started going to beautician school and worked as a manicurist for many years before she returned to the garment industry. Still in the "honeymoon" phase of her new marriage, Carmen is crossing her fingers and says that she is praying that God will give her "a second chance."[99]

Tina Mendoza says her husband has been very supportive of her involvement with Fuerza Unida. She just tries to make sure she has his meals ready and makes sufficient time for her family:

> I no longer have babies at home. My children are grown. My husband supports my work with Fuerza Unida. He wants me to be useful, not just staying home watching TV. I make sure I get my husband's meals ready and make his life easier. I try to spend as much time with the family as possible. He's a second level supervisor after working for the city for over 25 years. Where he works is unionized. Before the union came in there used to be a lots of discrimination against Mexicans. But thanks to the union, minorities have been able to raise their positions.[100]

Petra Mata also says her husband has been very supportive of her work at Fuerza Unida. Indeed, he has continued to work at two low-paying jobs to support the family, especially when funding runs out and she and her co-coordinator Viola Casares stop getting paid. She says that sometimes his friend rib him when they see her speaking at some demonstration on TV, but she says, "at least he can see what I'm doing."[101]

María del Carmen Domínguez takes pride in her scrapper stance towards her father, brothers, and schoolmates growing up, as well as in her children's strength:

My family made it possible for me to organize the strike at the factory and work here. (laughs) I started out fighting with my father. I fought in school. I fought with my husband. (laughs) *¡Aiiyaiiyaii!* Yes, because I am very strong! Come on! With the boys at school I played baseball. (laughs) First I wanted to bat, to pitch.... My daughter has some of the same personality as me. Well, I think, no, not only my daughter, but my boys, too, yeah. My daughter is a very, very fighting woman. (laughs) Yes, but she is also crying, fighting, crying.[102]

Carmen Ibarra López is both critical of her own upbringing as well as proud to break the mold in raising her daughter and son:

You know, I was born and grew up in a culture where the women didn't have a voice. So I said I'm not going to do the same with my children. I want to teach them to be different. I'm not the kind of a person who wants to do the same thing that my family does, did with me. No, I'm not. Especially with my daughter. You know my son is the oldest, and my daughter is the youngest. I taught my son how to clean house, wash dishes, and all kinds of tasks because I said, "Your sister is not going to be your maid. She is just going to be your sister and a human being." So they both respect each other very much. They are not just brother and a sister but very, very good and close friends. Yes, I don't want to keep doing the same thing that my family did. No, no way![103]

Through participation in their organizations and *el movimiento,* the women gained new skills and awareness, underwent major transformations, provided leadership to communities under siege, built working friendships with Asian immigrant women and other low-waged workers across the globe, and won victories.

During a protest at Levi's posh glass, steel, and brick corporate headquarters in San Francisco, to the surprise, consternation, then chagrin of management, *las mujeres* suddenly chain themselves to the front door. Calmly awaiting the arrival of police paddy wagons, over the bullhorn they issue a friendly Texas home-style invitation to their upcoming benefit dance with Dr. Loco's Rockin' Jalapeño Band. *Las mujeres luchando* inspire stanzas in the band's catchy *cumbia* rhythm, "El Picket Sign" (1992):

From San Anto to San Francisco Fuerza Unida has been saying
Desde San Anto hasta San Francisco Fuerza Unida anda diciendo
Don't buy Dockers or Levi's jeans and stop the Free Trade Agreement
¡Boicot Dockers y Levi's jeans y alto al libre comercio!

El picket sign, el picket sign
¡Que Viva La Mujer Obrera!
El picket sign, el picket sign
¡Queremos Justice for Janitors!
El picket sign, el picket sign
We say ¡Chale con Coors!
El picket sign, el picket sign
¡Porque la unión es La Fuerza! [104]

Carmen Ibarra López, María Antonia Flores, and María del Carmen Domínguez of La Mujer Obrera. This banner on their office wall reads: "Stop the Hemorrhaging of Our Jobs by NAFTA."
Photo by Miriam Ching Yoon Louie (1997)

María Antonia Flores

La Mujer Obrera Director,
Popular Educator

I was born in 1954 in Zacatecas, Mexico. My family moved to Ciudad Juárez in 1962. I have eight sisters and brothers, and I am the oldest. In Juárez my parents worked in maquilas, restaurants, [and] as vendors selling food.

I studied through middle school, then a year to be a secretary, and in a school for teachers. I was an adult literacy teacher while I was studying to become a teacher, but I didn't finish and get a diploma. I worked for two years as an educator, and later two years in a maquila.

The maquila was a rather large electronics factory called Centra Labs Components; about 400 people worked there. I was 19 years old then. For that period of time the pay was good—minimum wage, and one could earn 700 pesos, but it was very hard work. I started work at three in the afternoon, left at 11 p.m., and we worked Saturdays. I don't know the name, but we also used a paste, mixed like a dough to cover the capacitors, and it smelled really bad. We attached different components between the two edges so the current could pass through. Then we carried the capacitors and dipped them in alcohol or acetone. That work gave you a lot of headaches because sometimes when we handled such tiny capacitors, we had to use a big lens to see the small pieces well enough to grab them. After a while they changed me to a department where I worked at a machine that cut the capacitor wires, squared them, and sent them to be packaged in boxes for shipping. The majority of workers were almost *puras jovensitas* [all young women]; the supervisors were *puros varones* [all male].

I got married when I was 18, almost 19, on August 21, 1971. My daughter Paula was born August 18, 1972, a year after I got married. My son Gerardo was born in July 1973, my other daughter in February 1977, and my youngest son in July 1988. Now I have five grandchildren, four girls and one boy. [laughs] They're from my two daughters.

My husband and I came to the US from Juárez to El Paso in 1974 because his parents had residency here, and we lived with them for two years. Then he left the house and us to live with his mama until 1985, when I moved out of my in-laws' house. Already he had gone running around with other women. I was separated from him, almost since 1977. We got to know each other because he lived near me and came to a *fiesta* [party] at my house. He used to work as a factory operative in El Paso.

I came here when I was about 22, 23 years old. During the first years I was only a housewife, not doing anything but taking care of the family, the in-laws. But afterwards I started to work in small factory workshops, cleaning offices, doing homecare for adults. I got special training to take care of a sick person who could not move. I was with this person for two years and after that I worked at a factory for another year. Then I returned to cleaning offices and from 1986 to 1990 I did both jobs. During the day I worked in the factory, and at night and weekends I cleaned offices. [groans]

Aiiee! I never got any sleep! The garment factory was so difficult. I left my children home *solitos* [alone]. They went to school and we didn't see each other because I didn't get home from work until one or two in the morning.

The first factory where I worked was named Emily Joe. Later I worked at CMT and at other small shops, Elias Lavalla. The last one I worked at was Eddy Wad. With the first job I still didn't have my papers because my husband left me while he ran around with his friends and sweet young things. But because he was always working in these different industries he knew about jobs and told me where to go. On other jobs I had my own references, people that I worked with and knew. I always came with good recommendations. I found the last job because the factory was near where I lived.

After I got off from the factory I started coming to La Mujer Obrera. I volunteered because I enjoyed it. In March or April of 1985 a friend of mine who was a neighbor first brought me for a women's meeting on topics given by Cecilia [Rodríguez, La Mujer Obrera's co-founder], workshops on the oppression of *la mujer,* and planning for a festival for children. During those days I only participated in small meetings and visited, not as a member. In 1986 I became a member, worked on committees, then part of the leadership. After a year they started to organize special workshops to train me and two other compañeras, María del Carmen [Domínguez] and Eustolia [Olivas] as the first three organizers trained to advance the organization.

On some occasions Cecilia gave the training; at other times, Guillermo [Domínguez Glenn, Cecilia's husband]. People who came from different parts of the city, and political teachers, including from Mexico. They gave classes in politics and everything related to study, from Paolo Freire's methods to the political economy of Mexico. Trainings lasted two or three weeks, a month, three months, or sometimes daily when the teachers were here. What we got first from study we later put into practice.

Since about 1988 we began to develop more activities and a bit stronger membership. We started the first cooperative food project through a committee organized by María del Carmen. She also created the newspaper for educational work. It was about eight pages long and came out every month. María del Carmen developed all the educational material, leaflets and brochures, and gave classes. I was a teacher, yes, from my past training in Mexico.

There were big problems in the factories during this period so we leafleted them in 1988, 1990, 1991. We had over a thousand members, with educational meetings four times a week. Fifty workers came to every meeting. It was so busy! We were running *La Cooperativa* [the food cooperative] and also *La Clínica* [free workers health clinic]. Fifteen to twenty people helped us operate our educational program and the coop. There was a *huelga* [strike] in November. That's when we had all the problems with the union, the divisions.

I was in charge of political education. In 1995 and 1996 we also moved into economic development. I prepared the curriculum based on what we were planning, for the workers, volunteers, and people who came from outside El Paso. We even had a volunteer from Spain. We made presentations according to the needs of the group, whether it was religious, progressive, or more conservative.

We conducted political education in our *Escuela Popular* [People's School]. The courses lasted three months, two hours a week, with one hour in English or citizenship, and then one hour on economics, politics, and social issues. We made murals, drawings, and leaflets to reinforce the learning process. We do more murals and *dinámicas* [skits] and show videos. We developed plans for the *Comité de Lucha* and when the people developed as stronger leaders, they took on more responsibility for planning.

We have to design the curriculum so that everyone can understand. We do not rely much on writing because a lot of our people do not know how to read. Doing murals together is so people don't go to sleep like in church; they're so colorful. Workers come here tired and hungry so we have to capture their interest and keep them engaged. When people first come, we start with very basic stories and simple questions. If they go on to the second level, we cover more political economy and advanced topics. We talk about what money is, what transnational corporations are, why factories are closing, and neoliberalism. We draw pictures of the transnational corporations and their activities around the world and ask what does this have to do with us? We talk about what is happening to people in Chiapas and what that poor people's struggle has to do with workers in this community.

I love doing educational work! We started before the big garment factories started closing, while the women were still working. Then the different corporations began setting up twin plants along the border in the 1970s here in Juárez and El Paso; later the biggest factories started to leave. Through our relations with workers in Canada we learned more about the disasters workers went through in Canada and the United States. We made many trips and shared stories with other workers. One of the most beautiful of all experiences is when workers support each other. Different people from La Mujer Obrera participate in these exchanges. It sets a good base of information. But the governments still passed NAFTA.

We started working [in solidarity] with the [independent Mexican labor union federation] Frente Auténtico del Trabajo [FAT], founded in 1960.[105] The FAT works in four sectors. First, it works in the workers sector, which now has various national level unions, like the unions of iron and steel, farm, textile, and shoemaker workers, from northern Mexico to the southwest part of the central valley. Second, the cooperative sector organizes savings, credit, consumers, and producers cooperatives, including a glass factory that the workers won after a strike. Third, people living in the *colonias* [neighborhoods] developed similar consumer cooperatives; in the urban sector *colonia* residents organize around all kinds of questions, like water, electricity, and sewage. Finally, the *campesino* sector is conducting a survey of the people in the countryside to estimate the results of the harvest so they don't get exploited by some company. They work with the *ejidotarios* [owners of communal land]. The fundamental goal is to improve the conditions of life of all the people.

Our groups are organizing independently because we belong to no political party or government, and the workers themselves are the ones who feel this [is important].... The FAT had to develop completely independently from the unions [that are] working in collaboration with the government. We are based in self-determination where workers are the ones who decide what we want and who is going to represent us. The situation in Mexico is very different from that of US AFL-CIO unions; the CTM [Confederación de Trabadajores Mexicanos] is part of the official government and ruling party. The government's physical repression can't stop the workers, but does place many obstacles before them. For example, when workers really start organizing, the first thing they [the Mexican government] do is fire everyone [in the union]. Or the government labor commissions give false counts of the election votes. They bring in people to vote who really don't work there. Through these same laws and government bodies that are supposed to protect the workers, the administration carries out many tricks.

Since around 1963 they started to establish maquiladoras along the border and added many more in the 1980s and 1990s. So it became necessary for the FAT to establish a workers' center on the border, *Centro de Estudios y Taller Laboral,* to train women maquiladora workers about everything related to their labor rights to defend themselves whether at the individual or collective level. Especially here in the United States where there is no understanding of what an independent union or organization is, we want workers to know how things could be different.

In general people who work in the maquilas have no previous experience in these kinds of jobs. Some maquiladoras require that workers have completed primary school, but in others, many do not know how to read and write. Workers receive no study or training because all the work in the maquiladoras is very easy and routine, so one needs only a certain amount of manual aptitude. They contract mostly young people, from 16 to 35 years old, depending on the factory. If the work involves a lot of tiny pieces, they greatly prefer women's labor; when the work is a little more heavy, they contract more men. The ratio is about 60 percent women and 40 percent men. About 50 percent of the workers in Juárez are not from here, but from all the other states of the republic. Some 55 percent of the women also have children, averaging one or two. People often cannot secure the necessities of life. There are not enough childcare centers to accommodate so many people. Many times parents have to leave their children by themselves.

Most of the factories are transnational, headquartered in the United States, Canada, and Japan, [and more recently, subcontractors from South Korea and Taiwan] with also some Mexican-owned maquilas. The average pay is $4 a day. [exclaims] Yes, that's what it is! That includes bonuses for productivity, good attendance, punctuality, so that workers will work even harder to survive. They give some prizes, but the pay offered is so low because it benefits them to keep us needy. Many maquilas have people who worked ten, twelve years doing the same thing, but have not been trained to do anything else.

At La Mujer Obrera we have classes twice a week. We try not to lose hold of our education program, or we will have no power. We need to motivate the workers so they can struggle for their rights. Before NAFTA passed we helped organize a big march on the bridge between here and Mexico and had problems with the police. It was very cold! We stayed in the Plaza all night together with so many groups, including from Canada and Mexico.

Now the education we do is on the results of the crisis, the disaster, the unemployment, the people out in the streets, the treating of workers like they didn't exist. Workers are invisible in Mexico, here, and whatever part of the world. But how can workers become more visible and take on this problem? The problem we are having with NAFTA is not just a local one affecting El Paso; it is also the worldwide problem of neoliberalism. We have to educate workers, both immigrants and non-immigrants. We must understand the roots of the problems. We need to know not just that we don't have work, but *why* we don't have work.

Women are not the only ones who come for help, but yes, the working woman is the one who is in the worst need. You can hear it in our name, La Mujer Obrera [The Woman Worker]; it comes out in our methods of organizing, initiatives, development of women's leadership. La Mujer Obrera is a name people know so women come here directly to see how we can support them. When a woman comes with her needs, we should be ready to help her, whether she stays or not, because she is unprotected. But we also want women to participate in this organization because it is in our interest to strengthen the group to promote the development of women. We don't want to continue to be used as objects, like furniture, right?!

We have been through so many experiences that were good, strong, and brave. One of the most important things for us as leaders of this organization is to have the support of our families. One way they do this is by accepting our schedules, since there is no fixed routine. If a husband or children oppose our activities, we would have to leave our work only half done. Working together with women through hard times like the hunger strike or the organizing of Camp Dignity [a popular education, two-week summer camp LMO organized for NAFTA-displaced workers and their families] have been great learning experiences. [There] we saw how far each of us as an organizer could go and how the organization could grow. We have the experiences of building relationships among workers to better express themselves and communicate with others.

Now I can say what I want, what I expect, what I do or do not want done in the organization, in the family, for myself. But if you're only inside your home, you don't learn anything. Development is very important. Lots of good and bad things happen as one goes through life. The negative ones affect your health and psyche so we must be prepared to know how to get the strength to face problems and whatever lies ahead. If I know that my health could affect the organization, then I have to think not only of myself, but also of the group, of my co-workers. I think that once one joins an organization, one is not completely free because one has to think about the organization, the family, and the self. So you turn into many parts and you are not alone. You have to think about how you are going to respond to these different parts of your life because you cannot abandon them.

Our priorities for workers are in three areas: the economic, political, and ideological. In the future, I hope that we will reach our goal of having an economic base from which we can live and support the community and ourselves, so workers will be able to take care of their families. I hope that we will achieve the best for the workers, the dreams we've always had about creating a bilingual school and cultural plaza, which would be the greatest, most fabulous thing. Our political priority is to strengthen the workers to confront the bureaucrats to make them implement workers' rights. We must be conscious of what is happening so we can defend ourselves. We know what kind of politics we want and that we must exert efforts so that the voices of the community will be heard. Ideologically I will continue to uphold my ideals for the organization and my family to build a better future.

If the conditions of the community improve, then my family's condition will also improve. If the community's conditions do not improve, then my family will continue to live in the same poor situation they are in now. Without this organization we cannot have a better future for our children or our grandchildren. We have to keep fighting all three fights. If we are conscious of our goals, we won't lose our way, our vision. Any woman who is a real leader has to be in the forefront of continuing to struggle to better our conditions.

—El Paso, Texas, February 24, 1997

Petra Mata

Former Levi's Garment Worker,
Fuerza Unida Organizer and Miracle Maker

I was born on May 31, 1946 in a little town called Bustamente, Nuevo León, Mexico. My parents worked as farmers. When there was no more money in farming, they moved. My mother died at the very early age of 28 years old, when I was only 5. She had a baby in this small town they say is only a *rancho*. The hospital services were very poor, no doctors, nobody. In those days women had their babies at home. I think they did not take care of my mom very well, so she developed problems.

My little sister, the baby that my mom bore, died. A few days later my mom died, too. That left us five kids, my four brothers and myself. I was in the middle. When my mother died, my father felt lost. He couldn't stand that my mother had died, so he left us. After that, my grandfather moved me and my brothers to Nuevo Laredo. He took care of us kids until we got married.

It was sad for me. I made a lot of sacrifices and suffered when I was young because my ma died. I don't think anybody cares about you the way your mother does because you are born from her. That's what I tell my kids now, "You only have one mother in your life." I didn't have a mother. [eyes water] But in a way, my grandparents did something good for me because now I can live with dignity. When I was young I had to respect myself. I was always praying that I would not do something that was going to degrade me. I always tell my girls, "Respect yourself no matter what. You've got to have respect to receive respect."

After years and years my father came back and we accepted him. But I don't have the kind of love for him I would like to have because he never lived with us when we were little, when we needed him. When I got married I had all this sadness stored up in my heart that I had to let go of, that used to bother me. But now I have my family and a wonderful husband. He helps me a lot. I've got my four kids. My daughter turned 27 in August. My oldest boy is 26, my small boy is 22, and my girl is 17.

I met my [future] husband in *el mercado* [the market] in Nuevo Laredo when I was 15. Then I left to work in the United States for three or four years. We knew this family very well in Laredo, Texas. They asked my aunt if I could work for them. I worked in their house for two straight years without going to see my family. I had to clean the floors on my hands and knees and wash windows and change everything every month.

When I was 17, I was able to go home to Nuevo Laredo on the weekends, then come back to work by Monday. I went back and forth like that. I cleaned the house because I just went to six years of school in Mexico. At that time there was no opportunity to go to school or college. So I had to *¡Hijole!* work as a maid and serve them. They had two kids, and I had to put them to bed every night, give them their clothes, prepare them for school, make breakfast, and do all the housework. There was a wife, but of course I was the maid! [laughs] I only made $10 a week.

I went back to Nuevo Laredo to the same place where I had worked and started talking with my [future] husband. One time, when I was getting off from work, I called his house and asked, "What are you going to do today?" He said, "Well, nothing." I said, "Well, I'm going to go to the movies. Do you want to go with me?" He said right away, "Yeah!" My sister-in-law told me, "The day you called, we were all ready to go out, but he got so excited because he was going to go with you." So I'm the one who took the first step. [laughs] But it was only for that one day that he was just like a little chicklet with me. We have a very good relationship. We got married when I was 23 years old and Domingo was 27.

Three months later we came to the United States. All the kids were born here. I remember the first days were very bad because it was very cold. We didn't even have blankets to cover ourselves and the house didn't have any windows. Oooh! Then little by little we saved and began buying things. We are still in this house now.

After my third child was born I started working in a tortilla factory, counting tortillas on the night shift and taking care of my kids during the day. Then I moved to a restaurant where I was in charge of the kitchen and they paid me a very, very low wage, about $60 or

$70 a week. I was hired three years and worked 6am to 4pm every-day, even Saturdays, making tortillas and everything. I was unsatis-fied and felt like this was not all I could do.

People said that they were hiring at the Levi's factory on Zarzamora Street. The pay was very good. I said, "Well, wow! I would like to do this!" and decided to apply. I went one morning and took the test. I didn't even get back home before I already got a call. They told me to come in for an interview. So I went right away, and they hired me in 1976.

When I started working there, they were paying by levels A to D, with D getting higher pay—which I qualified for. I did the hard, more difficult operations, like sewing the pockets on the sides of the coat. For three and a half years I sewed this way before they put me on util-ity so I could do any operation. Then they made me a trainer to teach the new people. I liked working with the girls and helping out. Finally they made me a supervisor for eight years. I was very happy with my job because I got to work closely with my co-workers.

The layoff happened on January 16, 1990. The Friday before the Martin Luther King holiday, they told us that all the supervisors and trainers had to go downtown for a meeting. We suspected some-thing was wrong because we had heard a lot of rumors. Usually at Christmas they gave us a $500 bonus, but not that year. We found out later that they decreased our hours because they were planning to shut us down. Nobody got the benefit of a pay increase based on 40 hours because we were working less hours.

We [supervisors] went downtown to a very fancy hotel on Tues-day. Everyone sat down around tables in a big room. Then all of a sudden we saw a lot of people coming with folders. We thought, "What's going on?" Finally, the person from Levi's started to speak and said that they were planning to shut us down because Levi's had to be competitive in the market. Everything turned black. We started screaming and saying "Why?"

They already had the package ready, knew who we were, and took us to different, individual rooms. Then they start explaining, "This is what you're going to get." I was very sad. I started crying. They told us, "Yeah, yeah, calm down. I know how you feel, I know." Ahhh! I told her [eyes water], "How in the hell do you know how I feel?" I mean I *love* my job. After the 14 years I worked for this company, they just turn us out like this. Our jobs are over. "You're going to tell me you know how I feel? You still have a job!"

We came back and went outside. We hugged each other and said, "What are we going to do?" "Ahhh!" "I just bought my car." "I just got my credit card to buy Christmas gifts." A lot of people were buying houses, then lost them. They lost their cars. I had two cars at the time. We lost everything because we couldn't pay no more, *sabes* [you know]? When they turned us away they said, "Oh, we want you to cooperate with us. We want you to help us to work with the people tomorrow." Everybody went back and said, "Oh no! You want us to help you when you are doing this to us?"

They had a lot of advisors [who] told us, "You poor lady, you're going to be all right." They gave some money to the city to provide services, but those services did not help Levi's workers directly, but instead went to the whole city with close to 10,000 people out of jobs. They [also] mishandled that money by renting a big office and buying a lot of things. We didn't get anything. About 1,150 workers were displaced.

When Levi's closed, it was a disaster for most of the families. My husband has had to work at two jobs since they shut us down. In the evening he's a cook at the Marriott Hotel and in the morning he's working with vegetables in a lot of grocery stores. Before I lost my job I sent one of my kids to college. My two older kids had everything that they needed, not what they wanted, but at least what they needed. The ones who suffered most were the small ones. They remember that we could buy five pairs of pants, one for each day. When I lost my job my small boy said, "Mom, how come we can only buy two pants, one to use today and the other one tomorrow?" He asked, "Why did Junior have this and I cannot?" It was hard for them to understand.

About two months before they shut us down, they started reducing personnel. They paid us whatever they wanted. Workers didn't know how to calculate their pay. So we started comparing. "How much do you have?" "How much did you get?" And they said, "Well, look I got less than you and I was working more years." That's when we started to get together, decided to form Fuerza Unida, and declared the boycott against Levi's.

At first we didn't have any office. We did all of the work from Rubén's house. Rubén [Solís of the Southwest Public Workers Union] was the one who helped us start to put together Fuerza Unida. The first day they made the shut down announcement, Rubén was there protesting in front of the plant. We got a lawyer right away. We had meetings and formed the *Concilio* [Board of Directors]. The workers got involved, and we decided to put together our demands. Then we got a very little place at the Esperanza Peace and Justice Center on South Flores Street.

For six months we got unemployment benefits, $200 every two weeks. After that ran out, we felt very bad. We put more and more attention and time into Fuerza Unida. We put aside our personal and family problems. We used to cry *noches* [nights] to see the people with no food. We started having trainings and participating in conferences—locally, nationally, internationally. We moved again to 3946 South Zarzamora and stayed for almost two years until we moved over here [to 710 New Laredo Highway] where the rent is cheaper. We're low on income. The owner is a very good, cooperative man.

Viola, Irene [Reyna], and I were the co-coordinators at that time.... For the first year or two the people worked for free, nominated by the Board. First, there was Frances Estrella, Raquelina, and another lady whose name I don't remember, and Margie Castro, who volunteered so much. A lot of girls got involved and put in a lot of time. Then they decided to make Fuerza Unida a non-profit organization with papers and everything, and get a grant to pay full-time coordinators. They nominated Viola and Irene, and, because I was putting in my time volunteering, me in February 1992. We worked as a team, Viola, Irene, and myself. Irene had to leave when we ran out of money. I wish we had resources to hire technical assistance. We need someone to sit down and use the computer. Then we could move more quickly, with our sewing cooperative, food bank, and everything.

Every several weeks, we went to San Francisco to organize the campaign at Levi's corporate headquarters. We had to leave our families. It was good but hard. We needed to walk so far and learn to be good leaders to head the campaign. We have learned that if we want to do something, we just need to develop our own goals. I have a lot of friends who do not know what they can do. They see themselves as a wife and mother, washing dishes, cooking dinner, or making clothes only for their own families. A lot of women are heads of households; not enough attention is paid to the problems they face. San Antonio is very poor. Sometimes women fall deep down into that depression they must learn to cross so they can get to the other side. We also need to be motivated by other issues and aware of other people's problems to make changes. We tell women that if someone is trying to abuse you, you must speak up.

Of course, we learned these things. When we started picketing and going to protests, I held the poster up to cover my face. I was afraid. Now if people don't call me, I call them. If you are denied opportunities, you have to look for and create opportunities.

My two oldest [children] got married when I lost my job. I missed them a lot. With the two small ones I did not spend too much time at home. My son is very independent, but my little girl has always wanted to be with me. If I go to town and work late, she comes here to help me. It's hard for me to decide how many hours to work a day. You plan your day, but something comes up, people come in the door. Most of the time my family supports me. My husband's friends say, "Hey, I saw your wife on TV."

I learned so much at Fuerza Unida. This is the best school you could have, working with people, listening, chairing—all the things you have to understand to carry out the struggle. Here we are not just individuals. We go to support and participate in all struggles in the movement. We work with Asian, Filipino, African American, Mexican, white. We are part of the same vision, the same movement.

People come here to cry if they want to cry, complain if they want to complain, laugh if they want to laugh, and get recommendations and advice about what to do. We started a food bank two years ago, after the Levi's layoffs, to help people during emergencies with groceries. We didn't have many resources. We suffered and made sacrifices. We know what many people who are out of work need—flour, oil, rice, juices, canned goods, beans, crackers, laundry detergent, bread, tortillas. We pay 12 cents a pound to the food bank and give the bags away for free. People come to volunteer and sew in exchange.

We have a good group of volunteers working closely with us. The group is mixed between ex-Levi's and other workers. Our sewing coop sells ready-made items such as bedspreads, tablecloths, curtains, and aprons. We bought sewing machines after many fundraising events. We really need two more commercial machines with a single needle. We also need a new truck to pick-up the materials for the sewing coop and the food coop.

When sales are good, we try to give volunteers a little something for their gas expenses. Through our *Loteria Mexicana* [bingo] everyone can take something home. Everyone brings something in and we cook and eat together. Anyone who comes here goes away with something. When women get frustrated we tell them, "Hey, come over here!" They leave with a piece of material, bingo prize, advice, and friendship to make them feel good. We are trying to expand the work of the organization. Our dream is to make pants. Now we are making miracles.

We never knew we were going to be around this long. When we met with La Mujer Obrera years ago, we asked "how could you survive so long?" They told us, "You have to think about and plan how you are going to survive that long." We have survived this long. Six years from now, I would like to see a stronger, more established organization that can keep going boom, boom, boom! We need technical assistance to stabilize the organization. I want to see Fuerza Unida do not only local, but more global projects together with other women.

When we first came here my husband and I were undocumented. Then my husband got his citizenship. About two years ago I made myself a citizen, too, because I felt that it was not right for me to be in this struggle when I didn't have a voice, a right to vote. I got to be somebody in the United States. I want to continue to work for our people to have a better life. I want to teach my grandchildren to go to school and college, to be good citizens, and participate in making decisions. My health bothers me. I want to talk more with the people, to sew, to pray, and get the power to sit down for a while. But God knows what he's doing. Maybe he uses my health to make me slow down and take a rest. My husband and kids are in good shape. My husband works at two jobs. He does not go out to drink. He talks to me. He helps me clean house, wash, and cook. What else could I want? I only want to see Fuerza Unida become an established organization working especially for gender equality.

—San Antonio, Texas, October 7, 1997

1   English Translation:
     In the liberation fronts
     of working people
     There are women who are strong and valiant
     There are women who know how to struggle
     They are women developing
     In the city and the countryside
     Giving strength and vision to the people
     They are working class women luminous with struggle
     They are working class women for justice and peace
     Respect their culture and work
     With the force of their dignity
     They are garment workers demanding justice
     They are garment workers who know how to struggle
     They are the women displaced by Levis
     The strugglers of the great movement
     They are the seamstresses of La Fuerza Unida
     They are the seamstresses of liberation.
     Traditional music with lyrics adapted by Arnoldo García (1994).

2   Porfirio Díaz ruled Mexico with an iron hand from 1877 until the 1910
     Mexican Revolution.

3   José Martí, Cuba's beloved poet, writer, and leader who died May 19, 1895,
     fighting Spanish colonialism, coined this term and warned against US designs
     on Latin America. See Roig de Leuchsenring, 1967.

4   For example, while an estimated half million people of Mexican origin,
     including US citizens, were deported during the Great Depression, World
     War II brought Mexican workers back to the United States on a massive scale
     via the US government-sponsored "bracero" [working arms] program," a
     contract labor project designed to address wartime labor shortages in
     agriculture. In 1954 during the post-Korean War recession, the Immigration
     and Naturalization Services (INS) implemented "Operation Wetback,"
     which deported over one million undocumented Mexican workers. At the
     same time nearly five million temporary labor contracts were issued to
     Mexican citizens between 1942 and 1964, while apprehensions of Mexican
     workers without documents also numbered over five million. The bracero
     program ended in December 1964 due to strong opposition to abuses of
     migrant farm workers. (Hondagneu-Sotelo, 1994:22-23; Fernández-Kelly,
     1983:26). As of this writing, immigrant rights organizers feared that the
     George W. Bush administration will enact a new version of the bracero
     program to use guest migrant workers to work for one-year periods, making
     it difficult for them to organize without being deported, and forcing them to
     leave their families home in Mexico (Interview with Eunice Cho, National
     Network for Immigrant and Refugee Rights, February 26, 2001).

5   Fix and Passel, 1994:24-25.

6   Falk, 2001; McDonnel, 1999.

7   Ruiz, 1998:7; Hondagneu-Sotelo, 1994:20.

8 By the 1920's many growers sought a more stable supply of immigrant workers, including Mexican women and children. (Hondagneu-Sotelo, 1994:21-22). During the war years many Mexican and Chicana/o families migrated from Texas to California. As the population became increasingly urban, women moved from the fields into garment factories in the Southwest. (Amott and Matthei, 1996: 79-80; Blackwelder, 1997:71-72). For more on the role of Mexicana and Chicana labor, see feminist researchers like Zavella, 1987; Mora and Del Castillo, 1980; Ruiz, 1987 and 1998; Mary Romero, 1992; Leeper, 1993; Blackwelder, 1984 and 1997; Soldatenko, 1993; Rose, 1990 and 1995; Calderón and Zamora, 1990: 37-40; Vargas, 1997; Honig, 1996; Blackwelder, 1997:71-72; Ruiz, 1998; Amott and Matthei, 1996; and Fernández-Kelly and García, 1989and 1992; Fernández-Kelly and Sassen, 1991.

9 US Department of Labor, Women's Bureau, 1997:1.

10 US Department of Labor, Women's Bureau, 1997: 6-7. According to US government statistics, leading occupations for "Hispanic Origin" women were as cashiers, secretaries, sales, retail and personal service workers; janitors and cleaners; nursing aids, orderlies, and attendants; textile sewing machine operators, cleaners and servants in private households, and cooks in 1996. Segregation into lower-paying, secondary labor market jobs, layoffs and high unemployment, and lower educational attainment all combined to keep incomes low and poverty rates high for Mexicanas and Chicanas. The 1995 median incomes for full-time workers put Latinas at the bottom of the income scale averaging $17,178. While Mexicanas and Chicanas earned only half as much as Anglo men, their male counterparts also made only 61 percent of white male earnings in 1990 (Amott and Matthei, 1996: 91).

11 Interview with Refugio "Cuca" Arrieta, February 26, 1997.

12 Interview with Petra Mata, October 7, 1997.

13 Fernández-Kelley, 1983:4 and 19-46. For more on the border economy, see Southwest Network for Environmental & Economic Justice, 1996.

14 Interview with Celeste Jiménez, February 26, 1997.

15 Interview with Marta Martínez, October 9, 1997.

16 The neoliberal program was designed to address systemic problems of the 1970s, such as the falling rates of profit, global recession, oil crisis, slump in commodity prices and markets, and ballooning rates of foreign debt which international banks feared deeply indebted nations would be forced to default. See Martínez and García, 1997; Vickers, 1991; García, Arnoldo, 1996; Asian Migrant Centre, 1996b; Zamora, 1995; National Commission for Democracy in Mexico, 1997b.

17 See Sparr, 1994; Vickers, 1991; Rivera, 1996; Suárez Aguilar, 1996; Louie and Burnham, 2000.

18 Stephen, 1997: 115.

19 Chant, 1991:41, cited in Stephen, 1997:115.

20 Economist Intelligence Unit, 1994:13, cited in Stephen, 1997:115.

21 See Benería and Roldan, 1987; Stephen, 1997:111-157; and Thompson, 1999.

22 Interview with Refugio "Cuca" Arrieta, February 26, 1997.

23 Human Rights Watch, 1996:2.

24   Fernández-Kelly, 1994:263.

25   Bustos and Palacio, 1994:19; Louie, Miriam, 1998.

26   Fernández-Kelly, 1994:265.

27   Delegation meetings organized by National Interfaith Committee for Worker Justice and hosted by the *Comisión para la Defensa de los Derechos Humanos del Valle de Tehuacán, Cetilizchicahualistli* (Tehuacán Human Rights Commission), February 22-23, 1998. Interviews with "María" and "Araceli," February 22, 1998. See National Interfaith Committee for Worker Justice, 1998; Louie, Miriam, 1998.

28   Interview with Carmen Valadez and Reyna Montero, February 17, 1998 in Tijuana, Mexico. Interview with Beatriz Alfaro, November 8, 1998. See also Valadez and Cota, 1998. Valadez and Montero explained that their group chose the feminist name "Factor X," after the X chromosomes which distinguishes females from males.

29   Interview with Elizabeth "Beti" Robles Ortega, July 10, 1998.

30   Author interviews with Elizabeth Robles of SEDEPAC, July 10, 1998; Mathilde Arteaga of FAT, February 20, 1998; Carmen Valadez and Reyna Montero, February 17, 1998; and Beatríz Alfaro of Factor X, November 8, 1998.

31   Fernández-Kelly, 1983: 62-63, 70-71. Between 1995 and 2000, for example, more than 1 million Mexicans moved to the northern border, largely in search of work in the maquila industry (Thompson, 2001:A1).

32   Interview with María Antonia Flores, February 24, 1997.

33   Delegation meeting organized by the National Interfaith Committee for Worker Justice with the *Comisión para la Defensa de los Derechos Humanos del Valle de Tehuacán, Cetilizchicahualistli* (Tehuacán Human Rights Commission in Tehuacán), February 22, 1998.

34   Louie, Miriam, 1990.

35   Egan, 1997.

36   Gomez-Quiñones and Maciel, 1998:37-38.

37   Hondagneu-Sotelo, 1994:21.

38   Monto, 1994.

39   Interview with Celeste Jiménez, February 26, 1997.

40   Interview with María del Carmen Domínguez, February 24, 1997.

41   Interview with Carmen "Chitlan" Ibarra Lopéz, February 24, 1997.

42   Interview with Alicia and Carlos Marentes, February 25, 1997.

43   García, Arnoldo, 1996:6.

44   Fix and Passel, 1994:25. For more on militarization of the border see Palafox, 1996. See also Michael Moore's spoof on the inconsistencies of US immigration policy, "Not on the Mayflower? Then Leave!," 1996:33-42.

45   Cornelius, 1988, cited in Hondagneu-Sotelo, 1994:31.

46   Interview with Carmen "Chitlan" Ibarra Lopéz, February 24, 1997. The 1986 Immigration Reform and Contract Act contained provisions for an amnesty-legalization program for undocumented immigrants who could prove continuous residence in the United States since January 1, 1982, and for those who could prove they had worked in US agriculture for 90 days during specific periods (Hondagnue-Sotelo, 1994:26.)

47   Hondagneu-Sotelo, 1994:2-20.
48   Interview with María del Carmen Domínguez, February 24, 1997.
49   Interview with Petra Mata, October 7, 1997.
50   Interview with Lucrecia Tamayo, March 3, 1997.
51   Interview with Irma Montoya Barajas, February 28, 1997.
52   Interview with María del Carmen Domínguez, February 24, 1997.
53   Interview with Ernestina "Tina" Mendoza, October 8, 1997.
54   For more on second and third generation Chicanas' labor, see Romero, 1992; Zavella, 1987; and Ruiz, 1987 and 1998.
55   Interview with Viola Casares, October 7, 1997.
56   See Coyle, Hershatter and Honig, 1980; Honig, 1996.
57   Interview with Carmen "Chitlan" Ibarra Lopéz, February 24, 1997. For more on race and gender insensitivity and top-down leadership within the union during the Farah strike, see Coyle, Hershatter and Honig, 1980.
58   Interview with Refugio "Cuca" Arrieta, February 26, 1997.
59   Interview with María del Carmen Domínguez, February 24, 1997.
60   Interview with Petra Mata, October 7, 1997.
61   Bonacich and Walker, 1994:86-87.
62   Sweatshop Watch, 2000:1.
63   Kever, 1990.
64   See Bluestone and Harrison, 1982; Moore, 1996.
65   Interview with Viola Casares, October 7, 1997.
66   Interview with Petra Mata, October 7, 1997.
67   Colliver, 2000; Schoenberger, 2000.
68   Landler, 1998; Frost, 1998, Emert, 1998.
69   Emert, 1999.
70   Sweatshop Watch, 1998:1-2. UNITE had initially requested that Levi's and Liz Claiborne not be included in the original suit.
71   Verhovek, 1998.
72   For information on the lawsuit filed by injured workers at Levi's plants in El Paso, see Tanaka, Wendy. 1997.
73   Greater Texas Workers Committee, 1997.
74   La Mujer Obrera, "Desastre causado por NAFTA-caused Disaster," Flyer, 2000.
75   Interview with María del Carmen Domínguez, February 24, 1997.
76   Bonacich and Appelbaum, 2000:16.
77   Interview with Lucrecia Tamayo, March 3, 1997.
78   Interview with María del Carmen Domínguez, February 24, 1997. After becoming an LMO organizer, Domínguez in turn leafleted factory gates to inform workers of their rights during impending NAFTA closures.
79   Interview with María del Carmen Domínguez, February 24, 1997. See Centro de Trabajadores and La Mujer Obrera. 1993.

80   Interview with María del Carmen Domínguez, February 24, 1997. The independent union adopted as its name the day in 1985 when angry workers launched the group as Mexico City sweatshop owners retrieved machines first, instead of injured seamstresses trapped under the earthquake's rubble.

81   Interview with Carmen "Chitlan" Ibarra Lopéz, February 24, 1997.

82   Interview with Carmen "Chitlan" Ibarra Lopéz, February 24, 1997.

83   Verhovek, 1998.

84   Interview with Refugio "Cuca" Arrieta, February 26, 1997. LMO holds an annual awards dinner honoring outstanding women labor and community leaders.

85   Interview with María Antonia Flores, February 24, 1997. For discussion about popular education, see Freire, 1990; Bell, Gaventa and Peters, 1990.

86   Interview with María Antonia Flores, February 24, 1997.

87   Interview with Lucrecia Tamayo, March 3, 1997.

88   Interview with Viola Casares, October 7, 1997.

89   Interview with Viola Casares, October 7, 1997.

90   Interview with Marta Martínez, October 9, 1997.

91   Interview with Ernestina "Tina" Mendoza, October 8, 1997.

92   Interview with Obdulia "Obi" Segura, October 8, 1997.

93   Interview with Petra Mata, October 7, 1997.

94   Interview with Viola Casares, October 7, 1997.

95   Interview with Carmen "Chitlan" Ibarra Lopéz, February 24, 1997.

96   Interview with Viola Casares, October 7, 1997.

97   Interview with Viola Casares, October 7, 1997.

98   Interview with Remedios García, February 26, 1997.

99   Interview with Carmen "Chitlan" Ibarra Lopéz, February 24, 1997.

100 Interview with Ernestina "Tina" Mendoza, October 8, 1997.

101 Interview with Petra Mata, October 7, 1997.

102 Interview with María del Carmen Domínguez, February 24, 1997.

103 Interview with Carmen "Chitlan" Ibarra Lopéz, February 24, 1997.

104 Dr. Loco's Rockin' Jalapeño Band, 1992. Reprinted with permission.

105 The FAT started organizing on the northern border at the General Electric plant in Júarez in 1993. On September 28, 1996, the FAT inaugurated its new center for maquila workers, the *Centro de Estudios y Taller Laboral*, A.C. (CETLA) [Labor Workshop and Study Center]. Interview with Beatríz E. Lujan Uranga, CETLA organizer, Ciudad Júarez, February 25, 1997. Interview with Mathilde Arteaga, in charge of national women's organization within the FAT, Mexico City, February 20, 1998. For more information on the FAT, see Hathaway, 2000.

Rally in support of Nam Gang restaurant workers in L.A.'s Koreatown.
Photo by KIWA

Chapter Three

"Each Day I Go Home with A New Wound in My Heart"

Korean Immigrant Women Workers

On June 6, 1998, workers, their supporters, and Korean Immigrant Workers Advocates (KIWA) organizers embarked on a massive march demanding justice for Korean and Latino restaurant workers in Los Angeles' Koreatown. Snaking through mini-malls filled with surprised shoppers, the marchers' stomachs soon growled as the mouth-watering smells of *kalbi, bulgogi, kimchee, mae-un tang, dwenjang jikae,* and *pa-chun* wafted out the doors of their favorite restaurants. The march ended in front of the Shogun Sushi Restaurant where workers were paid just $2 an hour. Koreatown restaurant worker Han Hee Jin surged to the front of the rally and delivered a fiery speech. Just a week before, her boss fired her from a *naeng myon* [cold noodle] specialty restaurant when she complained about having to simultaneously wait tables, cook, and wash dishes. Han told the marchers,

> Even though we need each other, owners always treat workers with suspicion. And yet employers want to be treated as Master. Even in a small restaurant, we are always forced to call employers, "Yes, Boss," "Yes, Madam," while we are subjected to degrading comments such as "you are only a servant" or "you are made for carrying a tray all your life" or "you, waitress bitch." After seven years of being subjected to these and more degrading remarks, I stand here today to state that we will not tolerate them anymore.[1]

Han's impassioned appeal signaled a major new twist in a drama unfolding within the emerging Korean community. Despite blacklisting and censorship, women like Han have begun to break the silence and stand up for their rights. Like their Chinese and Mexican counterparts, many Korean immigrant women workers worked in global assembly line, service, and finance industry jobs before coming to the United States. As young women they served as the foot soldiers in South Korea's rapid march to industrialization and Four Dragon status.[2] They labored under the shadow of South Korea's militarized and globalized sex industry and within niches of the informal economy that sprang up from the ruins of their war-ravaged country. After immigrating, many Korean immigrant women found work in factories like those they had worked in at home; others started on the lowest rungs of the service industry, especially within the ethnic enclave economy that mushroomed with the jump in Korean immigration after 1965. Some brought their experiences with the independent workers movement in South Korea.

Women Finance South Korea's "Economic Miracle"

Many Korean women workers have grown up under a harsh gender regime expressed in the proverb, "the real taste of dried fish and tame women can only be derived from beating them once every three days."[3] Korea's traditional neo-Confucian ideology dictated women's subordination—first to father, then husband, then son under the *Sam Jong Ji Do* [triple order instruction]. Man was the *bakkat yangban* [outside lord] while woman was the *anae* [inside person] under the *Nam Jon Yu Bi* [man's predominance over woman]. Women's ultimate role was to serve as *Hyun Mo Yang Cho* [sacrificial mother and submissive wife].[4]

As the "inside persons" within *poor* families, Korean women's labor was central to family production, planting, weeding, harvesting, processing foods and fish, raising animals, collecting roots and ferns, and other time-consuming tasks such as making *kimchee,* soy bean and pepper paste, dried and salted fish, and creating cotton and hemp fabric, clothing, foot, and head wear. Korean traditional folk songs lament the hunger and hardship of farming and fishing people who harvested the land and sea. Women continue to cultivate the rice seedlings, red peppers, cabbages, squash, cucumbers, onions, and garlic. Along Korea's ample coasts and islands, women hang squid and seaweed on their clotheslines to dry in the spring breezes, while sesame leaves blanket the *shigol* [countryside]. Years spent working in Korean rice paddies and sweltering Koreatown kitchens have brought soft wrinkles to Paek Young Hee's smiling eyes and strong dark hands. In Los Angeles' tastiest *mandu* [potsticker] house, she deftly combines the secret ingredients of the succulent fillings and light wrappings and serves these treats steamed, pan-fried, floating in a garlic pepper broth, or cloaked in a steamed bun and christened *whang mandu* [emperor potsticker]. Like her Chinese and Mexican female peasant and working-class counterparts, Paek had less access to education than her brothers.

> Because I have little education, immigrant life here is very arduous. I went to elementary school in Korea for a little bit. But in the old days in the countryside it was customary for the people to only send their sons to school, not their daughters. Because life was very hard, there was not enough money to send all the children to school.[5]

The Korean proverb "when whales fight, shrimps' backs get broken" captures Korea's fate sandwiched between the great power rivalries of Japan, the United States, Russia, and China. Forcing the "hermit kingdom" into the global economy, Japan colonized Korea in 1905 and used it for the next 40 years as its combination rice basket, mine, railroad, factory, slave labor reserve, brothel, and bridgehead to conquer the Asian mainland.

The defeat of Japanese imperialism at the end of World War II left Korea as only nominally independent, with occupying forces from the Soviet Union and the United States. At US suggestion, the Korean peninsula was divided in half at the 38th parallel. The Soviets supported leftist guerrillas in the north, while in South Korea a US military government from 1945 to 1948 paved the way for rightwing conservative regimes to follow. The clashes between the south and north erupted in the Korean War, which killed a total of over 2 million Koreans and Chinese and over 50,000 Americans, and left the Korean peninsula still divided in 1953 and in ashes.[6] The leading role played by the United States in Korea's division and the war cemented its long-standing military, political, and economic penetration of South Korea and on-going state of war with North Korea.

Seeing South Korea as a bulwark against communism, the United States provided massive military and economic aid to a series of repressive military regimes. After seizing power through a military coup in 1961, General Park Chung Hee launched an aggressive program of industrialization that used state and military power to hot-house capitalism and build up the *chaebol* [giant family-run corporations] that control up to 80 percent of the Korean economy.[7] Women's underpaid labor, both as industrial workers and as sex workers, financed this process. In a pattern that was repeated in other developing countries, South Korean companies recruited *yo'kong* [factory girls] from the countryside to toil day and night in export-oriented industries, such as textiles, garments, electronics, plastics, wigs, food processing, and shoes.[8]

To assuage community fears about the temptations and dangers awaiting young country girls going to work in the "sinful city" and placate the "inside vs. outside person" dichotomy in gender roles, the government portrayed factory work as fulfilling one's national patriotic duty. Anthropologist Kim Seung-Kyung says that the state's call for *sanop chonsa* [industrial soldiers] stressed the women's loyalty and obedience, exploiting traditional messages of women as filial daughters willing to sacrifice themselves for the good of the nation.[9] Hierarchical gender relations were maintained at work via all male management, discipline, and sexual harassment, and employers portrayed factory work as only a temporary arrangement for women whose true vocation was marriage and motherhood.[10]

Koreatown restaurant worker Kim Chong Ok was one of the early *yo'kong*. Her story reads like the timeline of the development of South Korea's much touted "Miracle on the Han River."[11] Born into a poor peasant family, she and her older siblings migrated to Seoul as part of a family strategy to find work in 1971.

I helped my parents work on the farm a lot. I did whatever they asked me to do, whatever needed to be done, everything from tilling the land to sowing the seeds, to harvesting the crops. It was an extremely hard life. We often didn't have enough food when I was growing up. I'm sure a few people were able to live well, but everyone else survived on *jook* [rice porridge] and *kamja* [potatoes]. When times got really tough, you could take one bowl of rice and add enough water to serve four people for a couple of meals.[12]

Kim's work in the factories and sweatshops in Seoul continued through her marriage and the births of her children. Her husband worked as a chauffeur, driving elite government officials to their rendezvous and trysts.

After I got married, life was hard. I wanted to help out so I kept working. I did a little of everything. I never had [permanent] full-time work, but I kept myself busy to make money to survive. I worked in a factory where they made walking shoes. I made the holes for the shoelaces. I did homework making electric cords. I made flowers, too. After 1978, when I gave birth to my first child, I made envelopes while I was taking care of the kids.[13]

With industrialization came expansion of Korea's finance, retail, and service industries. In jobs demanding interaction with the public, employers often discriminated based on women's physical appearance and "attractiveness," a practice that has re-emerged among some Korean employers in the United States.

Sex Industry Shapes Service Sector

The sex industry is a huge part of South Korea's informal economy. Eight decades of military occupation and dictatorship—including sexual slavery as "Comfort Troops"[14] to the Japanese Imperial Army, compulsory military service and training in the use of deadly force for all men in Korea, and the continued occupation by 37,000 US troops—have made sex trafficking and violence against women intense.[15]

Cho Ailee, an English literature professor and member of the Research Center for Women's Studies in Korea, says that violence and sexual exploitation of Korean women is rooted in militarism.

You have to understand that Korea is a very violent society. We
have lived directly under military governments for 30 years. Even
though the [government] of Roh Tae Woo [1988-1992] was os-
tensibly civilian, in reality the military still wields power. For Roh
Tae Woo to reach the position of general, a lot of people had to
die. The military and police have killed people demonstrating for
democracy. *Kusadae* [Save the Company] thugs beat up workers.
In this violent military climate, men's violence against women is
sanctioned.[16]

During the Vietnam War, the Park regime developed the sex industry to entice foreign exchange out of Japanese businessmen and
US soldiers on "R and R" (rest and recreation) leave. Government
officials once again called on women factory and sex industry workers to sacrifice themselves "for the sake of the nation." Travel agencies offered "sex tours," which included air travel, hotel lodging,
transportation, and prostitutes.[17]

The exploitation of women sex workers spilled over to women
workers in other service industries. Korean women working in restaurants, bars, snack houses, and barber shops are often expected to
put up with male customers' sexual advances and harassment.[18] Korean Immigrant Workers Association (KIWA) organizer and former
restaurant worker Kim Seung Min recalled how her single mother
worked in a variety of odd jobs after her husband left.

> She used to work as a *don jang sa* [money lender].... She would find
> someone who needed money and a person who was willing to
> lend money for a high interest rate. She would be the middle per-
> son who connected people. I didn't like her business. It was ex-
> ploitative and led to a lot of people crying. But even though I
> didn't like the kind of business my mom was doing, that was the
> money she fed us with and that I grew up on. Isn't it ironic?
>
> Our father was a playboy. He was never home. Everyday a
> different woman would come to our house and ask, "Where is
> your father?" One time a woman came to my mother's home and
> kidnapped me. She used me as a kind of ransom to get hold of my
> father.... She threatened my mother, "If you don't tell me where
> he, is I'm going to kill her." I was only four or five then, but that is
> something that I'm going to remember my whole life.

We used to live in a house that my father built, but after he left we decided to move out. We didn't have much money so we moved into a rented room. There were times when for a month straight we only ate flour-based soup. Do you know *sujiebi* [flour dumpling]? Sometimes we would take a paper bag and go to the market and pick up potatoes and other stuff that the vendors left behind. My wish back then was to be able to eat all the rice and drink all the milk I wanted.[19]

Like many women working in service jobs, Kim's mother had to deal with sexual advances from male customers.

My mother would put us all to sleep early in the evening before she went away somewhere.... One day I pretended that I was asleep. I followed my mom when she left. I was afraid that I might lose her, so I ran to keep up. I saw my mom go into a *pochang macha* [outdoor tented restaurant], called *Sun Sul Jib* [Pure Wine House]. At that time I didn't know what kind of work she was doing. I peeked into the little grass window and saw my mom sitting next to a few men and drinking with them and singing some songs. They hit their chopsticks on the table in rhythm. [cries] I was staring in for a long time. Then I saw one of the men touch my mom's thigh. I was surprised and I screamed "Waaahhh!" really loud.

Then my mom dragged and spanked me all the way home from the restaurant. But after that my mom never went back to work there. I think it was very hard for a single woman to make a living in Korean society in those days. Maybe this was the easiest way for her to make money. When I was young I didn't hate my mom for doing these things. I tried to understand her situation.[20]

Minjung Workers' Movement

Labor organizing in Korea's formal economy has a long history of radicalism. The highly politicized and militant character of the South Korean *minjung* [mass or common people's] labor movement stems from the fusion between the militarized state and corporate capitalism. When demanding their most basic rights, workers immediately had to confront not only their bosses, but also the dictatorship and its agents, including the Korean CIA (KCIA), draconian national security and labor laws, police tactical squads called *baekgo'ldan* [White Skull Squadron], government-controlled unions, and ex-military company thugs.[21]

On November 13, 1970, Chun Tae Il, a 22-year-old garment worker set himself afire to protest employer and police repression of workers organizing for their rights in Seoul's Peace Market. Some 20,000 young women slaved in the one-block, four-story high maze of tiny cubicles for less than $30 a month each. As flames consumed his body, Chun grasped a copy of Korea's Labor Standards Act and shouted, "Obey the Labor Standards Act! Don't mistreat young girls!"[22] His mother, Lee So Sun, who witnessed his death, founded the Garment Workers' Union, *Chunggye Pibok,* immediately after his funeral.

Women spearheaded the democratic union movement throughout the 1970s.[23] Women workers at Dongil Textile Company waged a pitched six-year battle (1972-1978) to win their rights. They took on the company union and elected the first woman union president. Police beat up workers, company thugs smeared excrement on their faces, and bosses fired and blacklisted the leaders to smash the movement.[24]

Labor unrest continued to grow and in May 1979, police violence against women workers, including the death of Kim Kyong Suk, incited riots as far away as Masan and Pusan.[25] In May 1980, with US government and military complicity, the military regime of Generals Chun Doo Hwan and Roh Tae Woo dispatched some 40,000 troops to Kwangju City in South Cholla Province to crush citizens who had peacefully run their city for five days in hopes of a "democratic spring" after the death of dictator Park. Government troops brutally massacred hundreds of civilians. Horror at the army's brutality catalyzed the workers' and people's movements in Korea.[26] The government imposed martial law, completely suspended labor rights, and outlawed the Garment Workers' Union.[27]

During the 1980s, South Korea gained international notoriety for the world's longest workweek and highest rate of industrial accidents.[28] In 1985, the struggles of women workers in the Kurodong industrial estate on the outskirts of Seoul laid the basis for advances in the *minjung* labor movement. Kuro included large estates of shop compounds, which employed some 58,000 workers, including 38,000 young women who lived in company barracks, tiny rooms called *taak jang* [chicken coops]. Daewoo Apparel company got the government to declare its workers' strike for better wages illegal, and unionists were beaten, fired, and imprisoned. In a preview of the explosion that was to come, actions spread like wildfire as workers from other Kuro shops staged solidarity strikes, and women, student, religious, and human rights groups lent their support.

Launched in 1987 amidst the eruption of labor disputes across the country, the Korean Women Workers Association (KWWA) proved key in overcoming the fragmentation of women workers' struggles caused by state repression and forced retirement upon marriage and childbirth. KWWA organizer Yoon Hae Ryun started working in garment shops when she was 14, from 8 a.m. to 2 a.m. every day. She decided to join the 1985 cooperative strike in Kuro.

> When we started to strike, I told my family about it in order to prepare them for what might happen. They were shocked and cried and cried. I was the only wage earner in the family because the kids were in school and my father was too old to continue his job as a laborer lifting materials. I got arrested and spent six months in jail with workers and students. All of my friends from work were there. It was so crowded that there was no place to sleep. You had to sleep like a knife [draws arms close to her body to resemble a knife]. When I got out of jail I went back to the factory to work, but I kept getting dismissed from jobs. It got to the stage where I was blacklisted and could not get work. So together with other displaced women workers, I began to work with the KWWA to support women workers in their struggle.[29]

In 1987, Korea's federation of independent unions, *Chunnohyup,* seized world headlines as hundreds of thousands of students and workers demanding democracy battled with helmeted, baton-wielding police and government troops while blinding tear gas choked major cities. Some 1.3 million workers participated in over 3,600 strikes and organized 1,200 new unions.[30] In 1995, the democratic unions institutionalized their national structure as the Korean Confederation of Trade Unions (KCTU). Women workers played a significant role in the health workers' unions, particularly the nurses' union, as well as in unions of teachers, department store employees, and garment workers. Kim Seung Min explained that the 1987 *Pal Chil Nyun Nodongja Dae Toojaeng* [Great Workers' Struggle], was a "nationwide rebellion. Most people who had jobs during that period felt the impact of the uprising at their workplace because it was a nationwide rebellion, not just a union-based struggle at individual workplaces." [31]

As Korean workers unionized and raised their wages and working conditions, employers began to use migrant workers from China (both Koreans and Chinese), the Philippines, Vietnam, Indonesia, Nepal, and Bangladesh. Lee Jung Hee joined a democratic bank workers union during that period. She compares wages, working conditions, and treatment of immigrant workers in Korea and the United States:

> When I was in Korea I worked at a bank for about ten years. I was able to work my way up to a certain position within the bank.... There was a union that formed at the bank so I started wearing those special white T-shirts as a union member. I got paid 1,200,000 *won*. So it was more than [US]$2,000 a month. They gave me a lot of bonuses at the bank, too. I got vacation pay and I would get a bonus the size of my monthly pay.... In Korea you only had to work eight or nine hours a day. They never make you work 12 hours a day like here. Nowadays some of the Southeast Asian immigrant workers in Korea have to work 12 or more hours a day. I think their situation is very similar to what immigrants face here in the US. I feel like my situation here is very similar to those workers who are coming, almost like slave labor, to Korea.[32]

In 1990, Kim Seung Min was swept up in the *minjung* student movement while attending high school in Inchon, Korea.

> I became the leader of the third-year students. I thought "this strike is going to last for a long time so we'd better not make it boring." So I organized plays, singing, and games during the demonstrations. Students started coming out to watch the performances. Close to 2,000 students came out, almost the whole

school. So the real fight started with the 2,000 students. We used the public address system to call the students to come to the *undong chang* [sports stadium] to demonstrate. We slept in the stadium with the teachers. We brought sleeping bags and burners to cook. It was really fun. During that time we were able to spend a lot of time talking with the teachers about the society and how it runs. The teachers told us about the importance of what we were doing.

While we were at the school camping out, the police and our family members would come and ask us to go home.... A lot of the riot police use buses with barbed wire, like chicken wire. These buses are called *taak jang* [chicken cages]. They would park those buses outside the school and yell, "Those communists! Those reds! Why are you guys supporting them? Come out!" None of the students went out so the *baekgo'ldan* [White Skull Squadron], a special riot police, charged in and took away almost all of the teachers. They beat up the students and then stacked them one by one criss-cross on top of each other.[33]

In 1987, the police killing of college student Lee Han Yol set off nationwide demonstrations of workers, students, and many middle class people that forced Chun Doo Hwan to concede to demands for direct elections before the 1988 Seoul Olympics. Popular pressure on succeeding governments resulted in the November 1995 indictment of Chun and his collaborator Roh Tae Woo for corruption and the 1980 Kwangju massacre.[34] A Seoul district court sentenced Chun to death and Roh to 22 and a half years in prison. The Supreme Court later reduced the sentences, and in December 1997, after serving only two years in jail, the two were freed by a presidential pardon.[35] Koreatown restaurant worker Paek Young Hee comes from the Cholla province region that has suffered historic discrimination and where the Kwangju massacres were committed. Paek only had harsh words for Chun and Roh:

I am not satisfied with the judgment. First they got the death sentence but then it got changed to a life sentence. It is common knowledge that they killed many, many people. If they killed so many people, how can justice be served if they are still allowed to live?[36]

Second-Stage Capital Flight

During the 1980s, women workers launched determined campaigns against plant closures by Pico Products, Tandy, Control Data Electronics, and the Sumida Corporation.[37] In 1992, local Korean Women Workers Association (KWWA) branches united to form a national network, the Korean Women Workers Associations United (KWWAU), or *Yonohyob*.

As the labor movement gained ground, however, US and Japanese transnational corporations fled overseas to more fertile fields in Indonesia, Vietnam, China, Mexico, and Central America.[38] The companies discarded Korean women workers like old shoes, leaving many with crippling injuries. At the 1995 UN 4th World Conference on Women NGO Forum in Huairou, China, Choi Myung Hee, an injured worker, ten-year veteran of the shoe industry, and KWWAU organizer in Pusan detailed the devastating effects of this second-stage globalization.

> During the 1970s and 80s companies like Nike, Adidas, Reebok, and LA Gear flocked to Korea. We worked long hours with toxic glues and chemicals. Now 50,000 workers have lost their jobs. Those that can find work, can only do so in the service industry, in restaurants and the like.[39]

Nearly a million workers in Korea waged a general strike against new restrictive labor laws rammed through the legislature on December 26, 1996.[40] But by the end of 1997, the Asian financial crisis shattered South Korea's economic bubble. Economic growth came to a halt as the *won* plummeted, banks folded, and seven of the country's 40 largest conglomerates went bankrupt or were unable to pay their debts. Basic food and commodity prices skyrocketed. The December 1997 International Monetary Fund bailout package stipulated austerity measures that made the economy even more subservient to foreign capital.[41] In February 1998, the government legalized mass layoffs and the use of temporary employment agencies.[42]

Following the dictum of "last hired, first fired," women and migrants were hit hardest. More than a million workers, including some 622,000 women, lost their jobs.[43] The government repatriated over 270,000 migrant workers.[44] Union support for migrant workers shrank as unions focused on supporting local workers.[45]

In the wake of second-stage global restructuring and the 1997 financial crisis, KWWAU focused on the plight of displaced and contingent women workers. KWWAU won legislation to extend unemployment insurance to women working for small and medium-sized businesses and developed an employment and training center for displaced workers. On August 29, 1999, workers launched the Korean Women's Trade Union (KWTU), the first nation-wide, multi-industry labor union for women. Veteran labor activist and KWWAU director Maria Chol Soon Rhie says, "Now we've got two wheels to make our bicycle move faster—KWTU and KWWAU!"[46] KWTU has organized contingent workers such as women golf caddies, cafeteria and restaurant workers, and freelance writers for TV soap operas. KWTU president Choi Sang Rim says the union has a big job ahead.

> The present situation confronting women workers at the gateway to the 21st century can be summed up in the following facts: 64 percent are employed in workplaces with less than four workers; 70 percent are employed on an irregular basis.... [They] are the primary targets for dismissal [and] pressured to resign upon marriage or pregnancy.... The rate of organized women is only 5.6 percent.[47]

Since its inception, KWWAU has built ties between women workers in Korea and in other countries. Spurred by free trade policies like NAFTA and Asian Pacific Economic Cooperation,[48] South Korean subcontractors for US companies like J.C. Penney, Sears, Nike, and Reebok have moved into Southeast Asia, the Pacific Islands, Mexico, and Central America. A number of these companies use the same kind of abusive tactics overseas that have been employed against Korean workers since the 1960s.[49] Women workers groups in Asia and Latin America are increasing calling on KWWAU and KCTU for solidarity in fighting these Korean-owned companies.[50]

America Fever

Given the history of US intervention in Korea, it should come as no surprise that many Korean immigrants view the United States with a mixture of admiration, curiosity, anger, fascination, and disillusionment. Koreans call these ambivalent emotions *miguk yol* [America Fever] and *miguk byong* [America Sickness].[51]

Like many Koreatown restaurant workers, Chu Mi Hee comes home from work late. She looks great, despite having just come off a long work shift, and serves guests a tray loaded with cups of steaming hot tea and *anju* [snacks]. Mrs. Chu explains why she was drawn to *Miguk* [America/Beautiful Country].

> I came to the US in 1993 by myself. I wanted to try it out and see if this was the right place for me. In Korea, the US is still the object of admiration. My friend from church who is younger than me was living here. I came in July or August relying on that person's help. We lived together for about a month and a half.
>
> In Korea, I worked with a youth organization that was a subsidiary of a youth foundation. I worked as a clerk, more related to accounting. The pay was not bad considering I only had a high school diploma and not a higher degree. I was not married, so when I reached the age for marriage, I wanted some chance to improve myself. (laughs) I came to the US when I was 30.[52]

The disintegration of Korean feudal rule and rise of Japanese colonialism propelled the first wave of Korean migration to the United States between 1903 and 1905, principally to Hawaii for work as agricultural laborers.[53] Others, mostly students and intellectuals, were drawn by the influence of US Christian missionaries in Korea. Between 1910 and 1924, Korean women (called "picture brides") were allowed into the country to marry Korean men who had migrated earlier.[54]

In the 1950s, a second wave of migration included Korean wives of US servicemen and their children, war orphans, and professional workers and students.[55] Since the war, the US military has functioned as an economic enclave within South Korea, dispensing military contracts, jobs, and US surplus and commissary goods for the black market—that is, survival opportunities to an economically strapped population. Korean women's labor constitutes a central aspect of this enclave economy, through providing companionship, cooking, cleaning, translating, interacting with Korean institutions, and other services for US GIs. Prostitution, the sex industry, rape, and violence against women are all direct and inevitable byproducts of militarization.[56] The epithets leveled at Korean women with American men of *yang kongju* [western princess] and *yang nuna* [western sister] have come to be synonymous with "whore."[57] Despite this derogation, scholars estimate that Korean wives of US servicemen have assisted in the immigration of an additional 400,000 Koreans.[58]

The third and largest wave of Korean immigration to the United States occurred after the enactment of the Immigration and Naturalization Act of 1965. Between 1976 and 1990, from 30,000 to 35,000 Koreans immigrated annually to the United States. In the 1970s and 1980s, Koreans were the third largest group of immigrants after Mexicans and Filipinos.[59] Rapid industrialization, urbanization, the commercialization of agriculture, militarization, and political repression in Korea all pushed Koreans to immigrate to the United States. The South Korean government promoted Korean labor migration in order to earn foreign exchange and relieve employment pressures, as the Philippines and later Indonesia, Bangladesh, Nepal, and other countries were to do. The South Korean government sent workers and mercenary troops to Vietnam, male miners and construction workers to West Germany and the Middle East, female nurses to western Europe and the United States, and migrants to Latin America, some of whom later relocated to the United States.[60]

Since the war, Korean women have migrated to the United States at high rates in the Korean version of the feminization of migration. Girl orphans were preferred over boys by US adopting families.[61] Additionally, Korea sent more girls than boys given the higher value placed on sons than daughters in Korean culture.[62] By 1974, one-third of Korean immigrant professionals admitted to the United States were nurses. During the late 1960s Koreans were the second largest nationality group among US nurses.[63] The passage of legislation to discourage immigration of foreign health professionals in 1976 and 1977 drastically reduced immigration of Korean nurses.[64] Korean women nurses made a major contribution to establishing the US Korean community, first within the health industry, and later by starting small businesses with their husbands, many of whom they sponsored for immigration visas.[65]

Anthropologist Kyeyoung Park says that motivation for migration often differs based on economic strata: people from lower-class origins come for survival reasons; most middle- and upper-middle class people, for better well-being and capital investment; and others, like those who went bankrupt or were fired mid-career, for a new beginning. Some Koreans see the United States as a place where "all legitimate trades are equally honorable" in contrast to Korea.[66] Park also says that middle- and upper-class Koreans find it easier to manipulate immigration procedures, usually through sponsorship by relatives already here. But lower-class Koreans who have no kin to sponsor them may be smuggled into the United States by way of South America, Mexico, or the Caribbean.

Women-Centered Migration Chains

Many Korean women immigrants saw the United States as a place where they would be treated better than they had been in Korea.[67] Paek Young Hee's younger sister immigrated to the United States as a nurse and then sponsored the rest of the family. Because she—as the daughter of a poor farming family—had only been able to go to school for a couple of years, Paek worked hard in Koreatown restaurants to make sure that her children could take advantage of educational opportunities in the United States.

> That is why we made sure our children got an education after coming here. When we first came we stayed with my younger sister for about 20 days. After that we got a place in Hanin Town [Koreatown].[68]

Kyung Park, her parents, siblings, and children were able to start a new life in the United States with the help of her elder sister.

> I came to the US in 1990 without my husband. He stayed in Korea. At that time we were having big problems. He wanted a di-

vorce. We were separated for a while. After I came here I filed the divorce papers and sent them back to Korea. He treated me badly and had a lot of girlfriends. His job was terrible, hanging around with all of those women at night.... When I came to the US I lived with my family and my mom took care of me. I came in October 1990 and got a job after two months. [laughing] I've been working ever since.[69]

Kim Chong Ok immigrated at the invitation of her mother-in-law, who had obtained US citizenship.[70] Lee Jung Hee immigrated to the United States for the sake of her husband who had enrolled as a student. But the high cost of living in the United States coupled with unanticipated medical expenses for their daughter soon wiped out their savings. She ended up working in various Koreatown restaurants after the family bank account was depleted.

We sold our apartment in Korea in order to come here so we lived on that money for about one year. We didn't work at first because my husband was going to school and we didn't really know much about American society. We brought about $50,000 when we first came. But our daughter broke her leg so we had to pay for her medical bills. With the car and apartment payments we pretty much spent all the money we had saved in Korea within one year.[71]

Han Hee Jin immigrated to the United States after suffering a series of economic disasters in Korea. As an undocumented worker, she was vulnerable to her employer's abuse.

I was frank about my immigration status at the beginning of employment, but now the boss is trying to use this to silence me. I felt powerless and even more angry. The employer says she is a church-going Christian and cannot use bad words like I do. But she uses terms like "servant" to abuse me and the other workers. I don't know what kind of praying she does at church but she should self-criticize at home first. And, I hope her fellow church members are only made up of citizens and green card holders. I feel those who are hurt and truly need to be consoled are neglected by churches.[72]

Korean immigration to the United States peaked in 1987 at 35,849 and then began to decline. The number of Korean Americans returning to Korea rose from 848 in 1980 to 6,487 in 1992. Stories of hardship and long working hours in Korean small businesses in the United States fueled this trend, as did the return to civilian rule and the improving South Korean economy. In 1992, the backlash against the Korean community during the Rodney King civil unrest in Los Angeles also reverberated back to Korea, further slowing immigration.[73] In late 1997, the Asian financial crisis sent shock waves across the ocean to US shores. Many Korean immigrants in the United States sent US currency to relatives in Korea who had lost their jobs and homes and been sent to debtors' prison. In Los Angeles, some Koreatown employers cut back on wages, hours, and jobs, blaming the Asian financial crisis. As South Korean restructuring measures gutted gains by the labor movement, migration from Korea became attractive again as working people looked for ways to improve their lives.

Working Women

The model minority myth has obscured a sizable portion of the Korean community, namely low-waged workers, especially women. A greater proportion of US-born and immigrant Korean married women work for pay than do white women.[74] While 28 percent of all US women work in service or factory jobs, 40 percent of Korean working women are concentrated in these areas.[75]

A large portion of Korean women work in low-wage jobs in globalized industries, such as garment and electronics assembly, in hotels and janitorial services, and in ethnic enclave service jobs, such as restaurants, supermarkets, and stores. For example, in a study of Korean seamstresses working for ethnic Korean contractors in Dallas, Texas, sociologist Shim Ja Um found that more than 80 percent of the 74 women surveyed worked in poorly ventilated factories, averaging 53.7 hours per week, but sometimes more during peak seasons. Many also worked at home. These women workers did not have paid vacation leave, nor health insurance, and piece rates were low.[76]

Many Korean immigrant women living in San Jose and Santa Clara County, California, work as electronics assemblers. Of Silicon Valley's 172,400 electronics production workers—60 percent are female 70 percent are Asian or Latino.[77] Community activists estimate that 10 to 15 percent of the Asian production workforce is Korean, 10 to 15 percent South Asian, 30 percent Filipina/o, 30 percent Vietnamese, and the rest other Southeast Asians and Chinese.[78] Asians made up 47 percent and Latinos 21.6 percent of the semi-skilled blue-collar workforce, and 41.2 percent and 35.8 percent of the unskilled workforce within the industry.[79] Wages average $6 an hour, just above the minimum, without benefits, opportunities for raises, or upward mobility, even for women who have worked ten to fifteen years for the company. The women are pressured to work twelve-hour days and six-day weeks during rush seasons, but are let off without pay during dead seasons. Production lines are segregated by gender, immigrant status, and age, with older, limited English-speakers working the most hazardous and tedious jobs. Korean immigrant women assemblers commonly experience problems with repetitive stress injuries, poor vision, nausea, rashes, headaches, and miscarriages.[80]

Korean community organizers in Los Angeles estimate that half a million Koreans live in the greater LA area, constituting the largest concentration of Koreans in the United States. Some 70 percent of the immigrant population are workers, contrary to the popular view of all Koreans as business owners.[81] "Koreatown" covers a 20-mile square area filled with restaurants, markets, professional services, shops, churches, community and civic organizations, herb shops, Tae Kwon Do studios, and media outlets.[82] Koreatown serves as the diaspora's social and cultural center. Several thousand Korean women work as waitresses, cooks, hostesses, and cashiers in the 300 restaurants in the enclave.[83] Korean men work in Koreatown markets, and as janitors, handymen, painters, and construction workers.

While Koreatown functions as an ethnic enclave economy, Korean restaurant and market owners also employ Latino men to do a lot of the heavy "back of the house" work. Korean contractors in Los Angeles' downtown garment district employ Mexican and

Central American immigrants and some Korean women workers as pattern and sample makers. The practice of hiring Latino workers may have originated with Koreans who migrated to Latin America and worked in the garment industry before migrating to the United States.[84] Koreans constitute some 10 percent of all Koreatown residents, Latinos, 68 percent, and the remaining 12 percent, other Asians and African Americans.[85]

New immigrants from Korea find jobs relatively quickly in Koreatown. Women learn about jobs through friends, acquaintances, hometown contacts, and local newspapers. Lee Jung Hee says that the women restaurant workers' ages run from the early 20s to mid-60s, with the majority aged 35 to 40. The majority of women have children, and older workers also have grandchildren.[86] Adjusting to a new industry and country can be difficult. Chu Mi Hee was fired after working only two hours at her first job in the United States.

> After 15 days [from when she arrived in the US] I started looking for jobs here. I looked for *shik dang* [restaurant] jobs mostly, and I soon found different places. When I was honest about how short my immigration experience was, they wouldn't hire me. At one place I got hired for only two hours and then they kicked me out. I really didn't have any restaurant work experience. [laughs] I didn't say *oh so oh seyo* [please come in] and things like that to the customers. So I made mistakes.
>
> I continued to work in restaurants.... I worked at about four different restaurants, maybe more.... At first I was grateful to them for giving me a job since I had no other choice. I didn't complain even though the base pay was low. Once I started working at the big restaurants where I was paid by the hour, I learned the reality of what the pay should be. I tried to stick with the bigger restaurants. I didn't know any better when I first started. I really didn't feel that anything was wrong.[87]

Paek Young Hee found jobs in Koreatown through hometown friends and other acquaintances. As an older woman, she did "back of the house" labor in the kitchen and worked her way up from a part-time cook's helper to a full-time cook.

At first I worked at a *ddok jib* [rice cake house] owned by someone who came from the same area of Korea that I came from, a *kohyang chinku* [hometown friend]. The work was very hard so the owner recommended for me to go to some other restaurant to work. So I went there. I didn't know how to read the newspaper so it was only when other people told me about openings where I might go that I found out about jobs.

I worked in five or six different places. The other women working there were about the same age as me. People who are different ages work in different jobs. Usually the cooks are older and the waitresses are younger. At first I wasn't a full cook. I worked as a cook's helper, peeling potatoes, chopping vegetables, and things like that.[88]

Kim Seung Min also followed the trail of immigrant women to restaurant work in 1997.

My plan was to make lots of money for six months and then move to New York. [sighs] So I got hired at a restaurant where I worked ten days straight without any day off. Someone introduced me to that job. The owners told me that I didn't have much experience so I only got paid $15 a day from my share of the tips. After that they fired me, saying I wasn't fast enough. But it was all planned. The restaurant was always really, really busy. They just needed someone to cover for ten days, but they never told me that I was hired only temporarily. The day they told me not to come back anymore, the new worker who was supposed to start showed up. I got really upset. I said they couldn't use people like this, but they still insisted that I leave.[89]

Long Hours

By law, restaurant workers should get paid minimum wages before tips. In Koreatown, restaurant workers are often paid sub-minimum wages of just over $4 an hour at big restaurants. Twelve-hour days and six- to seven-day workweeks are standard. Depending on tips, Koreatown waitress can earn between $600 and $3,000 a month, and cooks, depending on whether the waitresses share tips, between $600 and $1,500.[90] Some women work split shifts, taking off between meals, and returning to finish up.

Thus, their waking hours are completely dominated by their work schedules. The long hours exact a toll on women workers, shortchanging the amount of time they have to spend with children, spouses, friends, or at church.

Paek took a pay cut to work for an acquaintance. She worked 12 hours a day, 6 days a week. When the business did not go well, the boss tried to lay her off without paying $1,200 owed in back wages. She eventually found another job, but the president of the Korean Restaurant Owners' Association tried to get her new boss to fire her for speaking out.

> I used to go to church but now I can't because I have to work on Sundays. The people I work with are my friends. But working so many hours, there is never enough time to socialize and spend with friends.[91]

Like many other restaurant kitchen workers in Koreatown restaurants, Paek works with Latino men who,

> wash dishes, lift heavy things, peel potatoes and things like that. How do we communicate? (laughs) By gesturing *son jit, pal jit* [with our hands and feet], our eyes and heads. They know a few Korean words and I know a few Mexican words so we point and show what we want. I have never had any problems communicating with the Mexican workers.[92]

Choi Kee Young found a restaurant job through the Korean newspaper. As with the case of many immigrant and African-American families where finding a job, even a low-paid one, can be easier for women than men, Choi was thrust into the role of the family "rice winner."

> It was really hard to get used to life here at first because I had to work pretty much 12 hours a day when I first started. Of course, my husband looked after our kids. But I'd come home so late that I couldn't really give my kids their baths. So during the summer, my daughter's hair smelled pretty bad!
>
> I lost a lot of weight since I came to America. I've really tried hard to gain weight, but I just can't because of the amount of work that I have to do. But if I don't live this way we can't survive. The apartment payment is the most important because we need a

place to stay. We need a car to get around and go to work. We need at least a thousand dollars a month to get by in America.

I work so late I can't look after my kids. If I could just work about six hours or so and I had the rest of the time to look after my kids I'd be OK. But in Koreatown all of the hours are so long that the potential for your kids to go bad are really high.... The biggest complaint that my husband has is that at night he has to get the family together and cook them dinner. It's very stressful for him so he doesn't really look after the homework of our children very well. He has turned to drinking by himself and he feels lonely. Sometimes he'll joke with me and say he's really missing Korea a lot, so that's why he's ended up drinking.[93]

Health Hazards

Low-wage Korean women workers in the restaurant, garment, hotel, and electronics industries face a number of health hazards. In the high-stress restaurant industry, women work with boiling liquids and hot stoves and dishwashers, and carry heavy pots and trays. In the poorly ventilated sweatshops of the garment industry, workers are engulfed by dust, threads, chemical dyes and sprays, and perform repetitive motions behind industrial machines for long hours in cramped spaces. In the hotel industry, women work with strong cleaning agents and perform heavy labor that can lead to back, shoulder, neck, and wrist injuries. In the electronics industry, women work with toxic chemicals, and often suffer from eye strain, dizziness, headaches, rashes, miscarriages, back and repetitive stress injuries, and cancers that do not become visible until years later when it is hard to hold employers accountable because the small shops have closed down and chemicals changed.[94]

Lee Kyu Hee worked at the luxurious Fairmont Hotel in San Francisco for nine years as a room cleaner before being promoted to the position of parlor maid and restroom-cleaner.

I started working there when I was 48 years old. The first day I cleaned seven rooms, the second day eight, then nine, ten, eleven rooms.... It took me one month to get up to cleaning 16 rooms. I didn't know I was on probation.... Now I get paid $8.20 an hour, every two weeks. I can't even think about quitting because I need to survive even though the work is hard.

I have problems only working part-time, but I have to since I'm not feeling so well. Sometimes I get laid off for a week or three days.... I went to see the doctor who took x-rays but couldn't find out the cause of the pain around my stomach. I went to the OB/GYN and internal medicine to take more x-rays. I have Kaiser insurance, but can't see a Korean doctor because they don't cover it.[95]

Lee Jung Hee described how she suffered serious back injuries, skin burns, and a miscarriage because of unsafe working conditions at the Sa Rit Gol Restaurant where she worked as a waitress. As in many other Korean-owned workplaces, her boss did not offer workers' compensation nor pay her medical bills for her injuries.

It's a very old restaurant so the tile is really, really slippery. There were no mats on the tile. They just kind of covered the floor with old boxes, like Budweiser boxes. When it gets wet a lot of people just slide on the boxes and fall down. Sometimes if you fall, a lot of people just laugh, not about the injury, but because it's so funny to watch people falling down.

I fell a lot and ended up hurting my lower back.... [I] was in a lot of pain, but I was afraid to tell my employer because I thought I would get fired. With few exceptions the restaurants in Koreatown are pretty much the same in terms of the work environment. So I just kind of tolerated the conditions because I felt that even if I went somewhere else it would be pretty much the same.

I also suffered a miscarriage when I was there...but I didn't tell my employer. A lot of my co-workers actually didn't have regular menstrual cycles either. A lot of times they would skip a month. There were four other women workers besides me. We went to the same gynecologist. My back was hurting a lot and I have a scar on my hand. A customer got drunk and pushed me. My entire hand was swollen because of that. But my employer didn't tell me anything about treatment or resting. Instead she just got annoyed that I was hurt so I told her, "No, I'm OK." I had no choice but to keep working. In the end my back hurt so much that I just couldn't work anymore.[96]

Sexual Harassment and Age Discrimination

Women complained about employers' expectations of women's physical appearance, demeanor, and conduct in restaurant and bar establishments. Women working for Korean employers sometimes confronted discriminatory gender practices "imported" from service industries in Korea. Kyung Park ended up leaving her restaurant job to escape the sexualized atmosphere.

> The manager was kind of jealous and didn't like me talking to the customers. Her title was manager but she was kind of like a madam, someone who sat and drank with the customers.... They had rooms sectioned off, and I saw her kissing customers and things like that. I didn't like seeing that and working in that kind of environment so I changed jobs right away. At lunch time it was half Korean and half American, but in the evening it was all Korean, all drinking.[97]

Lee Jung Hee described similar work experiences in restaurants, especially those selling liquor to male customers. Rituals of male "bonding," unleashing pent-up aggression, "letting it all hang out," drinking oneself into a stupor, and being served by and groping women in Korea and Japan and around US military bases throughout Asia is notorious.

> A lot of employers ask the waitresses to go out for a drink after work, stuff like that. If you don't do it, they won't think very well of you. Even while I'm working, employers will sometimes ask you to have a drink. Those kinds of things are very hard to tolerate, very hard to see. I've seen a lot of that around me. When I started working again, I applied to about four places. The first place I went to had a lot of customers who came to drink in the evening. The employer told me that because I looked like a traditional housewife I couldn't really match or play up to the atmosphere the male customers who came at night wanted so I wasn't fit for the job. That's why I had to leave that job.
>
> There was another job that I went to for about ten days and then I quit. That restaurant had these rooms where you can close the doors.... The sushi person told me if the owner asks you to go into that room late at night, don't go in because some bad things

go on in there. I was really scared after he told me that so I just quit the next day. I didn't see that with my own eyes, but I hear a lot of those kinds of stories.[98]

Koreatown restaurant owners often prefer pretty, young faces to attract male customers for drinks. Despite her youthful and attractive appearance, Park was repeatedly turned down by employers searching for younger women.

I went for interviews and the employers told me I was too old. I thought I was a good worker and I could get a job anywhere. But I was wrong. There's a lot of age discrimination against waitresses. Japanese restaurants especially prefer younger women because a lot of men come there at night to drink. I felt like crying every time I was turned down because of my age. Aughhh! *Nomu* [too much] hurt. I felt like I was deep down in a hole and I couldn't get out. They act like they're picking Miss Korea: they look at your face; they ask how old you are; they look at your body.[99]

Many Koreatown restaurant workers are treated like liars, thieves, and servants by their bosses. Han Hee Jin's boss called workers "servants" or "you, waitress bitch."[100] Lee Jung Hee's boss delivered a tirade on Korean-language radio calling Lee an ungrateful charity case who bit the hand that fed her.[101] Park said,

A friend of mine…worked at a restaurant that had sit-down rooms for guests. The employer told her that the mats that the customers sat on would get ruined if they were put into a washing machine, so he said that my friend should take them home and wash them by hand. She refused, and the employer started yelling and cursing at her. This is the reality for restaurant workers. My friend refused that work because after ten hours of demanding work, she knew that she would have no energy left to do anything except fall asleep when she got home. And yet, she was fired for disobeying her employer.[102]

Living in Post-Rodney King Los Angeles

On March 16, 1991—two weeks after the nation was rocked by video footage of Los Angeles police viciously beating African-American Rodney King—Soon Ja Du, a Korean-American grocer shot and killed Latasha Harlins, a 15-year-old, African-American teenager after a fight over a shoplifting charge for a $1.79 bottle of orange juice. The shooting was videotaped by an anti-theft camera and repeatedly played on TV, in what many saw as another mockery of the value of African-American life.[103]

A year later, the announcement of a not-guilty verdict for police officers who had beaten King ignited three days of what some have dubbed the nation's first "multi-racial riot."[104] During the April 1992 riots, Los Angeles' Korean community paid a high price for the African-American and Latino rage at a legal and economic system dominated by white racism. Over 2,000 Korean-owned stores were looted, burned, or both. One Korean was killed and 46 were injured. Korean merchants suffered almost half of the damages incurred, even though Koreans constituted less than 2 percent of Los Angeles county's population at the time.[105]

Korean Americans have wrestled with the causes of the riot and what the community could do to prevent such violence from erupting again. Koreatown restaurant worker Lee Jung Hee says that Korean owners must show more respect towards their workers and customers. She urges Koreans to be less status- and more community-oriented.

> In the LA Uprising, the question I ask is why is it that Koreans became the target? It's not something that hit Chinatown or Little Tokyo. When I talk to people who work in Little Tokyo I hear that the owners are very, very respectful of waitresses. The workers and the owners are on an equal level in terms of treatment. That's what I've heard.[106]

Finding Chun Tae Il in Koreatown

In March 1992, a mere month before the LA riots, progressives in the Korean community came together to address the rising tensions between Koreans and other ethnicities and to address the needs of working class Koreans. Korean Immigrant Workers Advocates (KIWA) was created as a place all Koreatown workers could come to when they ran into conflicts with their bosses. The workers' center organizes restaurant, janitorial, construction, garment, and other low-wage Korean and Latino immigrant workers who work for Korean employers. As a diaspora labor organization, KIWA shares a common heritage and perspectives with the Korean democratic labor movement.

In 1997, Kim Seung Min was looking for information about US labor law after getting laid off from a Koreatown restaurant. As a Korean democratic movement veteran, it didn't take her long to locate KIWA although she was skeptical that such a creature actually existed.

> I started looking through the Korean directory under service organizations. I saw Korean Immigrant Workers' Advocates. I wanted to know US labor law, not necessarily to get counseling. I was going out of my mind. I was crying. My boyfriend called KIWA for me. He told me that it was a movement organization. I called him, "*Babo yah!* [Hey, Dummy!] There's no movement organization in the US, only in Korea." But I said, "Let's just go there anyway." When I got here I began to gain trust because there was a picture of Chun Tae Il [the garment union martyr]. I came in November when KIWA was planning to have an event commemorating Chun Tae Il's life and had a flyer up. When I saw Chun Tae Il's picture I started crying. Oh, this must be an organization I can trust.[107]

After concerted pressure, the Korean Restaurant Owners Association signed an agreement with KIWA in October 1996 to set up a $10,000 workers' defense fund; conduct workers' rights seminars for almost all the KROA restaurants; post bilingual employment law notices; and initiate a joint research committee on working conditions. Lee Jung Hee, a former member of the democratic bank workers union in Korea, learned about KIWA when organizers conducted a seminar where she worked.

> I learned that there were maximum hour laws and minimum wages that I was supposed to get. That's the first time I learned that these things existed under US law. Before that if somebody had to quit, then the other waitresses had to put in 12-hour days with no rest days at all. Everyone puts in that kind of work. That's like the law in Koreatown; that's the rule people follow.[108]

In 1997, with KIWA's support, Lee filed a civil suit for a serious back injury she received because of dangerous working conditions. She talked about how KIWA could address workers' needs.

KIWA could do a lot in terms of teaching workers about what's going on in the US. But the level of knowledge of people who work in restaurants is limited to their work experience. It's not just that the work is bad, but we want opportunities to develop ourselves more, and be a bit more conscious about society. I need English skills the most. Ninety percent can't speak English, but I feel if people could learn English we could think a little more progressively. I think these kinds of problems are the most urgent for the workers.

I really, really agree with what KIWA's doing 100 percent. I'm doing this also for my children. [cries and pauses] There's a possibility that I'm going to keep living in the US without going back to Korea. In that case my kids could end up working in a restaurant. If the consciousness of Koreatown employers doesn't develop, I think my children would suffer as well.[109]

After resolving her own layoff case and volunteering at KIWA, Kim Seung Min joined KIWA's staff in November 1997.

I see workers outside of the meetings and try to spend time with them talking, eating, and having tea or coffee. I usually listen to what's on their minds and the difficulties they are facing at this point in their lives. That occupies a lot of my time. We talk about how to form an on-going workers association.

The biggest problem they have is standing up for themselves, because they feel that they are under the family system, under the husband. It's very difficult when they don't have the support of their husband and the family. Even though they think this work is very important, a lot of women cannot dismiss their husband's opposition. So the women face a lot of dilemmas and conflicts.[110]

After coming to the aid of restaurant workers in a number of disputes, KIWA began to lay the foundation for an independent restaurant workers association, the Restaurant Workers Association of Koreatown (RWAK). An outgrowth of KIWA's efforts to organize across race lines with Latino as well as Korean restaurant workers, this association is made up of two language components, one for Korean female workers and one for the Latino male workers. In addition to fighting for workplace issues like better wages and working conditions and workers compensation, RWAK is beginning to address the lack of healthcare benefits and childcare for the women who are working such long hours. RWAK is building a relationship with La Clínica Oscar Romero to provide health insurance for both its Latino and Korean members. The Korean membership component of RWAK is gathering resources to set up a childcare center for restaurant workers. Since many of the workers are undocumented, RWAK created its own ID card system for its members, in addition to a check-cashing program and micro-credit system.

Lee Jung Hee started working as an organizer for RWAK in May 2000. Her co-organizer, Kang Hoon Jung was active in the South Korean federation of student organizations, before migrating to the United States in 1992. Lee learned how to deal with employers and organize workers "on-the-job."

> Usually the problem we have when doing outreach to the restaurants is not with the workers, but with the employers. The workers sometimes act different when they are in front of their employers. Most of the information we bring is about labor, so the bosses want to kick us out. Lately RWAK has been trying to raise money for earthquake relief in El Salvador and the restaurants have been unexpectedly open to getting information. One employer that had a lot of claims against them said, "You're actually doing something good for a change," because of the information we had on immigration rights. That kind of thing appeals to the employers as well. Sometimes when we go to the restaurant, the boss just tears up the leaflets in front of our faces. But for the earthquake relief, one employer, even though he did not want to, put in a $20 donation.
>
> When I first started going to the restaurants it was really stressful. I was scared to go and would suffer. But now I am totally unafraid. Mostly I go by myself, but sometimes I go with the other organizers. I have worked on cases where I had to go represent a worker and I've done that on my own.[111]

Lee wants RWAK to combine labor and community organizing, which labor activists characterize as "social unionism."[112]

> What motivates me to do this job is when I think about what is happening to the Korean workers in the restaurant industry. They are working so hard for such long hours just to support their families. Because they are immigrants, they suffer for their whole lives. We need to work on a lot of the issues that surround and impact the lives of immigrants. I hope that RWAK can work on everything the worker needs. My second hope is for restaurant workers to become more a part of the community and do more work to build the community. When we do a lot of work together, good things happen and we can release the stress that builds up at work.[113]

Organizing Women, Releasing *Han*

Immigrant Korean women workers confronted gender and class oppression not only at their workplaces, but also within their families and the Korean community. In the course of organizing, the women began to develop a women's support network, and incorporate gender-specific education campaigns and services into their organizing work.

Despite Korean women's long work hours in the United States, they are still expected to perform almost all the domestic chores in their homes, while their husbands cope with either long hours or underemployment and a big drop in economic and social status, connections, and stability.[114] This creates a volatile environment in which alcoholism and domestic violence often erupts. A 2000 community needs assessment survey on the problem of domestic violence conducted by Shimtuh, the Korean Domestic Violence Program, found that 42 percent of the 347 respondents said that they knew of a Korean woman who had experienced physical violence from a husband or boyfriend, while 50 percent knew of a Korean woman who had experienced regular emotional abuse, and 33 percent reported that their father had hit their mother at least once.[115]

The combined gender and class oppression women face became evident during a sharing session held in April 1999 among some Korean women workers (who wish to remain anonymous). The women began by drawing charts plotting the highs and lows of their lives. One woman described the collapse of her husband's business, into which she had poured all of her labor and for which she had borrowed money from her family. She told of how her husband then fled to the United States, leaving her to close down the business and pay off its debts by herself. Once she arrived in the United States to start life over again, she found herself having to fight an abusive boss.[116]

Another woman, "Mrs. H.," told of how she and her husband, poor and hungry while struggling to survive in Korea, had planned a family suicide. They would drown themselves by jumping into the river while holding their kids. But she couldn't bear to pass the baby over the fence. Then her husband bolted. She searched for him for days. Since his body never turned up in the river, she began to suspect that he was still alive. He later appeared, and they eventually migrated to the United States with their children. Laughing bitterly and joking to make light of her story, she described how she went through many hardships because of her husband's drinking and gambling and her family's extreme poverty. Later when another woman recounted being beaten black and blue by her husband, Mrs. H. shouted out, "That's why I never left him in spite of everything; he never beat me."[117]

These stories released a flood of pent-up anguish, resentment, and tears, mixed with exclamations of *sei sang eh!* [what is this world coming to]" and other expressions of shock, sympathy, and support. Sometimes the women's faces glistened with tears; at other moments the room erupted in peals of laughter as they teased each other about the absurdity of it all.

The women workers' consciousness raising session combined popular education methodology and the cathartic release of *han*.[118] *Han* is the Korean term used to described accumulated suffering, sadness, and hardship. According to psychiatrist Luke Kim, *han* is an "individual and collective emotive state of Koreans, involving feelings of anger, rage, grudge, resignation, hate and revenge. [It is a] form of victimization syndrome of Korean people, with feelings of injustice and indignation suppressed and endured."[119] The "down side" of *han,* is the sadness, oppression, injustice, colonialism, war, tragedy, and cruel twists of fate suffered by Korean people. But the sharing of han between the women workers expresses the "up side" of *han,* a socially and culturally shared understanding that acknowledges and articulates Korean women's pent-up suffering, and *therefore,* facilitates and allows for its release through a collective process of support, solidarity, and sisterhood.

Joining the Movement

Korean women workers joined the movement when they reached the point when they could no longer tolerate their bosses' abuses. Some women organized together with their co-workers, while others started out fighting because of an individual grievance. Because of the close-knit character of the Korean community and ethnic enclave, women's decisions to stand up for their rights had immediate consequences. Restaurant owners quickly blacklisted some of the first Korean women restaurant workers who dared speak out. In addition to the bosses' attacks, some women endured censorship from their ministers and the ethnic media, and pressure from worried co-workers and family members who feared they would never be able to work in Koreatown again.

Chu Mi Hee worked at Koreatown's largest restaurant, Siyeon, as a waitress for two years. In 1996, she was fired and blacklisted after participating in a struggle against the boss.

> *Him dul ot jiyo!* [It was a strain, it was very hard] to work there. If things did not go his way, he [the boss] would use his fists. He would kick things, even people. The woman owner was about the same. She didn't use her fists, but she did the same thing with her words. They treated the workers very inhumanely. At first about 36 people worked there.... Then they started firing people they didn't like, and also to cut their labor costs. That's when our Mexican *chinku* [friends] started opening relations with KIWA....

Without me knowing, the owners found out and fired our Mexican friends.

We wanted to be treated with dignity and not have to work under physical and verbal abuse. Most of the Mexican workers and Korean waitresses united. With KIWA's help, we leafleted the customers. We made a wildcat strike that lasted one hour and demanded that the original promises be kept that the owners made when they opened.... I hoped that protesting, passing out leaflets, talking to people, all of these things would bring about good results. I feel that the things we were demanding were very basic. We were not asking for anything outrageous.[120]

After she was fired by Siyeon for fighting for a collective bargaining agreement, she took a new job at a coffee shop called Prince, which was owned by a cousin of one of the Siyeon owners. She was disoriented when Prince's manager and then her minister called her at home.

I was awakened by a phone call from the minister of the church where the manager and I went. The minister said, "I heard that you are suing [Siyeon] on behalf of the workers. How can you do such a childish thing?" The minister said he had gotten a phone call from the [Prince] manager and heard all about what was going on and that it was hard for me to continue working at [Prince]. Then I knew that I was being blacklisted.

When the Siyeon owner found out that I worked at Prince, he went to the Prince owner and asked, "How can you hire a person like that?" The Prince owner said, "None of your business." But the Prince owner wanted to consult with the manager because she was the one who referred me to Prince. The manager told me, "I'm very disappointed in you. How could you [participate in the Siyeon dispute]? Koreatown is really small. It's going to be hard for you to find another job." I demanded [that she] let me talk to the owner directly. She [the manager] said, "Let's all quit." At that time I felt really disappointed in humanity. After that incident I couldn't go back to church and face the [manager]. I found another job after resting for a while. To find a new job, I had to show my work experience, but to show my experience I had to talk about Siyeon. So I was afraid to go to places to look for work.[121]

The Siyeon workers had successfully negotiated a collective bargaining agreement in February and March of 1996, establishing wage scales, meal times, and the conditions for discharge, but they had to keep fighting for compliance. KIWA helped file lawsuits against the Siyeon and Prince operatives for firing and blacklisting Chu. On February 15, 1997, however, Siyeon went out of business and the case was subsequently dropped.[122]

Paek Young Hee worked 12 hours a day, 6 days a week, but her boss at Ho Dong restaurant blacklisted her for demanding unpaid wages in 1996. As with Chu, the owners association contacted Paek's next boss to get her fired.[123] Luckily, her new boss told her what had happened.

> One day when I was working at my new job, the owner called me into the office and asked why did I go against the restaurant where I was fired. I told him that it was only because I was not paid my rightful wage. The owner confessed that he had received a call from the Korean Restaurant Owners Association who told the owner to let me go because I was a troublemaker. But the owner ended up telling me that I was a great worker and that they needed me and were not going to fire me. I am still working at this restaurant now.[124]

Paek weathered a lot of criticism because she spoke up about the wages she was owed and how she was fired and blacklisted.

> I am very grateful because KIWA helps poor people who are powerless. I try to be active and help out all that I can.... But I feel a little ashamed. I feel like I have done something that I should not have done. All the people around me are telling me, "Why are you stabbing somebody from your own nationality? If they didn't pay you that well, you should have just accepted it, and left it at that. Why did you have to take these actions?" I tell them, "Why shouldn't I be paid for the work that I did?" But at the same time they give me dirty looks like I did something wrong.
>
> Both my children and my husband were not at all supportive of my actions...especially after they saw the news on the TV. The children said that the fact that I came out on TV might have a negative impact on their future as students. My husband was embarrassed because all his co-workers were talking about it. They

were saying it was a disgrace.... Although I was criticized,...I feel
that it was not right to let the owner of the restaurant do what she
did to me and the other people. I did it to stop her from continuing to do these things to people.[125]

Speaking Up for the Powerless

Immigrant women workers have said *ka ja!* [let's go!] and begun
to write a new chapter in Korean-American history. This story be-
gins with their labor struggles in their homeland and continues in the
kitchens, dining rooms, hotels, factories, and on the picket lines of
inner city barrios, tossed together like *chap chae* [mixed vegetables
and noodles] with their Mexican and Central American immigrant
co-workers. They have endured long hours, low wages, sexual harassment, age discrimination, insults, firings, blacklisting, censorship, criticism, and fear. They have been urged to be patient, endure,
and keep their mouths shut. Yet these pioneers are taking a stand
and beginning to change the climate and thinking within the community, winning respect for women workers' human rights, building
multi-racial solidarity, opening up new spaces for democracy, and
securing more justice within the Korean and other communities of
color within the United States.

The November 14, 1998 community town hall meeting of
Koreatown restaurant workers demanding "justice, dignity, and democracy" conveyed a tumultuous mix of images, languages, emotions. An angry gauntlet of restaurant owners taunted all seeking to
enter the towering union hall hosting the gathering. The owners'
ringleader boasted that he learned how to picket after being picketed
by workers and KIWA. Inside the hall the atmosphere was simultaneously welcoming, protective, and edgy as Korean and Mexican
restaurant workers delivered testimony to elected officials, government enforcement agencies, Korean, Spanish, and English language
press, community supporters, and family members. After describing
the abusive behavior by her ex-bosses, Kyung Park said:

> I go home every day with a new wound in my heart because of all
> the hurtful things that happen at work. I am a wife and mother at
> home, but at work, I am viewed sometimes as a servant, some-

times as a thief. This is the reality of restaurant workers. Not being able to get paid as we are supposed [to] and suffering through each day facing insults and curses—this is what makes up the lives of restaurant workers in Koreatown.... I would like to say to all the government leaders, media, workers, and all the other members of the audience present today: it is very possible that by coming forward today I may face the possibility of losing my job. But I have chosen to come to this gathering today in spite of all that. This is because I believe that unless someone speaks up for the rights of the powerless workers in Koreatown, we would have no choice but to go on living with bruises in our hearts.[126]

Kim Chong Ok

Economic Miracle Maker,
Koreatown Restaurant Worker

My memory's not so good. [laughs] I was born July 16, 1955 in Chungchong Namdo, Nomsan-kun, Yangchon-myon, Paramni Ilko. I went to school there, too. When I was 16, I came up to Seoul. I stayed in my older brother's house and learned some trades. My parents were *nongbu* [farmers]. They had their own piece of land. It was rather small, just big enough for us to feed ourselves.

There are nine of us kids, six daughters and three sons. I was the fourth daughter and seventh child in the family. All of my brothers and sisters turned out well. Actually, I'm the poorest among them. They all got married and had children. They never got divorced or had marriage troubles.

I went to school up to junior high school. Once you start asking me about what happened, I can't stop! [laughs] A lot of my older siblings couldn't even go to school. They learned *hangul* [the Korean alphabet] by themselves. Us younger ones were able to go to school and get some education.

When I got older, both of my parents and my older siblings all urged me to come up to Seoul. During that time people looked to Seoul as a better place to make a living than farming in the countryside. Farming is such hard work. Life is better in the city. While I was staying with my brother up in Seoul, I learned a trade, how to knit on a machine. My brother was a taxi driver. I stayed at different brothers' houses. My brothers took care of me because I was one of the youngest kids.

Life in Seoul was OK; at least it was better than farming. I did homework at someone else's home. It was like a private home, but they had machines there. A bunch of women would get together to make things. Maybe six or seven women worked there. The owner divided up the work between us. I was told that they would export these items, after we finished. We knitted sweaters for export. I also worked at a lot of small, small factories.

No regular hours were set for the homework. If you wanted to do more, you could; if not, you didn't. The hours depended on how much work you wanted to do, how much money you wanted to earn. The other workers were also young women. Everybody who worked there came from somewhere else. I lived in Mapo, Shinsu-dong, I think. The big factory area was in Kuro-dong dan. I lived close to there.

I came up to Seoul in 1971. *Bok chap hae* [that was a very complicated time]. I could write a book about it! It was too much. I worked at these different kinds of places until I got older and met my husband. I met him through friends. We girls had a kind of club where we got together to spend time and talk. Friends in that group brought guys to talk and introduced them. It was like a "meeting" [a group introductory date]. [laughs] One of the guys who came was my husband. He looked very old so I thought he was probably married. But it turned out that he got interested in me. He picked me and kept following me around. [laughs]

This was during the time of the Park Chung Hee regime. My husband was driver for one of the government officials. He did that for about a year. I criticized that job so he ended up leaving. I complained because even though we were married, he was still driving for these government officials. They would go to different women's houses. Then my husband had to stay out late to wait for them, and take them home. [sighs] Haaaahh, he was always coming home late because of that. After I criticized him, he never consulted me, he just quit. I hate to talk about this because people are going to think bad things about Korea.[127]

Through my husband, I was able to come to the United States. He had family members here. His mother was here and she had her [US] citizenship. We came November 30, 1985. Life here was very difficult. A month after I came I found work at Saint Joan's [a company in Los Angeles], that produced knitted sweaters and clothes. I think the company is very famous and big. I worked there for about a year. I lived on Olympic [Boulevard, in the heart of Koreatown] for six years. At first I didn't know how to get to work, so my husband took me back and forth to work. Then I learned how to take the bus.

I worked eight hours a day and got off on Saturdays and Sundays. Since I had the weekend off, I used the time to learn how to do garment work. When I got laid off from that factory, I was able to get a job sewing for four or five months. When Saint Joan's called me back to work, I decided not to go. I had problems understanding English and there were a lot of colors to remember for knitting the patterns. Also sometimes when I knit the needles would break and I wouldn't be able to get much done. When the work went smoothly it was fine, but when things went wrong, it was a big hassle. Sewing is much easier.

When I started working at Saint Joan's, the workers were trying to unionize, so I also participated. I didn't know all the details of what was going on, but the strikers were saying that we weren't getting paid enough. It was on Alvarado Street. I don't know exactly, but I think they couldn't unify fully because there were some older Korean ladies who were working there that did not want to participate. They did not do the knitting itself, but other kinds of work. They were afraid that they might lose their jobs there and not be able to find any other work.

I worked in the garment industry for about three years. My husband was a painter, so I followed him around and helped him for a while. At first I was scared to death to climb up on the roof. But after a while I got used to it. I got all sunburned with freckles on my face. The work was really hard. Later we opened a *baduk jang* [Korean chess hall], but the business didn't go very well. So we ran out of money and fell down. So then I went to work at the Korean Soup Restaurant. I stayed there a long time, from 1991 or 1992 until I quit in May 1998.

I was a cook's helper when I started. I worked as a cook's helper for about seven months and then became a cook. I started out at $1,400 a month, working more than 12 hours a day, 6 days a week. After I became a cook I got $100 more. The restaurant ran a 24-hour shift. I worked four days on the night shift and two days on the day shift.

We couldn't negotiate about our wages. Whenever we tried to negotiate, as soon as the words came out of our mouths, the employer would start cussing us out, and go on and on for days after that. We didn't want to face them. I didn't want to quit working there. It's not good to switch jobs too often. I figured that it was like this everywhere so I needed to just bear the hardship and keep working there. During this process I grew close to my co-workers. There were about four or five people who had worked there around ten years like me. Our friendship grew and we decided to stick together. My wages increased to $1,800 a month. But in April 1998, the employer complained that the business was not doing well. She said the IMF crisis was affecting the business over here in the US, and that they had decided to cut our wages. The cooks' wages were cut to $1,400 a month. So we decided to walk out.

Since the restaurant ran 24 hours, there were three cooks to work the three different shifts. We used to have dishwashers and cook's helpers. We really need that help to cook, but the employer cut three people out. So the cooks had to do everything in the kitchen. It was very hard on us and we already worked long hours.

The owner kept oppressing us and acting like she was doing everything within the law on wages and hours. But when we calculated how much we should have been earning, the figures just didn't match up. So we confronted the employer. She kept saying if you don't like it, you can always leave. She started [paying me] for eight hours of work but did not reduce my hours to that amount. So the problems started there.

The wage cut was a problem, but the employer also laid off people—for example, I worked four peoples' jobs. The employer reduced the wages and also demanded that we do all of the work [of the people who were laid off]. That upset me and everyone else. We talked about what we could do about this situation and it led to us taking action. We eventually went to KIWA for consultation because my employer emphasized that she was doing things by the law. She kept on saying "The law is this and that." So the workers decided to find out what our rights were.

KIWA [told us] about labor laws. For example, if workers work more than eight hours a day then they need to get compensated for overtime. Before going to KIWA , DOL [the US Department of Labor] investigated my restaurant [in 1998]. The Korean Soup Restaurant was operating 24 hours a day. But when the investigator came out, my employer told us not to tell our true work hours, but we were supposed to say whatever she told us to say. During the investigation, my employer got upset with us for not answering "correctly" to investigators.... [Eventually] the negotiations [between the workers and KIWA and the employer] broke down and we ended up suing the employers.

The KIWA organizers ask[ed] me to come to the meetings of restaurant workers so I participate[d].... I always think that whatever I can do to be of help, I will participate in.

The owners are the same wherever you go. They are not 100 percent satisfied with you. The treatment is, well, not the US law or the Korean law. How should I say it? It is half-half. The employers want to use you for their benefit. Do they allow us to take a day off on an American holiday? No. Even if there are no customers, the employers feel like, "Why should I let you rest when I am paying you?"

Well, I work from 10 a.m. to 10 p.m. Of course from the perspective of the employers, when the customers come in, they want to serve them even if it is past closing time. If I stay until the customers leave then who knows when I will leave? My legs cannot stand it after 12 hours. I tell my husband to pick me up at 10 p.m. So I leave. The employer also says to leave.

I feel that there is a division between the kitchen and hall workers. There needs to be an understanding between the kitchen and hall workers. For example, if the food does not come out in time, then it ruins the food. Both sides should be able to understand what [the] others' needs are.

When I first visited KIWA, I was so frightened. My heart started to pound and pound. But as I visited KIWA for the second time and the third time, I passed the frightening stage. Now we have become like neighbors. When KIWA [was] not in Koreatown, when [it was] so far away, near *Korea Times* [at their former office], it did not even occur to me to visit. But when KIWA was right in front of us, I got curious. I am sure a lot of people felt that way. I knew KIWA existed, but who knew where? I believe ever since [they] moved [their] cases must have increased.

I think KIWA is doing great work, *nomu nomu choun kot* [too many good things]. We didn't know what KIWA was doing before we came here. But now I have seen for myself that they're doing such good things. By coming here we've seen how much effort and energy they put into this work. In the future things are going to get better and we are going to see improvements in the working conditions.

—Los Angeles, November 17, 1998

Kyung Park

Koreatown Restaurant Worker and Fighter

I was born Christmas Eve, December 24, 1953.... My father was an electrician. He ran a medium-sized business. He used to lay out electrical lines from one mountain to the next. My mother helped him in his business for awhile, but later she became a full-time homemaker. I have an older sister and a younger brother and sister; I'm the second oldest. The second child is very bad you know. [laughs] They like to complain and never listen to their parents, like me.

I finished high school in Chun Chon. I didn't get accepted into school in Seoul, but I moved there after graduation from high school and worked as a hotel receptionist for almost seven years. The job was good and I was very happy. I learned about the job in the newspaper.

I met my husband during that time, when I was drinking coffee in the café. He was a musician, sang, and played instruments in clubs in downtown Seoul. We got married in 1984. After I got pregnant, I quit my job. My daughters were born in 1986 and 1993.

My sisters, brothers, and parents decided to immigrate to the US so I wanted to come, too. My elder sister came to study here after graduating from college in Korea, and she sponsored the whole family. I came to the US in 1990 without my husband. At that time we were having big problems. He wanted a divorce. We were separated for a while. After I came here, I filed the divorce papers and sent them back to Korea. He treated me badly and had a lot of girl-friends. His job was terrible, hanging around with all of those women at night. Looking back I think he might have come to the US if I had sponsored him. But then again, maybe he would not have come because he had something better going on in Korea.

[In the United States] first I worked as a furniture store sales person. Then I worked at *Joong-Ang Ilbo* [Korean Central Daily] on the directory, answering phones and so on in San Diego. Then I started working as a waitress.

San Diego was a very small community, so people knew me and

my family. I got my first waitress job through one of my sister's contacts. When she first came to study, my sister volunteered at this organization that helped immigrants who couldn't speak English.... One of the persons she helped worked as a head waitress. I went to an interview and found out that they knew each other and I ended up getting the position.

I worked in a Japanese restaurant and all of the customers were very friendly. The work was good because at that time all I had on my mind was earning lots of money because of my financial difficulties. I had just broken up with my husband and was wondering where I was going to get money to survive. I worked there until September 1993 when I became pregnant with my second child.

It's a very sad story. Do I have to tell? [laughs] Everything?! It's too much! The father of the second child is someone that I met in Korea and brought to the US. I was working here before he came. So I saved up some money and won $26,000 of *kyeh don* [money from a mutual credit union]. I bought a car and had everything ready for him. But when he came, he just couldn't adjust to American life so we went through a lot of hardship. Then I got pregnant and couldn't work anymore. He ended up spending all my money. He worked, but his income was not enough so I had to work, too. He beat [and] cursed me and called me names. I think his frustrations came from making less money than me. Everyone in my family told me to break up with him, but since we had a child we wanted to try to make it work once more so we moved from San Diego to Orange County. But that didn't work out either. So I ended up moving to LA.

While we were married, we used credit cards to pay the bills and we ended up owing $10,000. Since the cards were under my name, he said I had to pay for it. So I ended up having to pay off the debt and leaving my kids at my parents' and sister's house. I got separated from my kids. The second relationship was even harder than the first.

I moved to LA in 1996, maybe in March. I didn't have any friends in LA, only an acquaintance. I started working right away in a Japanese restaurant inside the Radisson Hotel. Since I didn't know anyone, I learned about the job through the newspaper. I got paid minimum wage. When I worked holidays, I got holiday pay; when I worked overtime, I got overtime pay. So everything was OK.

I stayed there for about eight or nine months. The other waitresses couldn't handle their tables, so even though I was getting the same pay, I had to help cover them too. It was OK at the beginning, but I was having a hard time myself.... After that job I worked at another Japanese restaurant. It was good because I had only wanted to work at night and I was able to get that position. My hours were from 5 p.m. to midnight, six days a week. At a lot of the Japanese restaurants you had to report to work in the morning then take a two- or three-hour break midday, then go back to work. I would rather rest during the day, then go to work all at once. Night is when the restaurant is busy anyway. A lot of people who go to work during the day have kids, so they don't like to stay to close up. They want to go home early. I didn't have my kids staying with me, so I was able to work at night.

I never made a mistake at that restaurant except just once. When the customers order a la carte they get a little receipt. I was supposed to ring that up, too, but I forgot. I think it was about $12. The manager kept following me around demanding that I pay half and saying it was my fault. I got upset because he should have talked to me about it after the shift instead of bothering me while I was working. So I said, "I'll pay the whole thing and I'm quitting." It's not like I made that mistake all the time, just that once. So after five months working there I ended up quitting.

After that came the hard times. [laughs] I went for interviews and the employers told me I was too old. Ehhhh! I thought I was a good worker and I could get a job anywhere. Uhhhh! But I was wrong.... I'm going to count how many owners turned me down. Maybe it was five or six owners.

Before that I was hired at a different restaurant briefly through a head sushi man I knew. I got fired because the relationship between the sushi man and owner turned bad, and the sushi man left the restaurant. I tried to stay, but after a month I had to leave because the owner didn't like me since I was brought in by the sushi man, so she started giving me a hard time. My co-workers told me, "Try to endure and bear it. Let's just work together." I wanted to continue but the employer said she couldn't work with me.

I got rejected by so many Korean restaurants that I didn't want to deal with Koreans anymore, so I went to a Japanese restaurant. Yet it was also owned by a Korean. My friend who worked at this restaurant said, "I'm moving to Texas so why don't you come and replace me?" So that's how I got this job where I'm working. The hours are OK and the owner is only in the restaurant briefly, so it's good.

At one restaurant I received hourly pay; at another I wasn't paid by the hour, but I think the pay was pretty close to minimum wage. I got about $700, I think it was about 46 hours a week, sometimes 42 hours per week, with some 49-hour weeks. I reported to work from 5 [p.m.] to midnight for four days. Then for two days I reported to work in the morning, got off at midday, and then reported back to work. We ended up picketing this restaurant because I didn't get paid for three days of work. After I quit, they said they wouldn't pay me.

I kept on calling the restaurant and demanding my pay. Even if I quit, I deserved to be paid for the work I had already done. I got so upset that I couldn't sleep. A co-worker there told me, "Why don't you try calling KIWA?" So that's why I called. KIWA does good work. They helped me do something that I couldn't do by myself. I think it's very powerful to have this organization. Before this, I felt I was not important, that the work I did in restaurants was very meaningless. But now I'm able to stand up for my rights.

When I went to the restaurant to demand my back wages, one of my other co-workers said, "Why don't you just give up, what can you do?" The owner had a lot of power and money and was well-known in the community. But I felt that I really needed to get this money because I had worked for it.

I received the check from one of the business partners, not from the actual owner. Sometimes the partner who paid still comes to the restaurant where I work now and tells me that I did the right thing. She said that it's good that I stood up for my rights, and that even if I run into her partner I should be strong and tell her that I only did what I had to do and there's nothing to be ashamed of. Their partnership broke up. So she still asks how I'm doing and sometimes we have coffee together.

Since that time I have been participating in KIWA activities. Because of KIWA, I realized that so many people are working under worse conditions than me. I'm just coming out to meetings and things like that. I hope that this is helpful. [laughs] After I retire I can come out full-time. I think that by looking at what KIWA does and the kind of people who work with the organization you can better understand why the world goes around and how justice can be served. It's very easy to just think about yourself and get on with your own life, but there are people who work hard to win some justice. This is really good and important work and I'm proud to be a part of it.

It didn't take long for me to decide to speak out [at the community town hall meeting]. I decided in about five minutes when someone came to our house to ask me about it. It's something that had to be done, so I decided just to do it. There's a Korean saying that it's better to get whipped first. [laughs] I was like that in school. When everyone in the group was getting scolded, I would be the first one to go up there to get punished. I hated the pain of waiting. It was pure torture! One part of me is worried that my picture came out in the newspaper. But the other part of me is saying I didn't do anything wrong. I want justice and I only said what was true. But even though it's true, the employers won't be too happy when they see it. They're not going to like it.

My family in San Diego doesn't know about the hearing yet. My husband here in LA kind of joked and said, "Hey, that's how you become a star!" [laughs] I asked him, "What am I going to do if I get fired?" and he said to go to the labor commission and sue. *Karuchi!* [That's so!] My daughters, ahhh! The younger daughter doesn't exactly know because she's too small. But I have brought my daughters to the picket lines before. At first they were very hesitant and scared, but we chanted in English and people explained things to my older daughter so she has a better sense of what is going on. After the rally she would say, "That was a very bad owner." She also complains how it's unfair for me not to get time off for Thanksgiving or Christmas. My older daughter is very proud that I spoke at the hearing. *Omma jal haet dako.* [She said, "Mom, you did well."]

[Chants:] "Who's got the power? We got the power!" Sometimes the two of them play by chanting.

My husband also works in the restaurant business, but not here in Koreatown. He hates Koreatown. He's Korean, but he's tired of working for Koreans.... My children came to live with me again this year, after two years of being separated from them. I have paid all my debts and for my credit cards. Now I even make $20,000 a year. [laughs] My husband helps me a lot and I've got my own money.

In the beginning when I first left my children I cried everyday. I think time is the medicine. It's better now. *Kasum sokeh* [inside my chest] it really hurts to think about the two years that I wasn't there for my children. *Kunyang* [that's how it is]. I'm satisfied now; my children are with me.

Whenever I come to KIWA, they are always busy; they need help. They don't complain. [laughs] But I feel someone needs to donate a lot of money to them. Right now KIWA is looking into health insurance plans that workers can join. One of the workers passed away from cancer. It's hard to go to the doctor because it's so expensive. Once a year women need to go for a checkup. I think KIWA does good work, not only on our individual cases, but also by helping us to deal with other issues. Life is hard so we need to do other things besides being waitresses all day, all of our lives.

The media coverage about the restaurant workers' justice campaign [in 1998 was] terrible. Korean newspapers here are different from the ones in Korea. They run the papers through advertisements. Since the restaurant owners advertise, they have a bigger say. The media should be in the middle or give more say to the powerless, but that's not the way it is. I was upset after reading today's [November 16, 1998] *Korea Times* article about the hearing with my picture. The coverage was not fair, not objective. All of the news coverage, even the *Radio Korea* interview, concludes that KIWA is the one creating the problem. What I want to say to the media is that they should go work at the restaurants they are talking about for at least a week. They must go experience how it really feels to work in that situation to tell the story right. I don't get the sense that the media even knows where we are coming from. For example, until you go inside a mine you don't know what it's like to be down there. After you go in and sweat and breathe all of that black dust into your lungs, you will know how it feels to be there.

Even when the business is not doing well, employers are still in a better situation than the workers. It's very important to share with people who don't have as much. It's something that employers should remember, that must become a part of their thinking.

—Los Angeles, November 16, 1998

1   Han Hee Jin, Speech delivered in front of Shogun Sushi, Koreatown, Los Angeles, June 6, 1998.

2   Called the "Four Dragons," "Four Tigers," or the East Asian Newly Industrialized Countries (NICs), South Korea, Taiwan, Singapore, and Hong Kong experienced rapid economic growth since the 1960s based on their special relationship with the United States and Japan, and a system of state-directed capitalist development (Bello, Walden and Rosenfeld, 1990:1-16).

3   Tieszen, 1977:50.

4   Kim, El-Hannah, 1998:23-33. Scholars assert that Yi dynasty (1392-1910) rulers in Korea promulgated a brand of neo-Confucianism that even outdid China in severity. A woman's own name was not entered into her husband's family register, nor could she take her husband's name. She was often referred to instead as "so-and-so's mother," "so-and-so's wife," or "third daughter," etc. (Kim, Yung-Chung, 1976:85). See Kim, El-Hannah, 1998 for a lively feminist critique of Confucius "the Man."

5   Interview with Paek Young Hee, March 27, 1997.

6   Spence, 1990:530-531; Associated Press, 2000. For critical views of the US role in Korea's division and the Korean War see Stone, 1988; Burchett, 1968; and Cumings, 1981 and 1990; Spence, 1990:530-531; Associated Press, 2000.

7   South Korea is often promoted as a model for developing nations. But its "economic miracle" was created within a particular historical juncture during the Cold War. South Korea's *chaebol* [family-run corporations] benefited from US "favored nation" status, contracts during the Vietnam War, preferential treatment proffered by the South Korean government, and super-exploitation of its workers, backed by the Park, Chun, and Roh regimes. In the post-Cold War era these conditions are not so easy to duplicate for developing nations as more and more countries flood the global competition to sell their exports on the world market.

8   Koo, 1987:105.

9   Kim, Seung-Kyung, 1997:2-9.

10   Kim, Seung-Kyung, 1997.

11   South Korea's rapid industrialization under the Park government was called the "miracle on the Han River." The Han runs through the heart of Seoul and out into the West Sea. Ogle, 1990. Cumings, 1997

12   Interview with Kim Chong Ok, November 17, 1998.

13   Interview with Kim Chong Ok, November 17, 1998.

14   See Howard, 1995; "The Stories from the Comfort Women," www.hk.co.kr/event/jeonshin/w2/e_jsd_1.htm; and Puente, 2000.

15   See Howard, 1995; Lie, 1991; Louie, Miriam, 1995a. Some 40 US bases remain on Korean soil. An average of 2,000 altercations between local Koreans and US military personnel occur each year, often involving Korean women (Interview with Lee Yeung Hee, Seoul, May 27, 1992). South Korea has the world's third highest rate of sexual assault according to a 1989 study by the Korea Criminal Policy Institute (Korea Sexual Violence Relief Center, 1991:11).

16   Interview with Cho Ailee, Seoul, May 23, 1992.

17   Haruhi, 1985; Lie, 1991; Louie, Miriam, 1989.

18   See Chang Pil-wha 1986:255-281.

19   Interview with Kim Seung Min, November 16, 1998.

20   Interview with Kim Seung Min, November 16, 1998.

21   Ogle, 1990:86-92.

22   Ogle, 1990:72-75.

23   See Committee for Asian Women and Korean Women Workers Associations, 1992:6-7.

24   During the 1970s, women workers also fought for their rights at the Sygnetics, Bando Songsa, Pangrim, Hankook Mobang, Dongsu, and Yanghaing companies. See Committee for Asian Women and Korean Women Workers Associations, 1992; and Korean Women Workers Associations United and Korean Women's Trade Union, 2000.

25   Seoul's Y.H. Trading Company had closed down when its president ran off to the United States with the company's assets, throwing 500 women out of work. Police clubbed and arrested protesting workers, killing Kim Kyong Suk, one of the strikers. On October 26, 1979, while discussing ways to handle the riots, KCIA head Kim Chae Gyu assassinated dictator Park Chung Hee, and on December 12, 1979, the military regime of Generals Chun Doo Hwan and Roh Tae Woo took power (Ogle, 1990:92; and Cumings, 1997:374-390).

26   For an eye witness account of the Kwangju Uprising and subsequent massacre, see Lee, Jae-eiu, 1999. For a critique of US complicity in the massacre see Shorrick, 1996.

27   Chun Doo Hwan dissolved the union in January 1981, just before he was received as newly elected President Ronald Reagan's first foreign dignitary (Cumings, 1997:379).

28   Bello and Rosenfeld, 1990:25

29   Interview with Yoon Hae Ryun, Seoul, May 28, 1992.

30   See http://www.nodong.org/english/index.htm.

31   Interview with Kim Seung Min, November 16, 1998.

32   Interview with Lee Jung Hee, February 1, 2001. See Asian Migrant Centre, 1996b:30 and Varona, 1998.

33   Interview with Kim Seung Min, November 16, 1998.

34   Cumings, 1997:386-391.

35   ToBak Yi Theater Company (of Kwangju), "Kumhi's May," Program Booklet, performed May 31,1996, Wilshire Ebell Theater, Los Angeles.

36   Interview with Paek Young Hee, March 27, 1997.

37   Committee for Asian Women, 1993:12; Liem and Kim, 1992: Ogle, 1990:172-175.

38   South Korean chaebol are also exploring investment prospects in free trade zones in North Korea. The collapse of the economy after the fall of the Soviet camp trading partners in 1989, followed by a series of floods and draughts since 1995, led to widespread famine in North Korea. North Korea's Kim Jong Il and South Korea's Kim Dae Jung met during a historic summit in June 2000, and family and other exchanges between the two nations were slowly increasing before George W. Bush's administration.

Perhaps in the future, North Korean workers may provide yet another source of low-waged labor for South Korean chaebol and subcontractors. Korean migrants from Chinese provinces bordering North Korea already make up a large proportion of South Korea's undocumented migrant workers.

39 Committee for Asian Women, 1995b.

40 See Asia Monitor Resource Center, 1997:1-6.

41 See Lee Jai Yun, 1998:17-19.

42 Varona, 1998:10-11.

43 Interview with Maria Chol Soon Rhie, Korean Women Workers Association office, Seoul, May 24, 1999.

44 Lee, 1998:19.

45 Varona, 1998:11-12.

46 Interview with Maria Chol Soon Rhie, February 9, 2001.

47 Choi, 1997:7.

48 APEC is a ministerial forum involving 18 countries and territories around the Pacific Ocean, from Asia to Australia, Latin America, and the United States. APEC's mission is reduction of trade barriers, promotion of investment between members, and borderless trade within the region by the year 2020. See APEC Labor Rights Monitor, 1996.

49 See for example, Greenhouse, 2001.

50 Interview with Maria Chol Soon Rhie, February 9, 2001.

51 See Kyeyoung Park's insights on the complexities of *miguk byong* and cultural colonialism, 1997:29-33. The interpenetration of the South Korean and US economies, military structures, and cultures since the country's division in 1945 forms the basis for *miguk yol.* For example, one of South Korea's main TV channels is the American Forces in Korea Networks (AFKN), which features popular "stateside" shows and tips for US military personnel and an opportunity to listen to English spoken by "native speakers." During the 1970s and 1980s, many brand name "American" products were actually manufactured by Korean workers.

52 Interview with Chu Mi Hee, March 25, 1997.

53 Hurh, 1998:33.

54 Kim, Warren, 1971:4; Hurh, 1998:37; Chai, 1988:51-63.

55 Hurh and Kim, 1984, cited in Hurh 1998:35.

56 See Sturdevant and Stoltzfus, 1992.

57 See Lee, Daniel, 1991:304-316.

58 Lee, Daniel, 1991:301. Despite stigmatization and ostracism, Korean wives of US servicemen helped sustain extended families and communities in Korea and the United States. Lee says the women's human services in supporting immigration and settlement are immeasurable, and that it is easy to find kinship groups of 30 to 40 relatives, including parents, siblings, and their in-laws, in many US cities all connected back to one woman who came as the wife of an American serviceman. Yet many wives of US servicemen have a tough time isolated on military bases, facing language and acculturation barriers, and domestic violence and spousal abuse, while bereft of the support of Korean family and friends. See also Kim, Bok-Lim, 1981.

59 Min, 1996: 3.

60 Kim, Ilsoo, 1981:52-53 and Light and Bonacich, 1988:103 cited in Park, Kyeyoung, 1997:15 footnote.

61 Min and Song, 1998:52.

62 South Korea exported tens of thousands of orphans, principally with through church agencies after US christians Harry and Bertha Holt initiated the process in 1955, campaigned Congress to pass the Holt bill on international adoptions, and launched the Holt International Children's Services. South Korea became the largest supplier of children to the developed world. The South Korean government began to take steps to slow the sending of orphans after massive criticism of the practice, which had persisted decades after the war. Many Korean adoptees have worked to develop a distinct sense of identity, community, and support networks. US couples also adopted children from Vietnam, and more recently from China, especially in the wake of the one-child policy and preferences for boys over girls. See Liem, Deann Borshay, 2000.

63 Ishi, 1988:36, cited in Park, 1997:15

64 Min and Song, 1998:55.

65 Park, Kyeyoung, 1997:15.

66 Park, Kyeyoung, 1997:15, 25-34.

67 Park, Kyeyoung, 1997:31, 94-138.

68 Interview with Paek Young Hee, March 27, 1997.

69 Interview with Kyung Park, November 16, 1998.

70 Interview with Kim Chong Ok, November 17, 1998.

71 Interview with Lee Jung Hee, November 16, 1998.

72 Korean Immigrant Workers Advocates, 1998a:13.

73 *Korea Times Chicago,* 1994; and *New York Times,* 1995, both cited in Hurh, 1998:46-47. Within the Korean community, people hotly debated whether to call the April 29, 1992 "Sa-I-Gu" response to the Rodney King verdict a "riot" or "rebellion." KIWA uses the middle-ground term "civil unrest."

74 Seventy-two percent of US-born Korean-American married women, in contrast to 61 percent of US-born white women, worked in the paid labor force. Among immigrants, 61 percent of Korean immigrant married women and 52 percent of Euro-American immigrants worked for pay (US Commission on Civil Rights, 1988. *The Economic Status of Americans of Asian Descent: An Exploratory Investigation,* p. 37, cited in Paik, 1991:256).

75 Moon, 1998:43.

76 Um, 1996.

77 Kadeskey, 1993b:517. See also presentation by Lenny Siegal of the Pacific Studies Center to Southwest Network for Environmental and Economic Justice Network's High-Tech Core Group Committee and Asian Immigrant Women Advocates, Oakland, California, May 5, 1996; Kadesky, 1993a; Ewell and Oanh Ha, 1999a; and Ewell and Oanh Ha 1999b.

78 Interview with Jennifer Jihye Chun, February 8, 2001.

79 Pacific Studies Center, US Equal Employment Opportunity Commission, 1990 US Census cited in Abate, 1993.

80 Interview with Jennifer Jihye Chun, February 8, 2001. Asian Immigrant Women Advocates (AIWA) organizes Korean electronics assemblers and offers workplace literacy classes, a Peer Health Promoter Network, and an immigrant women workers health clinic. See Asian Immigrant Women Advocates, 2000a.

81 Interview with Paul Lee, February 1, 2001. Other cities with large Korean populations include New York, San Francisco, San Jose, Washington, DC, Chicago, Philadelphia, Seattle, Honolulu, Baltimore, and Dallas. See www.asianmediaguide.com/korean/k_p.html.

82 Hurh, 1998:118-120.

83 Interview with Lee Jung Hee, February 1, 2001.

84 See Min, 1996: 59-61.

85 Yu, Eui-Young 1993, cited in Hurh, 1998:120.

86 Interview with Lee Jung Hee, February 1, 2001.

87 Interview with Chu Mi Hee, March 25, 1997.

88 Interview with Paek Young Hee, March 27, 1997.

89 Interview with Kim Seung Min, November 16, 1998.

90 Interviews with Chu Mi Hee, March 25, 1997; Paek Young Hee, March 27, 1997; and Kim Chong Ok, November 17, 1998.

91 Interview with Paek Young Hee, March 27, 1997.

92 Interview with Paek Young Hee, March 27, 1997.

93 Interview with Choi Kee Young, November 16, 1998.

94 Interviews with Helen Kim, April 25, 1994, and Jennifer Jihye Chun, February 8, 2001. Kim says that over 2,000 chemicals are used in the electronics industry.

95 Interview with Lee Kyu Hee, September 21, 1989.

96 Interview with Lee Jung Hee, November 16, 1998. She filed a suit against her employer in 1997 and says that such cases usually take about five years to resolve.

97 Interview with Kyung Park, November 16, 1998.

98 Interview with Lee Jung Hee, November 16, 1998.

99 Interview with Kyung Park, November 16, 1998.

100 Speech delivered by Han Hee Jin in front of Shogun Sushi, Koreatown, Los Angeles, June 6, 1998.

101 Interview with Lee Jung Hee, November 16, 1998.

102 Korean Immigrant Workers Advocates, 1998b:3

103 At first facing 11 years in prison, Du was sentenced to five years probation, 400 hours of community service, and a $500 fine for killing Harlins. See García, Robert, 1990.

104 See Kwong, Peter, 1992; Chang and Leong, 1994; and Abelmann and Lie, 1995.

105 Min, 1996:90 cited in Hurh, 1998:133. Forty percent of the damaged businesses were Latino-owned. Pastor, 1993:1 cited in Navarro, 1994. Of the people arrested, 51% were Latinos, 38% were black, 9% were Anglos, and 2% were Asian Americans or "other" (García, Robert, 1990.)

106 Interview with Lee Jung Hee, November 16, 1998.

107 Interview with Kim Seung Min, November 16, 1998.

108 Interview with Lee Jung Hee, November 16, 1998.

109 Interview with Lee Jung Hee, November 16, 1998.

110 Interview with Kim Seung Min, November 16, 1998.

111 Interview with Lee Jung Hee, February 1, 2001.

112 Interviews with Peter Olney, May 1, 1997; Arnoldo García, April 21, 1997; and Roy Hong, March 26, 1997.

113 Interview with Lee Jung Hee, February 1, 2001.

114 See Song and Moon, 1998b:161-173.

115 Shimtuh, 2000. See also Korean American Coalition to End Domestic Abuse, 1999; and Song and Moon, 1998b:162-163. Song and Moon's 1987 study that found that 60 percent of Korean immigrant women reported having been battered by their spouses.

116 Meeting of Koreatown restaurant workers, April 3, 1999.

117 Meeting of Koreatown restaurant workers, April 3, 1999.

118 Popular education is the process through which people process direct lived experiences as the knowledge base from which to make connections with and analyze broader relations in the society and economy. See Freire, 1990; Bell et al, 1990.

119 Kim, Luke I., 1991, cited in Kim-Goh, 1998:230. The cultural sector of the 1980s *minjung* movement helped reclaim and transform the practice of *kut* and *han puri,* Korean shamanistic exorcism and *han* release rituals, such as those dedicated to the memory of the Comfort Women and the martyrs of the Kwangju Massacre. Luke Kim says that Korean psychotherapists and theologians have grown more interested in exploring the concept of *han* as it sheds light on problems facing their clients and parishioners (Kim, Luke I., 1998:219.)

120 Interview with Chu Mi Hee, March 25, 1997.

121 Interview with Chu Mi Hee, March 25, 1997.

122 See Korean Immigrant Workers Advocates, 1997.

123 Korean Immigrant Workers Advocates, 1996.

124 Interview with Paek Young Hee, March 27, 1997.

125 Interview with Paek Young Hee, March 27, 1997.

126 Korean Immigrant Workers Advocates, 1998b.

127 The interview took place during the Clinton-Lewinsky scandal.

Chapter Four

Extended Families

Small and spry, Mrs. Yu Sau Kwan is the mother of four strong women in their twenties. After immigrating from Hong Kong in 1972, she toiled in unionized Chinatown factories for over two decades, developing deep pains in her back, hip, and fingers from sewing 900 zippers a day. Neither the union nor her employers let her know she was entitled to Workers Compensation for her on-the-job injuries. After seeing the hard work and suffering their mother had to endure, Mrs. Yu's daughters Betty and Virginia joined their peers gravitating to the Chinese Staff and Workers Association (CSWA). Virginia eventually participated in a 7-day hunger strike protesting the Jing Fong restaurant owners' treatment of the workers in 1995.

The passionate identification of her daughters with the restaurant workers in turn drew Mrs. Yu to CSWA. Yu says, "I wondered, 'What kind of organization is CSWA that it would make my daughter want to fast?' So, I decided to go take a look. I ended up joining myself!"[1]

She now organizes her immigrant women worker peers as a member of CSWA's Board and Coordinating Committee of its Brooklyn Center. As a co-founder of the Garment Workers' Health and Safety Project, she works not only with injured Chinese workers, but also Latina/o, Caribbean, and Polish workers. Betty and Virginia continue to work with CSWA as well.[2]

Workers' centers draw their organizers and activists from two different generational pools of the ethnic immigrant community: low-wage immigrant workers and their "extended family members," both figuratively and literally. The women workers' extended family members join the movement out of anger over the discrimination, exploitation, and health risks that the women in their families and communities confront. At the same time, these family members have their own set of grievances with the power pyramid and their own dreams of how they want to live individually and in relationship to their elders. And just as in women's families, their movements often include the stray Japanese, Filipino, Salvadoran, African-American, white, or Puerto Rican "in-laws" and friends in the mix. This chapter introduces some of the family members who work alongside the women in their organizations and movements, and examines the role this generation plays as translators and the fusion between women like Mrs. Yu and their extended family members.

"We Are the Children"[3]

The children and grandchildren of immigrant workers are often thrust into the role of translators and intermediaries between US institutions and their elders. The youth often feel responsible for repaying their families and the broader immigrant community for the sacrifices the older generation made so their children would fare better in this country. Sometimes the parents are proud of their descendants' community activism; in other cases they grumble that they wish their kids used their bilingual abilities and organizing skills to get jobs with higher pay and prestige.

These 1.5, second, third, and fourth generation activists come from a range of class backgrounds. Those of working-class origin may have worked or played alongside their immigrant mothers in sweatshops, doing piece work at home or farm work in the fields. Others put in long hours of unpaid labor in small family-run "mom and pop" businesses. Some raised younger siblings while their parents worked late at electronics factories, restaurants, nursing homes, sweatshops, or in private homes as domestic workers. A number spent time working within these industries themselves. Some of the younger generation family members were swept up with the immigrant women into labor and community movements. Had their mothers, grandmothers, or great grandmothers stayed in China, Korea, or Mexico, these working-class leaders, both the youth and their elders, might well have been swept up in workers', peasants', and poor peoples' movements in their home countries.

The labor movement sees working- and middle-class youth as a great resource to be developed. Ethnic workers' centers have put forth many youth campaigns, such as CSWA's Youth Group and its off-shoot National Mobilization Against Sweatshops, AIWA's Youth Build Empowerment Project, youth and student organizing initiatives of the US Commission for Democracy in Mexico, KIWA's Summer Activists Training program, and Fuerza Unida's links to student organizations such as MEChA (Movimiento Estudiantil Chicano de Atzlan), LASO (Latin American Student Organization), and La Raza Student Organization.

The younger generation women who have worked alongside the immigrant organizers profiled in this book include women like Julia Song, a 1.5 generation immigrant who assists her mom at the family gift shop on her only day off from KIWA. She shows gentle respect, laughter, and awesome *onni* [big sister] skills in her work with Koreatown restaurant workers. Her "running buddy," first-generation immigrant Kim Seung Min said:

> At KIWA now, we have woman power. We take power. Julia's nickname is *dabalchong*, the da-da-da-da! machine gun. My nickname is *baksapo*, the boong-boong-boong! bazooka. We fight the owners and sometimes the customers who cross the picket line. Julia goes *da-da-da!* and I go *boong, boong, boong!* We challenge so many stereotypes because we're young and we look like high school kids to them. Especially when women speak up, they can't stand it. Yeah, fantastic![4]

Trinh Duong was born in Vietnam and immigrated to the United States with her Chinese parents in 1980, when she was six years old. Duong chuckled that when she first tried to join the picket line in front of the Jing Fong Restaurant, the largest restaurant in New York's Chinatown, she was inadvertently swept inside to the owners' tea party, causing workers to suspect her of being a spy. Now an organizer for CSWA, Duong and others received death threats from a sweatshop owner angry over the organizing of workers slaving over 100-hour weeks.[5]

Cecilia Rodríguez is a third-generation Chicana born in El Paso's *Segundo Barrio*. Her father, a US citizen, was deported to Mexico during the mass deportations of the Hoover years. His family's land in Arizona was seized and he used to cross the river illegally, mistakenly believing that he was undocumented. Rodríguez says, "The Farah strike was going on while I was still in middle school and it shook the whole city. My parents moved out of the neighborhood and I spent high school watching skirmishes between whites and Mexicans." Joining the Texas Chicana/o movement in El Paso, she later moved to the lower Rio Grande Valley and organized auto workers and community residents around services and health needs.

Rodríguez helped co-found La Mujer Obrera (LMO), initially with support from the US-Mexico Border Program of the American Friends Service Committee, before LMO spun off as an independent organization. After serving as LMO's Director for many years, Rodríguez left behind a strong core of immigrant women worker organizers and moved on to build sister movements with the Zapatistas in Chiapas through the National Commission for Democracy in Mexico.[6]

Helen Kim is a 1.5-generation immigrant from Korea whose mother worked in Chicago for 18 years as an electronics assembler, principally for Motorola. Kim's mother soldered printed circuit boards that went into radios and the first generation of cell phones. She complained of headaches and came home with teary eyes from peering through the microscope all day, with her clothes smelling of chemicals, and hair speckled with filament wires and fibers. She sometimes brought her work home, including different log sheets to be completed, as well as the stresses and tears triggered by competitive relations fostered between the women.

Kim says that she first stumbled into work at AIWA as a volunteer. Kim nurtured national support for AIWA's Garment Workers Justice Campaign and the Jessica McClintock boycott. She simultaneously built AIWA's Silicon Valley workers leadership project, organizing, inspiring, and breaking bread and *kimbab* [seaweed wrapped rice] with Korean electronics assemblers like her mom. Kim said the involvement of AIWA members' children in their mothers' movement warms her heart. She reflected:

> This is the best thing I could have stumbled into. It was the starting point for me to put together the different pieces of my life—as an immigrant, as the daughter of an electronics worker, regarding the role I should play within the immigrant community, of how I could utilize my language skills.[7]

Geri Almanza was born in the United States to Mexican immigrants, childhood sweethearts from *campesino* families in Guanajuato, Mexico, who immigrated to work in Los Angeles' nurseries. Almanza's mother worked as an electronics assembler in Silicon Valley. An organizer for PODER, an environmental justice organization in San Francisco's Mission District, Almanza first encountered Fuerza Unida as an intern at Southwest Network for Environmental and Economic Justice (SNEEJ).

> Viola [Casares of Fuerza Unida] reminded me so much of my aunt Juanita who helped raise me. But then she was born here just like me. I saw how Viola and Petra [Mata] were doing all this work to create this big family that reminded me so much of my own.[8]

Yrene Espinoza is a third-generation *Tejana* [Chicana Texan] who grew up in San Benito in south Texas' Rio Grande Valley. Her mother assembled parts for computers and moved to Minnesota to find more stable work, while her father worked at various part-time jobs in the school system. Her mother got her GED and always wanted to go back to college and get involved in the movement, but had a hard time as a single mother. Espinoza visited La Mujer Obrera, started volunteering, and now "runs with *las mujeres* 24/7." She serves as the assistant to ex-garment worker and La Mujer Obrera's director, María Antonia Flores, whose story was featured in the earlier chapter on Mexican women workers. Yrene explained:

> It wasn't until I started working here that I began to better understand what was going on. Even if you come from that family background, it does not necessarily mean that you understand. I started to see what is happening to our people.[9]

Pamela Chiang's mother worked in Hong Kong, Shanghai and Taiwan before immigrating to San Francisco in 1965. Pamela's grandmother used to clean house for the matriarch of the Koret family of garment industrialists. Once Pamela enrolled in the University of California at Berkeley, she co-founded *Nindakin* [we are part of the earth], a students of color environmental justice group, and discovered SNEEJ and Fuerza Unida after volunteering at AIWA. Chiang helped develop the campaign that brought *las mujeres* of Fuerza Unida to Levi's San Francisco headquarters. She now organizes Laotian and other immigrant communities against toxic polluters.

> De facto growing up in an immigrant family you end up being the negotiator for your family, like "Where do I go to get the senior citizen bus passes for my grandparents?" Hey, those were the days of "Suzie Wong." All that racist and sexist stuff I saw getting dumped on my single mom felt pretty yucky when I was a young girl growing up.[10]

Nellie Casas and Brenda Mata are the daughters of laid-off Levi's workers Rosa Casas and Petra Mata, respectively. Nellie volunteered at Fuerza Unida, worked there as a SNEEJ youth intern, and served as a *promotora* [organizer] when the campaign focused on Levi's corporate headquarters. Brenda was nine years old when Levi's announced the plant closure. As the youngest child, her parents sent her to Delaware to live with her married sister for a year, so the entire family unit could absorb and weather the immediate crisis. Brenda says that period of her life was really hard, and her mom tells her that she left as a child and came back as a teenager. After that, her mom was always there for her.

Brenda used to play with the other kids during Fuerza Unida meetings and, by the time she was in middle school, she started understanding more about the struggle. She remembers being at Levi's San Francisco headquarters, playing the role of an elf in a skit about Levi's being the Grinch who stole Christmas, and the fear she felt when the women and their supporters were driven from the plaza by the police. "Whenever we go to demonstrations, I still ask my mom if we're going to be arrested. I tell her, 'Mom, I can't get arrested now; I have a baby!'"

Growing up, Brenda accompanied Petra and the other women to San Francisco and on other organizing road trips, kept her mom company at the Fuerza Unida office after school when she worked late, and started speaking at events. Now Viola Casares' grandchildren Amanda and Joseph Benítez and Stacy Olivares are doing the same thing. Brenda says her mother refused to let her boyfriend enter the house the first time she brought him home because he was wearing Levi's brand Dockers pants. He asked, "Are you serious?" But she made him go home and change his pants. Brenda wants to go to college, but is still contemplating what field of study could both help her parents and kindle her own imagination. She says,

> I learned so many things from Fuerza Unida, especially about all the rights you have. Before that I didn't know anything about women's rights. I was born in Mexico where men tell the women what to do, although my family was never like that. I learned about US history. When they talked about the supposedly great history of the Levi's company at school I said, "I don't have to listen to this," so I got sent home. I learned to speak up when people are not treated equally. None of my friends wear Levi's or Dockers. They don't want to get me started![11]

These are just a few of the talented young women who have graced the movement. They have wisdom beyond their years because of the responsibilities they shouldered in their families and organizations.

Talented Tenth and Working-Class Youth

Some organizers and activists in the movement come from privileged class backgrounds. W.E.B. DuBois dubbed these middle-class educated activists in the African-American community the "talented tenth."[12] The radical movement in China called these young radicals "patriotic intellectuals." Having chosen to throw in their lot with the common people/*minjung*/*lao pai hsing*/*gente*, these young people stand in stark contrast to the "comprador class," those ethnic intermediaries who act in the interests of the outside elites: the "good Hispanics," the "Asian model minorities," or in more pungent community parlance, the *"vende patrias,"* "sellouts," "running dogs," "bananas," or "coconuts."

In the United States the ranks of the "talented tenth"—and the hopes raised among the other, under acknowledged "nine-tenths" —of all racial groups, female and male, expanded with civil rights victories that ended legal segregation in education, employment, and housing. At the same time the removal of racist quotas on immigration in 1965 and the change in preferences to encourage greater migration of skilled workers, professionals, and business people, also broadened the ranks of the educated middle and upper classes of immigrants. Additionally, due to reasons of history, policy, and geography, the East and South Asian immigrant populations in the United States now have a relatively larger proportion of the "talented tenth" than the Filipino, Southeast Asian, Mexican, Central American, and Caribbean immigrant groups.

During the social upheavals of the 1960s and early 70s, many working- and middle-class youth got swept up in the social movements for change.[13] Some promoted grassroots struggles. Some, like the Black Panther Party for example, also romanticized the "outlaws" from the system.[14] Other middle-class youth responded to the hypocrisy of what President Dwight Eisenhower called the "military-industrial complex" by choosing to "tune in, turn on, and drop-out." By the mid-1970s the gains of the civil rights and other movements encountered a period of backlash and many middle-class activists either retreated to climb the corporate ladder or retrenched by starting nonprofits in order to institutionalize their movement organizations. In contrast, working-class youth were split between those who scrambled for a good education, stable job, and upward mobility and those who have had to endure decreasing access to quality education, declining wages, and increasing rates of incarceration and slave labor in the globalized economy.

These United States-based immigrant workers and working- and middle-class youth have counterparts in the movements back in their homelands. For example, in Korea, the April 19th student movement toppled dictator Syngman Rhee in 1960 and helped oust General Chun Doo Hwan in 1987. Enraged at the repression of pro-democracy student demonstrators, workers constituted the majority of those who took to the streets and were cut down by government troops during 1980 Kwangju and 1989 Tiananmen uprisings. In Mexico, after the army massacred students protesting in 1968 in Tlatelolco Plaza, survivors fanned out into various left, labor, poor, and indigenous movements. Thirty years later, the offspring of Tlatelolco can be seen in the strength of the anti-globalization activism initiated by the independent labor group FAT in 1991, the indigenous Zaptista rebellion in Chiapas beginning in 1994, and the historic electoral defeat of the PRI in 2000.

Youth Spice Up Movements

Maria Rhie of Korean Women Workers Associations United said, "The student movement's relation to the workers' movement is like *mi-won* [MSG/monosodium glutamate]—adding a little enhances the flavor of the dish; too much ruins it."[15] At the same time, students in the United States and the women's homelands are also class stratified, between those based in elite schools and those in community colleges and vocational schools.[16]

Because of the language barriers they face and their lack of familiarity with US institutions, immigrant women workers often rely on English-speaking, sometimes younger generation co-organizers to help develop the workers' movement. These co-organizers struggle hard to not take short cuts and substitute themselves and their own partial knowledge, experience, and position for the immigrant workers' consciousness, leadership, base building, and experience organizing against the sweatshop structure.

How to skillfully manage the tension between the different generations and classes that make up the workers' movement remains an ongoing challenge not only for workers' centers, but also for unions and community organizations. In the 1990s, many AFL-CIO unions and community groups started hiring organizers straight out of elite colleges, while failing to invest in the leadership development of rank-and-file workers, grassroots community people, and working-class youth. The politics of privilege in a complex movement with members hailing from varying combinations of generations, classes, races, genders, sexual orientations, nations, citizenship statuses, and language groups must be consciously confronted—or these inequities will be mirrored in the movement and can end up hurting movements, organizations, and individuals.

Code Switchers, Bridge Builders, Border Crossers

While the children and grandchildren of immigrant workers often play the role of translators for their elders, this function is often performed under duress. Being forced to play this role from an early age shapes the particular challenges that confront these 1.5 and US-born generation organizers and activists. In a powerful piece about the role of child translators within the social history of Tejana farm workers, historian Antonia I. Castañeda asks:

> What cultural issues are at stake for child translators? How do they interpret for themselves the cultures they must translate for others? What are the politics they confront each time they translate cultures? How do they negotiate their culture of origin, which cannot protect them and in which the roles of parent and child are inverted as children become the tongues, the lifeline, the public voice of parents, family, and sometimes communities. How do they negotiate the culture they must translate for their parents: the culture that assaults and violates them, their families, and their communities with its assumptions and attitudes about them as well as with its language and other lethal weapons?... [T]hey and all children in the United States are steeped in lessons about rugged individualism, democracy, "American" nationalism, equality, justice, merit, and fair play. What do children of color, children of farmworker families, and other working class children, whose daily experiences belie the national myths, understand and know about these myths?[17]

The challenges facing the extended family members who join the women's movements expand from acting as the translator for one's immediate family to playing that role for many workers and families. This broadening of consciousness and action is the corollary of the transformation women described—from looking out only for their individual families to accepting responsibility for other workers and families within their own and sister communities. This leads to the mixed response immigrant parents sometimes have to their children's involvement in the labor and community movements.

Those families who have not yet decided to join the movement themselves have often invested in their children all their hopes for the advancement of their own family. While angered at the derailing of their plans, some are fiercely proud of their kids for their ethics in valuing people over profits in their work. In contrast, for those children of immigrant workers who have grown up on the picket line holding on for dear life to the protective arms of the women and riding on the broad shoulders of the men in their families, the challenge may be having the right to decide for themselves—with the same bristling, hard-headed independence of their parents and grandparents—exactly when, where, how, and whether they want to participate in a movement they can claim and fashion as their own.

Of course, joining the movement does not require that middle-class youth drop out of school and take low-waged jobs or that working-class youth make their way through college. Down through the decades, however, many radicalized youth the world over decided to jump off the track and gain a world of experience by walking a different path. Whatever the case, being part of the movement means linking up with other people to fight for justice, exercising accountability, and challenging pyramids of power and privilege *wherever* one works, studies, and lives.

As Castañeda indicates above, translation demands not only bilingual language fluency, but also the acquisition of different ways of thinking and knowing, of speaking and listening between different ethnicities, nations, genders, and classes. Because borders are used to control and oppress particular sets of people, a crossing can be fraught with danger for some while no more than a tourist shopping junket for others. What the child translators value in their families and communities may be despised when they cross into the outside world. While a worker may lack English fluency or formal education, that tells one nothing about her actual knowledge, communication skills, organizing capacity, and life experience. To bend the stick in the other direction, a college and professional education may also not tell much about a person's knowledge, communication skills, organizing capacity, and life experience. Of course, one type of experience, knowledge, and training is derided, while the other is valued.

The children of workers are confronted with the polarized dilemma: either destruction, mutilation, and trauma via dropping out of school, dead-end jobs, unemployment, drugs, incarceration, and violence, or a definitely more comfortable form of mutilation in the form of escape from the ghetto/barrio/Chinatown/Koreatown via the corporate or nonprofit professional ladder, during which they learn to think like, work like, and talk like those already in the upper echelons of the power pyramid. Those who, like the activists who've come before them, have experienced that moment of rupture from the myth, who have glimpsed the big picture and decided to join the labor and other resistance movements, still face the continual struggle against professionalization and corporatization of the labor and community movements. The reproduction of hierarchy and stratification within the movement is not just a matter of individual willpower or personal failing—it is simply an occupational health hazard of working "inside the belly of the beast."

Combating these tendencies is particularly difficult when the resistance movements are weak and have not yet been able to build a positive alternative vision, method, and infrastructure based in the participation of workers and grassroots people. The movements must develop strong counter-measures that prevent workers' translators from turning into elite professional organizers who orchestrate workers' struggles top-down and use grassroots people to leverage their own positioning within the power pyramid. In the worse case scenario, within some labor unions and community organizations, these spokespeople, who may have even started out in the rank-and-file and were democratically elected to "represent," start acting like internal colonial police who get pissed off when the base threatens to jeopardize their well-paid buffer negotiating gigs with the elite. At the same time, the workers and grassroots community organizations are crying out for the kind of programs that build the leadership skills necessary for poor people to defend themselves from violation of their rights by well-heeled and well-connected elites, and to create alternative visions, viable programs, and sturdy movements for self-determination.

The role of translator and bridge builder is not limited to bilingual and English-speaking extended family members, but also lands right in the laps of the women themselves. These working-class organizers are themselves the translators and bridges between the organizations and movements they are building and the broader base of unorganized workers and community people that they are trying to convince to join them. As seen in their stories, at certain moments the women were confronted with ruptures that forced them to see the big picture of the pyramid they were working in. During those moments they had to decide whether they wanted to see more, confront this power structure, and subject themselves to the punishment that was sure to come for their actions. Their ability to know and do more depended on their own resources and those of their co-workers, extended families, communities, organizations, and movements. The women who were not immediately rebuffed, exhausted, or crushed had to keep remaking the decision about what they were prepared to do and the price they were prepared to pay.

But as the women tell us, their experiences in the movement were also not just doom and gloom. The women got animated talking about what energized them, nourished their spirits, and schooled them. And part of what they were thirsty to learn, even as they sighed and shook their heads in frustration, was the primary language of the land where they worked and decided to raise their children and grandchildren. They are learning and transforming the English language like the African Americans who have bestowed upon this country the gift of Black English, a vibrant example of fusion. The women are enriching this polyglot rainbow nation's language, food, style, labor, culture, and identity.

And as the women build their organizations together with their extended family members and get exposed to the new ways of working, thinking, and learning that the other generations, classes, and races bring to their movements, they are challenged to not get separated from, but stay closely connected with the women in their home communities. The elites in their industries and communities have warned the other women to shun and silence them. But the women continue to organize and build the power with their peers, and help these women translate their life experiences into the analysis and action that will include even more of their peers, partners, children, and neighbors.

The fusion of different generations and classes within the immigrant workers' movement is a complex, ongoing process of tension and mutual interaction between these different sectors of the community. It requires a struggle and transformation across both sides of language, culture, and generation borders to produce a new, more durable entity. When workers and their children break through the deadening constraints of poverty, overwork, alcoholism, substance abuse, violence, and all the other oppressive mechanisms through which the system entraps poor people, they may not use the language of the "talented tenth" and intellectual class, but they show the potential power of the "neglected nine-tenths."

Workers have their own life experience, knowledge, skills, and language through which they can access the broader analysis and build the power to liberate themselves and the broader society alongside and above them—from the bottom of the sweatshop pyramid. If the radicalized "talented tenth" can refuse to be bought off, intoxicated, suffocated, and neutralized by their privilege, and instead cast their lot with the workers and the poor, they can bring the many skills that privilege and access have given them to really "serve the people" and help reshape power relations. And this call to bridge generations and classes reaches far beyond the borders of the immigrant community, to include those who have spoken English and have lived in this country for generations, like the Black elders, youth, and children who made up the rank-and-file leaders, workers, and intellectuals of the civil rights movement.[18]

The challenge facing these translators and fusion artists is learning to code-switch and move smoothly back and forth across borders—in the service of the people. The delight and danger in honing this role with sharper consciousness and skill is in multiplying the sheer numbers and collective finesse of ever more border crossers, bridge builders, translators, code switchers, and leader-organizers.

Fusion has produced some bumpin' music, screamin' food, knockout fashions, and kick-butt movements that can invigorate one and all. Fusion is a creative art form that indigenous peoples, slaves, immigrant laborers, and their descendants, have experimented with since they were thrown together on this continent. Now that we have met some of the women and extended family members, let us look more closely at some of the organizations and movements that these fusion artists have created.

1   Chinese Staff and Workers Association, 1997.

2   Chinese Staff and Worker Association, 1998.

3   Ijima and Miyamoto, 1970.

4   Interview with Kim Seung Min, November 16, 1998.

5   Interview with Trinh Duong, October 21, 1997.

6   Interview with Cecilia Rodríguez, February 21, 2001.

7   Interview with Helen Kim, March 17, 2001.

8   Interview with Geri Almanza, April 24, 2000.

9   Interview with Yrene Espinoza, June 4, 2000.

10 Interview with Pamela Chiang, April 24, 2000.

11 Interview with Brenda Mata, March 28, 2001.

12 DuBois, 1903.

13 Elbaum, 2001.

14 The Panthers and a number of other revolutionary youth organizations debated how the lumpen proletariat, rather than the overall Black working class would lead the struggle. See Lusane, 1997. His insightful chapter "Thug Life: The Rap on Capitalism" analyzes this perspective as it has resurfaced and been commodified and globalized within gangsta rap.

15 Interview with Maria Chol Soon Rhie, January 25, 1991. Some US trade unions also use the term "salting," or sending in organizers to "spice up" workers organizing to get a union at their shop.

16 Omatsu, 1999.

17 Castañeda, 1997.

18 Carson, 1981; Grant, 1998; and Branch, 1989 and 1998.

Chapter Five

Movement Roots

The Ysleta-Zaragoza international bridge just southeast of El Paso, Texas, and the Mexican city of Juárez is the mainline NAFTA artery pumping products, trade, cultures, and people in both directions. Juárez houses a huge concentration of maquilas and some 300,000 workers, many of whom commute to jobs in El Paso. But on a blistering summer day in 1997, the teeming flow of traffic came to a screeching halt as NAFTA-displaced workers seized control of the bridge. Facing the pending cut-off of job training money for Mexican immigrant and Chicana/o workers whose jobs had run across the border to Mexico, the workers' action served notice that business as usual was unacceptable. The workers were soon overwhelmed, arrested, and hauled off by SWAT commandos. While the workers were not unionized, they belonged to La Mujer Obrera and its fraternal organization, the Asociación de Trabajadores Fronterizos [Association of Border Workers].[1] These two groups represent modern-day descendants of the *mutualistas* [mutual aid organizations] formed by earlier generations of Mexicans as they fanned out across the Southwest border region and along the seasonal migrant worker trails.

By linking the *mutualistas* and other ethnically based independent labor organizations of yesteryear with those of today, the "big picture" expands from a single frame shot of a current struggle to a rolling documentary film that also encompasses the ethnic- and gender-based labor organizing that preceded today's movement. Reclaiming and elaborating this work-in-progress is important for all groups, but especially for immigrants, due to the compression of historical time and confusion of social meaning that occurs when one crosses a border. Immigrants experience tremendous disjuncture when their life- and movement-related experiences prior to migration are invisible to the non-immigrants and other ethnic groups with whom they work and live. Another aspect of this split is that immigrants who do not know about the history of US race, national, class, and gender relations can walk straight into the middle of an ambush without so much as a warning.

This break in historical continuity impacts immigrants of all classes and people of all races. For example, skilled professional immigrants who work in glass ceiling jobs in corporations, live in the suburbs, and send their children to ivy league schools may mistakenly believe that their access to the "good life" and the "American dream" is only a result of their individual talents and struggles. Since history is largely told by the conquerors and not the vanquished, national myths such as "the United States is a meritocracy" serve to hide from communal knowledge not only the memories of the hounding and beatings of economic miracle workers in immigrants' home countries, but also the genocide, enslavement, criminalization, and murder of indigenous, Black, and other folks of color who have not "risen" within this illusion of equality.

Fortunately, new ethnic- and race-conscious labor histories are beginning to be produced. Yet much labor history, old and new, remains to be told. This chapter will touch on how immigrant women workers' ethnic- and gender-based labor organizing is rooted in the history of prior movements, especially how the five workers' centers featured in this book are rooted in particular sections of sweatshop industry workers' struggles and in earlier stages of the Mexican/Chicano, Chinese, and Korean radical labor and community movements.

Earlier Stages of Immigrant Organizing

Today's workers' centers are being built on the foundation of the two prominent periods in 20th-century US social change organizing—the 30s and the 60s—as well as the preceding labor history.

Before immigration from Europe was restricted in the 1920s, many Jewish, Italian, German, Irish, and other European immigrant workers organized themselves along ethnic lines. Immigrant workers' organizations often fused radical political traditions from home with new organizing currents in the United States. Anti-racism was not necessarily one of those traditions and some of the craft-oriented, European immigrant-based unions attacked workers of color whom they saw as competitors, for example spearheading campaigns to exclude Chinese immigrant and newly emancipated Black workers.[2]

Most mainstream labor organizations mirrored the American Federation of Labor's (AFL) racist exclusion of immigrants of color and African Americans. Left to fend for themselves, these workers formed ethnic-based organizations such as the Mexican *mutualistas,* the Chinese Seamen's Union formed in 1911, and the Chinese Hand Laundry Alliance formed in the 30s. In order to revive business and reduce widespread unemployment stemming from the Depression, the Roosevelt administration enacted legislation that guaranteed workers the right to organize, join unions of their own choosing, and bargain collectively with employers, leading to a wave of labor organizing.[3] The creation of the Congress of Industrial Organizations (CIO) in 1935 ushered in another wave of rank-and-file organizing that began to break with the practice of racist exclusion.

Unskilled first- and second-generation immigrants from southern and eastern Europe, as well as Mexicans and Asians in the Southwest and West, and Blacks in the South became the core of industrial unionism in the 1930s. Second-generation children of immigrants predominated among CIO activists.[4] Many Black workers during this period were racialized internal migrants, joining the Great Migration to urban centers within the South and to the North spurred by the increased demand for labor and grinding conditions in Southern agriculture during the World Wars.[5] Puerto Rican and Cuban immigrant cigar rolling workers in New York organized their own unions, as did other Latin American, Asian-American, and African-American workers.[6] By 1945 unionized labor had reached a high of 35.5 percent of all US workers.[7]

Labor organizing during the 1930s and 1940s looked different among Latina/o and Asian workers depending on the gender composition of the particular wave of immigrant workers at the time. For example, given the focused recruitment of Chinese male laborers, the Chinese Exclusion Act, and skewed composition of male to female ratios, Chinese worker organizations consisted of immigrant men fighting for their rights practically alone within a racially segregated environment.[8] Once immigration policy changed to permit the immigration of women workers, a multi-generational community grew to reinforce the workers' organizations.

In contrast, given the higher proportion of women within the Mexican-American communities, that period also saw struggles by Mexican and Chicana women food packing workers, and *extended family support* for the struggles of Mexicano workers. According to historian Zaragosa Vargas, Tejana worker leaders like Manuela Solis Sager, Minnie Rendon, Juana Sanchez, and Emma Tenayuca played leading roles in Depression Era organizing in San Antonio. At the time young and single Tejanas made up 79 percent of that city's low-waged garment, cigar, and pecan-shelling workers. Tenayuca emerged as the leader of the 1938 pecan-shellers' strike, which included over 10,000 strikers, and was the largest labor strike in San Antonio's history and biggest community-based labor struggle among the nation's Mexican population during the 1930s.[9] Mexicanas and Chicanas, the wives of male strikers, played a pivotal role in the strike by 1400 members (90 percent Mexican) of Local 890 of the International Union of Mine, Mill, and Smelter Workers against Empire Zinc in Grant County, New Mexico between October 1950 to January 1952—the longest strike in New Mexico's history.[10] This struggle inspired the production of *Salt of the Earth,* the internationally known film that was banned in the United States but can still brings tears to the eyes of those who borrow it from their local Chicano or Labor Studies library.

Social unionism[11] severely threatened big capital, but during the McCarthy era the government and right-wing elites smashed the center-left alliance and purged leftists from the labor movement. A tamed labor and a chastened capital both endorsed a social pact promising ongoing raises in some workers' standard of living in exchange for worker compliance. Under the new "business unionism," workers exhibited more passivity toward bosses and supported the government's chauvinistic foreign policy. This period coincided with an extended interval of US economic growth following the country's rise to superpower status during World War II.

"Young, Gifted, and Brown"

Since the 1960s, three demographic explosions rocked the US workforce: massive Asian and Latina/o migration after the removal of racially discriminatory quotas; growing paid labor force participation of women of all races, including women with children; and the reverberations of the civil rights revolution through employment and education practices.

The workers' centers featured in this book all have linkages back to sections of the Asian and Latina/o radical movements that erupted in the United States and internationally in the late 1960s and early 1970s. In those adrenaline-filled days, many young folks of color (the equivalent of singer Nina Simone's "young, gifted, and Black") connected with first generation immigrant workers and other grassroots community people to develop "serve the people"[12] programs and organizing drives within the key racial, national, class and gender justice battles of the period. The struggles of immigrant farm, garment, and restaurant workers inspired and galvanized that generation of Latina/o and Asian-American sweatshop industry labor organizers. For example, the Filipino independent Agricultural Workers Organizing Committee kicked off the 1965 Delano, California grape strike and teamed up with the Mexican National Farm Workers Association (NFWA) to form the United Farm Workers Organizing Committee.[13] Some organizers who emerged in these movements later joined AFL-CIO unions, while others co-founded workers' centers and other grassroots community organizations.[14] Many of the workers and youth active in these struggles, including those who got jobs working in unions and community organizations, eventually returned to "civilian life" after both winning some victories and getting trounced by the reactionary backlash during the

Reagan/Bush administrations. The mustered out troops continued to use their movement-acquired consciousness and skills at work and school, and in their families and communities.

Battered by the rupture of the social pact and economic decline of the 70s, and the subsequent deindustrialization, economic restructuring, and globalization, the proportion of unionized workers shrank to a mere 13.5 percent of the US workforce by 2000.[15] *Today some 86 percent of US workers are not unionized.* During the mid-1970s the neoliberal assault on workers, the poor, people of color, immigrants, women, lesbians, and gays shifted into high gear leading to the founding of workers' centers. Many movement organizations dissolved and those that continued were forced to adjust to a harsh new political climate.

Today's workers' centers emerged in response to this vacuum. By the 1990s, in grappling with an economy and workforce transformed by immigrant workers and globalization, some sections of the broader labor movement had begun to raise many similar questions and experiment with new approaches. In the late 19th and early 20th centuries, new organizing initiatives among immigrant workers from Asia, Latin America, and Europe flagged major shifts in the US economy and new stages in the development of the broader labor movement. In the late 20th and early 21st centuries, independent, ethnic-based organizing among immigrant sweatshop industry workers provided an early warning signal both of the deleterious effects of global economic restructuring on the most vulnerable workers and of the means through which these workers can organize to defend themselves.

Below are brief "work visa" snapshots of the five workers' centers, in terms of their initial origins; worker and intergenerational ethnic community base and ties; and victories and accomplishments. The centers are listed by order of their founding year.

Chinese Staff and Workers Association: Organizing Sewing Women and Kitchen Men

CSWA was born in 1979 "when a group of Chinese restaurant workers met at a hamburger joint in Chinatown and discussed their desire for rights and dignity in the workplace."[16] Some of CSWA's founding members had accumulated experience in various mass struggles including the marches of tens of thousands of Chinatown residents in 1974 and 1975 voicing support for low-income tenants' rights; the campaign to break racist hiring practices in the construction industry; and campaigns against police brutality, for quality health care and nutrition programs, and for normalization of US relations with China.[17] CSWA reflects the radical perspectives and methods of workers and youth from across the Chinese diaspora.

Chinese immigrant men in New York have tended to take low-waged jobs in the restaurant industry. In 1980, after being spurned by the Hotel and Restaurant Employees and Bartenders Union, Local 69, former workers from the Silver Palace Restaurant formed their own union with the support of CSWA. They named it the 318 Restaurant Workers' Union, in honor of the day, March 18, on which they had been fired for protesting against the restaurant's management.

In the 70s and after, Chinese immigrant women followed a well-beaten path to garment sweatshops, revitalizing New York's then sagging rag trade, and yielding profits and start-up capital for Chinese and other entrepreneurs and real estate developers. The majority of Chinese garment workers became members of the International Ladies Garment Workers Union (ILGWU), Local 23-25, after the union reached agreements with the manufacturers and contractors top-down in 1974. Chinese immigrant women hit the streets 20,000 strong to defend their contract against the machinations of the Chinatown bosses in 1982. When ILGWU (and later UNITE) failed to harness their energy or adequately support their interests, many turned to CSWA.[18]

CSWA has won many precedent-setting victories. They successfully brought shorter working hours to many New York City Chinatown restaurants and garment factories. They've forced government and social institutions to allocate more space and support for child care programs critical to Chinatown's working women. In 1985, CSWA led the Concerned Committee of the Chung Park Project to call for community space, including a day-care center. That

year it also began organizing the first group of Chinese homestead-
ers on the Lower East Side, who won a building that houses 12
low-income co-op units, the Latino Workers' Center (originally a
CSWA project), and the Committee Against Anti-Asian Violence
(CAAAV). In 1989 CSWA helped Chinese workers at the Chinatown Planning Council (CPC) and African-American construction
workers protest underpayment of workers under a federally funded
CPC training program. These workers finally won a $2.15 million
settlement in 1994. CSWA helped workers send employers to prison
when they failed to pay. They have organized injured workers and
fought for safer working conditions, and for workers to have more
control over their time and lives.[19]

La Mujer Obrera: ¡La Unidad Nos Hara Fuertes! [Unity Will Make Us Strong!]

A "handful of women, tempered by the painful experience"
with the Amalgamated Clothing and Textile Workers' Union
(ACTUW) and the Farah strike founded La Mujer Obrera in 1981.
Nine years earlier some 4,000 workers had walked out on strike at
Farah demanding to be represented by the ACTWU.[20]

> In those days [the Farah workers] sought out the tool best known
> to them in order to defend themselves: the labor union. After
> many months of struggle they learned that the union, especially
> when it was governed by laws which favored big business and
> which allowed it to be controlled by corrupt leaders, was not the
> solution for all their problems. Then they sought to preserve their
> struggle through a workers' center, an independent organization
> where they could not only defend themselves against the bosses,
> but also defend their right to be organized, a right which the "un-
> ion" continued to deny them. This right to be organized was even
> more important for a sector which suffered a great deal of dis-
> crimination: the women who made up 80 percent of the garment
> labor force.[21]

Additionally some of the founding members of La Mujer
Obrera had worked in the Rio Grande Valley in South Texas, which
served as a focal of point for organizing by the Texas Farm Workers

Union; in community struggles against racism, police, INS, and Border Patrol assaults; and for decent housing, public utilities, sanitation, education, and health care. With the birth of the modern Chicana/o movement, Tejana/o activists organized in border cities across the region. La Raza Unida Party registered and rallied voters, electrified the Chicano movement, and "pissed off red necks," when it swept the Board of Education and Crystal City and county elections in 1970.[22]

Given the special bi-national character of the border region, Mexican and Chicana/o activists have created "sister movements" and organized against the negative impacts of neoliberalism. The army and death squads' massacre of students in Mexico City's Tlatelolco Plaza on October 2, 1968, ten days before the opening of the Olympics, shocked and radicalized Mexicans on both sides of the border. Organizing spread among the urban and rural poor, indigenous peoples, and within the church, via liberation theology. La Mujer Obrera taps into these Chicana/Tejana/Mexicana radical labor, community, and indigenous movement roots.

Over its 20-year history, La Mujer Obrera has enabled immigrant workers to organize themselves to both win many disputes and develop programs to meet their basic needs in the face of massive deindustrialization. In 1990 LMO members chained themselves to their sewing machines and staged a hunger strike, outing the underground sweatshop system and flight of large companies. In 1991 the organization unionized three factories and one laundry (Sonia, DCB, H&R, and Apparel Conditioners Corp.), helping workers win collective bargaining agreements, including pay, vacation, and minimal health package increases. The nine-month strike, which included a hunger strike during which a 60-year-old garment worker fasted for 23 days, won broad support from labor, community, and church groups, as well as elected officials. It also prompted all five of El Paso's state legislators to immediately draft, lobby for, and win a bill that established criminal penalties including imprisonment, for non-payment of wages. LMO's efforts also convinced Texas' Attorney General to prosecute various subcontractors, efforts which eventually recouped over $200,000 in back wages owed to women garment workers.[23] La Mujer persuaded the El Paso government to invest $367,000 in expanding child-care services and economic opportunities for low-income women workers. It also took part in local, state, national, and tri-national mobilizations against NAFTA and organized workers facing impending plant closures to fight for severance pay, benefits, and job retraining. In 1997 with the help of LMO, NAFTA-displaced workers won a $3 million extension in government funded training for laid-off workers in addition to the original $4.2 million allocated. In addition to running its own Popular School and women's organizing projects, LMO has generated independent organizations, including the Asociación de Trabajadores Fronterizos. Another spin-off, El Puente [the Bridge], focuses on development projects that create an economic base for the community, such as the Rayito del Sol Daycare Center, Café Mayapan Restaurant, and other low-cost housing and job training and creation projects.[24]

Asian Immigrant Women Advocates: Community Transformational and Organizing Strategy

In 1983, Asian Immigrant Women Advocates (AIWA) emerged in Oakland, California from discussions between Korean hotel room cleaners; first and second generation Korean-American activists Young Shin and Elaine Kim of the Korean Community Center of the East Bay (KCCEB), a Korean community-oriented social service organization; and Chinese-American Local 2 union organizer Patricia Lee. KCCEB, AIWA's co-founder, was the local Korean version of the "serve the people" programs that young progressives co-founded with immigrant elders to deal with pressing language, social, and economic needs of their emerging communities. As in other ethnic communities, women played a central role in these community service organizations, as part of their "triple *jornada*" [triple shift], of labor on the job, in the family, and in the community.

In the 1970s and 80s, San Francisco's hotel industry was undergoing a tremendous change, with growing numbers of "back of the house" Asian and Latino immigrant workers and "front of the house" college-educated waitresses, waiters, and receptionists. Despite this influx of non-English speakers, the Hotel and Restaurant Employees and Bartenders Union (HERE) Local 2, employed no organizers fluent in the Korean language. Thus Korean hotel workers at the exclusive Fairmont Hotel atop Nob Hill in San Francisco, although members of the union, could neither understand the union contract nor participate in union activities.

After unseating the local's 35-year entrenched leadership, hotel workers went on strike in 1980 for better wages and improved working conditions. Local 2 emerged as San Francisco's largest union and a hotbed of radical organizing, with Filipina and Latina hotel maids comprising some 95 percent of strike picketers.[25]

As AIWA began organizing Asian garment workers in Oakland and Korean hotel room cleaners in San Francisco, the Asian Law Caucus argued the cases of garment workers and worked with Reverend Norman Fong of Cameron House and the Presbyterian Church in Chinatown to develop a San Francisco garment workers center that, like AIWA, offered English classes, information on labor, housing, and immigration law to workers, and social activities for the women and their families.[26] Many of the young people active in immigrant worker organizing, including at AIWA, had also been politicized and influenced by the 1968 strikes for ethnic studies programs at San Francisco State College and the University of California at Berkeley; the fight to defend the International Hotel, which had housed many low-income residents of San Francisco's Manilatown/Chinatown before they were brutally evicted on August 4, 1977;[27] the activities of the Chinatown Workers Sewing Coop, housed in the I-Hotel storefront of the Asian Community Center (ACC); [28] the struggles of Jung Sai garment workers and Lee Mah electronics workers who worked under ILGWU and Teamster contracts for Esprit and Faranon respectively;[29] and the Filipino farm workers who invited young Filipina/os and other Asians to join them in the United Farm Workers Organizing Committee fight against the growers.

In October 1990 AIWA also launched a project targeting a new set of sweatshop industry workers—electronics assemblers in Santa Clara County's Silicon Valley. Tens of thousands of immigrant women from Asia and Latin America worked in shops, ranging from large factories to small fly-by-night shops set up in garages by subcontractors. The women often worked up to 14-hour days handling hazardous chemicals and inhaling toxic fumes as they assembled, cleaned, and tested printed circuit boards for "everything from watches to warheads."[30]

AIWA is strongly committed to developing grassroots women's leadership. The group's many accomplishments include providing workplace literacy and citizenship classes for immigrant women workers in Oakland's Chinatown and in Silicon Valley; organizing worker-led leadership development institutes and peer trainings around workers' rights; and leadership and organizing training for the children of garment and electronics workers.[31] In 1990, AIWA initiated an environmental health and safety project for Silicon Valley electronics workers, to help workers protect themselves from toxic chemicals and other industry hazards. In 1992, they launched the Garment Workers Justice Campaign, which resulted in an unprecedented settlement holding manufacturers accountable to their women workers and community. In 1997, AIWA pressured three more manufacturers to establish multilingual, confidential, and toll-free hotlines for garment workers to report violations of women's rights in the workplace. In 2000, AIWA co-sponsored the Asian Immigrant Women Workers Clinic to address the health needs of electronics workers.

Their work has developed concrete strategies for advancing immigrant women workers' leadership in the struggles for economic and social justice, and has catapulted women workers into various networks of workers' centers and grassroots organizations fighting for environmental and economic justice.[32]

Fuerza Unida: *La Mujer Luchando*

Fuerza Unida was founded in 1990 by "early victims of NAFTA," non-unionized workers laid off by Levi Strauss and Co.'s plant in San Antonio, Texas on January 16. The laid-off workers first met at Our Lady of Angels Church on January 30, then launched the organization on February 6. Within a month the organization began negotiating for the workers. By May 1990, Fuerza Unida had elaborated a detailed list of 15 demands ranging from a statewide study about the feasibility of re-opening the plant to transferring ownership of the facility to laid-off workers, providing a specific severance package, and offering retraining programs. Marta Martínez, one of the laid-off workers recalled back in 1991

> First we organized 15 women, then 30, and then each month it's been getting larger. After 18 months we now have 650 members. They have regular meetings, committees taking up different responsibilities, a general council where decisions are made and a small coordinating committee. It doesn't work perfectly, and we're learning a lot about democracy as we go along.[33]

Fuerza Unida launched a national boycott of Levi's labels and carried out hunger strikes and pickets. The group filed two lawsuits against the company, one alleging pension fund violations, work injury claims, especially for carpal tunnel syndrome, and the other, racially discriminatory layoff practices towards the primarily Latina women workers. The work injury suit was denied by the right-to-work state of Texas and the discrimination suit by the federal district court, which discouraged many of the workers.

Many Latina/o and some white labor, community, church, and legal advocates offered initial support to the laid-off workers. When Levi's first announced the layoffs, the Southwest Public Workers Union (SPWU) demonstrated at the factory and met with workers. SPWU represents custodians, school cafeteria, hotel, and restaurant workers. SPWU's founding members Rubén Solís and Chavel López had been involved in the Centro de Acción Social Autonoma-Hermandad General de Trabajadores (CASA-HGT), a mass-based undocumented workers' rights organization active during the 1970s.[34] CASA-HGT served as basic training camp for many labor, immigrant, and civil rights leaders and organizers. During the 1980s at the height of US intervention in Central America, ex-CASA and other Tejana/o activists worked in Chicanos Against Intervention in Latin America (CAMILA), an organization that fused the Chicana/o support for national liberation struggles with a critique of the racial blind spots of the white-dominated, anti-intervention

movement.[35] During the 1990s, much of the energy of the anti-intervention movement shifted from military issues to the exploitation of women inside proliferating maquiladoras in Mexico and
Central America and the impending passage of NAFTA. Tejana/o
anti-interventionist activists introduced Fuerza Unida to women
workers networks in those regions, with whom the women shared
language, cultural, religious, and class commonalities.

Fuerza Unida enjoyed support from the Esperanza Peace and
Justice Center, the American Friends Service Committee, the Southwest Network for Environmental and Economic Justice, and the
MEChA, many of whose members had organized against US intervention in Central America. Each of these organizations in turn is
rooted in different sections of the Mexican, Chicana/o, and Latina/o
women's, lesbian, cultural, anti-intervention, solidarity, environmental justice, and student movements. Organizations like Mexican
American Legal Education and Defense Fund, the League of United
Latin American Citizens, and elected officials like Henry B. Gonzáles and Ciro Rodríguez also endorsed Fuerza Unida's campaign,
then became the object of intense lobbying by the corporation seeking to dampen their support for the women.

The women of Fuerza Unida are recognized as early grassroots
leaders of the national campaign for justice in the garment industry
and against NAFTA and corporate globalization. Their organizing
has scored impressive victories including the creation of a women
workers' resource center for low-income residents of San Antonio's
South and Westside barrios. They've developed women workers'
leadership through a Promotora Leadership Development Campaign and peer group trainings. In 1996, they worked with other local organizations to force the city council to adopt pro-worker
legislation and legislation that requires companies to support and
pay taxes for job training and other programs.[36] Fuerza's voice has
been heard worldwide through their success in improving settlement packages for laid-off workers in the United States, Canada,
Belgium, and France. While the group was born fighting against the
world's largest garment corporation, Puerto Rican feminist activist
Luz Guerra says that the group "is now engaged in what may be

their biggest battle yet: to establish themselves as a community-based organization dedicated to supporting and empowering
the poor and working-class women of San Antonio, on their own
terms."[37] Reflecting on how the refusal of the Amalgamated Clothing and Textile Workers Union (ACTUW) to help the laid-off Levi's
workers may have been a blessing in disguise, Fuerza Unida's Petra
Mata explained,

> We have to be independent to be happy. We don't want people to
> tell us what to do and what not to do. Through Fuerza Unida we
> can speak out and say whatever we want, whatever is in our
> hearts. A lot of people go where the money and power is. Yes,
> money helps. But money is not everything. It depends on your vi-
> sion and what you have in your mind. We have learned to be
> strong and we know how to struggle.[38]

Korean Immigrant Workers Advocates:
Organizing *Minjung* Diaspora

Founded in 1992, one month before the Rodney King civil unrest, Korean Immigrant Workers Advocates (KIWA) in Los Angeles, California, organizes restaurant, janitorial, construction,
garment, and other low-waged Korean and Latino immigrants who
work for Korean employers.

KIWA grew out of the Korean progressive community that had
spawned, a decade earlier, such Korean-American organizing as the
intergenerational community campaign to free Chol Soo Lee,[39] and
the initiatives launched by first generation immigrant youth shaped
by the Kwangju Uprising, such as Young Koreans United.[40] The legacy of these early efforts of the Korean progressive community include an ongoing identification with the history of progressive
organizing in South Korea, support for peaceful reunification with
North Korea, and opposition to US neocolonial policies on the Korean peninsula. KIWA also received early support from former
members of the Korean Labor Association in Los Angeles, which
had previously organized in support of immigrant garment workers'
wage claims and against the South Korean military regime.

KIWA had inside experience with the strengths and weaknesses of different AFL-CIO unions' approaches to the rights of immigrants, women, and people of color. KIWA founders Roy Hong and Danny Park had organized Korean janitors at the San Francisco airport, and Hong had worked as an organizer for Service Employees International Union (SEIU), at both the local and international levels. SEIU launched its innovative Justice for Janitors campaign in Los Angeles in 1988.[41] Hong and Park had also assisted HERE Local 11 in Los Angeles when Korean owners bought the Hilton Hotel and tried to fire its worker leaders. After an 11-month campaign, workers succeeded in keeping their jobs and winning a collective bargaining agreement.

Los Angeles has been been repeatedly rocked and resegregated through race and class conflicts, making KIWA's cross-race organizing all the more important and noteworthy. The 1965 Watts rebellion was followed by deindustrialization and massive labor migration from Latin America and Asia. Ongoing racial and class tensions were manifested in the 1992 Rodney King civil unrest, the first "multi-racial riot." Through its many victories, KIWA has served as a cutting-edge example of cross-racial worker organizing, building coalitions between Korean workers and other communities of color, including fighting to raise the state minimum wage, lower bus rates for the poor, maintain the state's affirmative action programs, and in solidarity with hotel workers and janitors fighting for jobs and dignity.

KIWA is also known for its role in co-organizing a campaign in defense of 78 Thai and 55 Latino workers from the El Monte "slave shop" where workers won a $4 million settlement with retailers. One of its first successes was in organizing 45 workers displaced by the April 1992 civil unrest, demanding inclusion of workers in relief fund distribution and winning $109,000 from conservative business owners. KIWA pressured the Korean Restaurant Owners Association members to join the California Workers Compensation Fund and participate in creating a community mediation-arbitration board to resolve workers disputes with employers. KIWA also raised over $30,000 for North Korean famine relief; supported the independent workers' movements in South Korea and Mexico; and organized Korean immigrant voters to collaborate with other communities of color to impact electoral politics.

In sum, the women's struggles and workers' centers are rooted both in resistance to sweatshop industry exploitation and in the accumulated experience of prior labor and community movements. The workers' centers represent a fusion of the different generations of workers and their expanded family members. The women in this book described how they were often compelled by the sheer force of anger and crisis to join or help create such organizations and take on leadership roles with the help of extended family members, often the descendants of prior generations of immigrant workers. In these positions, they took on powerful, well-entrenched institutions, and developed skills they never dreamed they could. They have won thousands of dollars in back wages, slowed the pace of layoffs, secured better settlement packages, strengthened legislation demanding greater corporate accountability to workers and their communities, increased visibility about industry abuses, and offered programmatic alternatives to employer greed. By example, the women showed their peers and communities that change is possible and worth fighting for. Although largely unsung heroines, these risk-takers and their organizations constitute the bleeding edge of anti-corporate movements in the age of globalization. Their perspectives and experiences constitute a treasure trove of lessons on how to organize the most disenfranchised sectors of their communities and create a more just society. We will unpack more from this chest of organizing lessons and movement building in the next chapter.

1   Interview with Guillermo Domínguez Glen, April 3, 2001.

2   Saxton, 1971 and Douglass, 1892 (1962 revised edition).

3   Gómez-Quiñones, 1994:105

4   In terms of European ethnic immigrant workers see Cohen, 1990:324-25 and Friendlander, 1975 both cited in Milkman, 2000:4-5. For more on Mexican, Asian, and Black workers organizing linked to CIO unions see Gómez-Quiñones, 1994; Ruíz, Vicki L., 1984; Vargas, 1997; Acuña, 1988; Yu, Renqiu, 1992; Kwong, Peter, 1979; Scharlin and Villanueva, 1994; Yoneda, 1983; and Kelley, 1990 and 1994.

5   Kelley, 1990 and 1994. Kelley analyzes CIO and left-related organizing among Black sharecroppers and steelworkers.

6   Vega, 1984; Yoneda, 1983; Scharlin and Villanueva, 1994; and Kelley, 1990 and 1994.

7   Gómez-Quiñones, 1994:333.

8   Yu, Renqiu, 1992:51-52. In the case of the Chinese Hand Laundry Alliance of New York, the workers hired progressive lawyer, Julius Louis Bezozo, the son of Polish-Jewish immigrants, to represent the workers' in legal cases. He was assisted by CHLA's English Language Secretary, the only CHLA official to receive a regular salary ($40/month in the 1930s). Yu says that the function of the English Secretary was to deal with city authorities and serve as spokesman of the CHLA to the English-speaking world. He also translated the regulations and ordinances related to the business and their lawyer's explanations of these documents to members, served as the lawyer's interpreter, and accompanied members to court. The CHLA's Chinese Language Secretary coordinated the CHLA's intervention in the fractious class politics within the Chinese community. Many immigrant workers' centers still carry out the dual functions of the CHLA's English and Chinese Secretaries, though with a broader infrastructure of support than did these early male pioneers.

9   Vargas, 1997:553-580. See also Ruíz, Vicki L., 1987; and Calderón and Zamora, 1990.

10   Acuña, 1988:278-279.

11   Social unionism addresses both the connections between workers and their broader communities, and the process of labor organizing as part of the broader fight for social and economic justice. In contrast, business unions often engage in winnable fights to improve the terms of the deal workers get from bosses, build up the financial assets of the union, and lobby, finance, and influence politicians and other institutions, without regard to the interests of their mass members, unorganized workers, and the broader community. In alliances between labor and community organizations, social unionism and social justice community organizing builds relations on the basis of mutual respect and solidarity to advance the overlapping interests of all partners within the movement against corporate control, etc. Under business unionism and narrow self-interest community organizing, each party organizes on the basis of its own direct self-interest and only links up with others in order to use the other party to advance its own agenda.

With the suppression of the left within the labor and other movements and fragmentation between movements, an elite form of professionalization has come to dominate many sections of the movement. The distinctions between the terms "organizer," "leader," and "activist" represent this type of professionalization: "organizer" has come to mean college-educated, middle-class, professional organizer; "leader" signifies a worker or grassroots person being cultivated and trained by organizers; and "activist" applies to other random people who volunteer their time in these movements. In another indication of the purge of the left in the resistance movements, the terms "ally" and "supporter" have replaced what used to be called "sisters and brothers in the struggle." Where in the past an "ally" was seen as someone who acted in "solidarity" in shared battles against oppression, now it is often reduced to those who can be used to leverage single-issue tit-for-tat. Now "solidarity" and "support" sometimes mean nothing more than "charity" to help "victims" somewhere else.

12 The concept of "serve the people" was advocated by revolutionaries in China. Young radicals of color identified with Third World national liberation movements in the 1960s and 70s, such as the Black Panther Party, Young Lords, I Wor Kuen, Wei Min Sei, Katipunan Ng Demokratic, and others developed US inner city versions of serve-the-people-style free breakfast, health clinics, low-cost housing, and other programs. For example, see Louie, Steve.

13 Gómez-Quiñones, 1994:47-59; Yu, Renqiu, 1992; Kwong, Peter, 1979:116-130; Scharlin and Villanueva, 1992:27-42; and Acuña, 1988.

14 I hope that more Asian and Latina/o AFL-CIO union organizers will document the history in that section of the labor movement, including the stories of low-waged immigrant union members.

15 Bureau of Labor Statistics, 2000, cited in Moberg, 2001.

16 Chinese Staff and Workers Association, 1999a:1.

17 Kwong, Peter, 1987:137-173; Ho, Fred, 2000; and Louie, Steve, et al.., 2001 (forthcoming).

18 Kwong, Peter, 1987:137-159.

19 Chinese Staff and Workers Association, 1999a.

20 La Mujer Obrera, 1996a:3.

21 La Mujer Obrera, 1996a:2-3.

22 Acuña, 1988:339 and 387, Gutiérrez, 1998.

23 La Mujer Obrera, 1991:1 and 7; and Marquez, 1995: 68-78.

24 La Mujer Obrera, 1996a; author interviews with María Antonia Flores and Cindy Arnold, December 9, 1997 and Guillermo Domínguez Glenn, May 5, 2000; presentation by Jena Camp and Yrene Espinoza, June 4, 2000; White Polk, 2000; La Mujer Obrera, 2001.

25 Interview with Lora Jo Foo, April 11, 1997. Wells, 2000:109-129.

26 Interview with Lora Jo Foo, April 11, 1997.

27 Toribio, Helen, 2000; and Habal, Stella, 2000.

28 Interview with Bea Tam and Harvey Dong, May 4, 1997. Ironically, the Coop's first contract was with garment manufacturer Jessica McClintock; in

English classes, Coop members practiced how to say, "You're too cheap!" during negotiations over piece rates.

29 Interview with Bea Tam and Harvey Dong, May 4, 1997.

30 Asian Immigrant Women Advocates, 1993.

31 Shin, 1995:48-50; and Louie, Miriam, 1992.

32 AIWA, 1998:5-6; see also Shin, 1997.

33 *Canadian Tribune,* 1991.

34 CASA sought to develop a general *hermanidad* [brotherhood] of Mexican workers *sin fronteras* [without borders]. CASA combined two demographic pools: immigrant workers and young Chicana/o radical students, activists, and professionals who used their newly acquired skills to manage the organization's service programs. CASA was particularly strong in California, Texas, Illinois, and Washington, i.e., states with large Mexican immigrant worker populations during that period. See García, Mario, 1994:286-320. Interviews with Arnoldo García, April 21, 1997 and May 6, 1997; and Rubén Solís, October 8, 1997. See also Ruíz, 1998:99-126 about Chicanas' roles in the movement and struggles against sexism, particularly within CASA and La Raza Unida Party.

35 Interview with Antonio Díaz, December 7, 1999. See also Guerra, 1990.

36 Fuerza Unida, 1998:5-6.

37 Guerra, Luz. 1997:2.

38 Interview with Petra Mata, March 20, 2001.

39 Chol Soo Lee was on San Quentin's death row, convicted of a Chinatown murder he did not commit, and a killing while in prison. With the help of Korean community elders lawyer Jay Kun Yoo and newspaper man Kyung Won Lee, his case served as a rallying point for the Korean-American community during the late 1970s and early 80s. See Jay Kun Yoo's story in Kim and Yu, 1996:282-293.

40 Sim, 2000.

41 Acuña, 1996:184-188; and Fisk, Mitchell, and Erickson. 2000.

Chapter Six

"Just-in-Time"
Guerrilla Warriors

Immigrant Workers' Centers

Rojana "Na" Cheunchujit delivered an impassioned speech to some 20,000 workers who jammed the Los Angeles Sports Arena at an AFL-CIO rally on June 10, 2000, demanding the end of employer sanctions and unconditional amnesty for undocumented workers. In March 1999, she testified before the California Assembly Committee on Labor and Employment in support of a bill to crack down on sweatshop abuses in California's $30 billion garment industry.

The sports stadium and state legislature halls are a long way from the El Monte sweatshop where Cheunchujit and her Thai co-workers were imprisoned behind razor wire—a long way, also, from the Immigration and Naturalization Service (INS) detention center where the workers were reincarcerated after their "liberation" by government agents. They are half a world away from the Bangkok garment factories where Cheunchujit sewed as a teenager and the village where she was born and planted rice seedlings with her parents as a child.

Cheunchujit was one of the 72 Thai workers imprisoned as sewing slaves in a sweatshop in El Monte, California which had opened in 1988.[1] When government agents stormed the factory on August 2, 1995, the workers' terrified faces made front-page headlines and prime-time TV news across the nation. Their case shocked many

who thought that sweatshops were something that existed overseas—not within US borders. The workers' subsequent campaign
provoked scrutiny of brand name retailers and manufacturers and
helped spur the creation, in August 1996, of a presidential task force
to reform the garment industry.[2]

When asked whether workers feared demonstrating against retailers after their release, Cheunchujit laughed. "Participating in the
campaign was not scary, not after what we'd been through!... This
campaign might help to redistribute the wealth." Cheunchujit had
participated in a strike as a young garment worker in Thailand. She
found her bearings amidst the confusion at the INS detention center
and threw in her lot with the Thai Community Development Center,
the Asian Pacific American Legal Center, and KIWA who came to
get the workers out of jail. She says the groups "really helped us to
overcome the terrible things we went through. We felt like we were
part of a larger family of people who really cared for us, people who
loved us, whom we could trust."[3]

The ethnic-based workers' centers reach, organize, and defend
the immigrant, low-waged, ethnic minority women workers who are
not protected by the trade union movement. During moments of crisis, workers like Cheunchujit and her co-workers at the El Monte
slaveshop, the Korean and Latino restaurant workers in LA's
Koreatown, the Mexicana garment workers in El Paso and San Antonio, and the Chinese garment and restaurant workers in New York,
Oakland, and San Francisco reached out to these centers.

"Just-in-Time" Methods

The transformation that the women make from sweatshop industry workers to sweatshop warriors is expressed in the development and maturation of the organizations they build to carry out
their battles. Like the women's lives, their organizations are shaped
by the contradictions and tensions unfolding within the sweatshop
industries where the women work and the ethnic communities
where they live with their families. The women's position at the bottom of the sweatshop pyramid frames the demands, methodology,
culture, look, and feel of their organizations and movements. Even

the modest storefronts and community centers that house their centers often resemble the hole-in-the-wall garment shops where the women toil or the shuttered factories where they used to work.

In many ways, the low-waged immigrant women workers' organizations are the flip side of the "just-in-time" production methods pursued by corporate management. Based on the successes of Japan's auto industry since the 1980s, just-in-time production methods reduce inventory and workforce size via subcontracting out "small batches" of goods, based on closer tracking and categorization of consumer tastes as "special niche" or "micro markets," and quick response to customers trends. The successfully tested products and services of small business innovators are often copied or absorbed by big businesses, who may buy out, subcontract to, or out-compete the small fry. Employers extol these methods with such code words as "flexibility," "lean and mean production," "diversification of risks," and "right sizing." For workers, these methods spell increased competition with and between subcontracted workers, plummeting wages, shrinking benefits, runaway shops, layoffs, temporary work, loss of job security, speed-ups, increased injuries, and heightened discrimination.[4] In short, subcontracted workers act as on-call shock absorbers for the just-in-time system.

Mirroring and intersecting with this restructuring of production within the sweatshop pyramid, the workers' centers respond with just-in-time methods to organize "small batches" and "micro markets" of immigrant, women, and ethnic minority workers segregated at the bottom of the "new economy." These workers are fragmented and divided through the subcontracting system, by ethnicity, gender, and immigrant status, and at times, also by the globalization of their industries. The sweatshop industry workers are joined by workers from larger facilities "downsized" through restructuring who end up scrambling for sweatshop-type jobs where they invariably get paid lower wages with less benefits—if they can even manage to land a job. The women live in poor communities with other people of color. These "niche markets" of low-waged immigrant women workers have often been passed over by the broader labor movement—but not by the "brown bomber" barrio organizations who recognize these women as family.

Just as corporate management extols "lean and mean" businesses with the "flexibility" to quickly adapt to changing "market conditions" and "environments," so do the sweatshop industry workers' organizations learn to maximize scarce resources and "use what they got to get what they need."[5] Low-waged workers' organizations do not have much room for error or to squander resources. Like small business innovators within the corporate setting, the workers' centers within the broader labor movement have to hustle to understand and anticipate changing conditions, while developing their long-term perspective, strategy, and infrastructure to ride out the bust and boom of capitalist business cycles and "keep their eyes on the prize."

In this respect workers' centers are a bit like small guerrilla warriors fighting a more heavily armed opponent. They are relatively small, lack resources, and fight class forces with considerably more firepower to both punish those who challenge the status quo and reward the "good Hispanics," "Asian model minorities," and other "team players" who rush to the bosses' defense. These sweatshop warrior organizations are flexible, move quickly, maximize limited resources, organize "outside of the box," and utilize tactics and strategies based on their ethnic backgrounds—like "war of the flea," *tai chi, jujitsu, habkido,* and the ideas of Gandhi, César Chávez, and the Zaptistas—techniques that deflect and toss their more powerful opponents' weight back at them. Sometimes Korean and Chinese groups have also been known to use *tae kwon do* and *gung-fu*-like tactics where both opponents just kick and punch each other until one goes down.[6]

From inside the ethnic enclaves, the centers "give props" to workers to take on their co-ethnic bosses as well as the hegemony of large US corporations. The centers offer workers an infrastructure that enables them to take advantage of the experiences and expertise accumulated in prior struggles, develop their consciousness and leadership, connect with other workers and organizations, act as part of a broader movement, and begin to alter the power relations within the industries and communities where they work and live.[7] The women's organizations operate like "fish swimming in the sea," sharing the common language, culture, history, and interests of the broader base of workers and their communities.

The just-in-time organizations defend workers' rights through different stages of industrial restructuring while simultaneously pursuing independent strategies and alternatives that enable workers to stabilize their lives and movements through the vicissitudes of the market and profit-oriented economy. Because the centers are based within particular ethnic communities, they stick with the workers through thick and thin. They follow immigrant workers into expanding industries and accompany them through deindustrialization, runaway shops, and layoffs. Community-based labor organizing demands a long-term commitment to the workers and community, an accurate grasp of shifting conditions, and development of independent strategies and tactics that enable workers to build their organizations and power not just in defensive/reactive, but also in offensive/proactive ways.

Successfully organizing the growing proportion of female workers requires bringing gender consciousness to labor organizing. Gender oppression plays a huge role in shaping the lives of low-waged immigrant women workers, and the problems they face as women are compounded by their class, race, and nationality status. Immigrant workers' organizations are either women's groups or have gender-specific initiatives within a mixed-gender organization. Thrust into positions of major responsibility, the women in this book fought uphill battles individually and collectively to develop their skills and assert their leadership. They learned to make difficult decisions, run their organizations, and not be stymied by racist, classist, and male chauvinist assaults on their personhood. Like women in other movements, they often encountered sexist practices that devalued their opinions and contributions, a lack of commitment to providing child care and negotiating family responsibilities that impact their participation, and sexual harassment, among other challenges. Those women who shouldered these struggles often had to deal with defensiveness, guilt,

trivialization, backlash, and charges of divisiveness for outing sup-
posedly taboo topics. Nevertheless, through their centers and committees, these battle-scarred working-class pioneers for women's
liberation have knocked down doors so that more of their sisters can
enter and stay in these movements.[8]

Cross-Fertilization within the Labor Movement

The concurrent reemergence of ethnic-based *mutualistas* and of
sweatshops is happening during a stage when some of the labor
movement's "standing army battalions"—large trade unions—are
in the process of massive rethinking and retooling. When the guerrilla and standing army units share a common perspective and strategy, they can compliment and increase each others' effectiveness in
organizing workers across race, gender, industry, and nationality divisions. In today's world of subcontracting, labor market re-segrega-
tion, and global economic restructuring, workers will continue to
need community-based workers' centers and independent unions.[9]

Today's workers' centers represent an updated version of the community labor linkages and social unionism that characterized the
struggles of the earlier waves of immigrant workers and the birth of
industrial unionism. Just as the AFL-CIO eventually incorporated
more diverse ethnicities, the innovations of ethnic workers are often
adopted by industry unions, which are always on the lookout for
new dues-paying members.

The global economic restructuring process and shifts in the
composition of the US workforce since the mid-1960s built up underground, geyser-like pressures that sporadically erupted on the
surface of the broader labor movement. Labor radicals have debated
and written thoughtfully and persuasively about the need and basis
for change in the trade union movement and provided examples of
innovative organizing among particular sectors of unionized workers, including immigrants.[10] They analyzed the significance of the
1995 victory of John Sweeney, Richard Trumka, and Linda
Chávez-Thompson; the dismantling of the cold war vintage American Institute for Free Labor Development; the movement of many
radical labor activists into the AFL-CIO's national organizing, edu-

cation, and women's departments; labor's role in the Congressional defeat of NAFTA fast tracking in 1997; labor's participation in the Seattle protests against the World Trade Organization in 1999 despite tremendous pressure from the Democratic Party not to embarrass the moderate presidential candidate Al Gore; and the February 2000 AFL-CIO shift to oppose employer sanctions and call for unconditional amnesty for undocumented workers.[11]

Immigrants make up a growing proportion of the US labor force and movement, especially in states like California, Texas, New York, and Florida. According to the 2000 Census, Latinos have grown to 12 percent of the US population, and 32 percent of California's, while Asians make up 4 percent and 12 percent respectively.[12] California is returning to its pre-Mexico annexation, and pre-anti-Asian exclusion acts demographic mix.[13] According to the *New York Times* labor reporter Steven Greenhouse, the Los Angeles labor movement, by focusing on organizing immigrant workers, is bringing in new members faster than unions anywhere else in the country. In 1999, 74,000 LA home care workers, most of whom were Latina/os, voted to unionize in the largest successful US organizing drive since the 1930s.[14]

The just-in-time guerrilla groups have influenced segments of the trade union movement, especially in those industries and cities where the workers' centers operate. The relationship between the centers and unions depends principally on the politics of the particular union, including its stance towards employers; its willingness to fight for the rights of workers; the weight it gives to organizing, education, training and promotion of rank-and-file leadership; and its relationship with community and other social movements. Since many of the unions themselves are highly fractured internally, at times the relationship between the workers' centers and unions also depends on the stance of key leaders and organizers representing different political perspectives and constituencies within the unions. In some cases the relationship is more contentious,[15] but in others, more cooperative.[16]

Collective bargaining agreements, workers' centers, and unions, whether independent or AFL-CIO, are all tools that workers must hone to sharpness. When a tool grows dull, or when the environment or task changes, tools can cease to be useful. Many labor veterans inside and outside of the AFL-CIO critique organized labor's stagnation; indifference toward immigrants, women, and people of color; and degeneration into profit-making institutions investing and managing workers' pensions, benefit funds, and fixed assets.

Like AFL-CIO unions, workers' centers can also fall into cautious, service-oriented, toothless groups if they do not develop workers' leadership, link up with other campaigns for justice, and alter power relations within the sweatshop pyramid. The workers' centers must also struggle against accepting the premises and structures of ghettoization and segregation imposed on immigrant, women, and racial minority workers from the bosses and, all too often, accommodated by other institutions inside and outside the labor movement.

In an effort to define the methodology that would enable workers' groups to maintain a militant, worker-oriented, bottom-up character, CSWA and La Mujer Obrera initiated the National Consortium of Workers' Centers in 1994, which invited workers to build a "new labor movement." The consortium principles called for organizing workers across trade lines; bringing together community and workplace struggles; building leadership from the bottom up; raising workers' capacities, skills, consciousness, leadership, and communication through the fight for basic necessities; not being service agencies; and fighting sexism, racism, and discrimination.[17] The following campaigns highlight some of the organizing innovations of these immigrant workers' groups.

Anti-Corporate Campaigns

Much of the day-to-day work of the centers is assisting workers in fighting disputes with employers around violation of their wage, hour, and safety rights. But when large corporations have shrugged off responsibility, the centers have launched anti-corporate campaigns to force them to the bargaining table. Employers have access to many corporate "hired guns"—management consultants, financial institutions, government agencies, elected officials, academic associations, and mainstream media advocates to assist them in running their businesses, including "handling labor problems." To effectively deal with employers, workers also need to develop their own set of relations with other groups and institutions with whom they share common interests. Often, immigrants' children and subsequent generations act as bridges between the sweatshop warriors and other sections of the US population, as well as other workers at the bottom of the sweatshop pyramid. In some cases, workers' campaigns have even won over employers who were trying to treat their employees fairly and also felt squeezed by manufacturers and retailers.

The use of boycotts, sit-ins, freedom rides, non-violent civil disobedience, and mass mobilization by the civil rights movement in the 1960s provided valuable lessons for immigrant workers of color. The United Farm Workers Union (UFW) launched its national grape boycott in the 1960s to broaden the front pressuring the growers to negotiate with the Mexican and Filipino farm workers. The campaign trained farm workers and youth "on-the-job" by dispatching them to cities around the nation to seed and grow boycott committees in diverse communities to support *la causa*.[18] A young generation of Chicana/o and Filipina/o activists cut their teeth on this struggle. During the 1970s, Chicana/o and Chinese activists also developed anti-corporate campaigns in support of striking Farah and Jung Sai workers.

In 1990, Fuerza Unida was the first of the workers' centers featured in this book to launch a nationwide boycott. AIWA launched the Jessica McClintock boycott and Garment Workers Justice Campaign in 1992; KIWA and their Sweatshop Watch partners launched the Retailers Accountability Campaign in 1995; and CSWA and NMASS initiated the DKNY "girl"cott in 1999. Each campaign merits its own book, but will be briefly spotlighted below.

Levi's, Button Your Fly: Your Greed Is Showing

Fuerza Unida's campaign against Levi's represented one of the major fightbacks by laid-off workers against deindustrialization and runaway shops during the 1990s. This campaign was organized and led by *non-unionized*, Mexicana and Chicana garment workers, with help from a small, local independent union, the Southwest Public Workers Union. Hundreds of thousands of auto, garment, shoe, electronics, plastics, and other manufacturing workers had lost their jobs by the time of the 1990 San Antonio layoffs. Fuerza Unida helped create a bridge linking the plant closures movement of the 1970s and 1980s with the anti-sweatshop, anti-corporate movement it helped bring into prominence in the 1990s.

Beginning with emergency mass meetings at Our Lady of the Angels Church in San Antonio's Southside barrio, Fuerza Unida went on to launch a national boycott that garnered solidarity from labor, community, religious, economic justice, student, and youth organizations around the country and overseas. Thousands of supporters sent sheared off Levi's labels to company CEO Robert Haas.[19] Workers organized community tribunals in San Antonio and San Francisco and the women took turns traveling to San Francisco to bring the campaign to Levi's corporate headquarters. Actions included the first protest at the exclusive San Francisco Pacific Heights home of Levi's corporate family patriarch and protests and hunger strikes in front of Levi's outlets in cities across the nation.

While the company continued to stonewall San Antonio workers, its second round of layoffs in 1997-1999 revealed how many "goodies" Fuerza Unida's "piñata-busters" had knocked loose from corporate coffers. When Levi's announced plans to lay-off some 6,400 workers at 11 US plants in 1997, the supposed generosity of its severance package was heralded by UNITE as "by far the best severance settlement apparel workers have ever gotten."[20] Levi's acknowledged that "There's no denying that San Antonio in 1990 had something to do with the development of these benefits in 1997," and that Levi's had failed to anticipate how much criticism it would receive from the San Antonio community.[21]

Fuerza Unida's struggle may have also delayed the layoff of thousands of workers by several years. Levi's had fired thousands of US workers—in 1982, 1984, 1985, 1986, 1988, 1989, before it hit the San Antonio workers in 1990. A seven-year lull followed before the company resumed layoffs in 1997, 1998, and 1999, dumping half of its US and Canadian workers and 20 percent of its European staff. Simultaneously, management announced plans to expand production in China, Mexico, and the Caribbean.[22] Fuerza Unida's campaign also caused the image-conscious corporation to dole out more money to community organizations through its Project Change diversity initiative, ironically located in communities where Levi's plant closures disproportionately hit people of color.[23] Fuerza Unida may have also helped ACTWU/UNITE get into Levi's plants, since it was likely seen as a "team player," business-oriented union that would cooperate with the company. In 1994 during the merger between ACTUW and ILGWU, and the negotiations with Levi's to gain the company's voluntary recognition of the union's card check agreement, ILGWU cut a deal with the management to get other local unions' to stop supporting Fuerza Unida.[24] Two days into Fuerza Unida's 21-day hunger strike at corporate headquarters, Levi's and ACTWU announced their joint partnership.[25] Yet the company soon dumped many UNITE members during its 1997-1999 layoffs. According to *Labor Notes*, a progressive labor magazine:

> The new closings come just three years after UNITE (then ACTWU) entered a labor-management partnership with Levi Strauss in 1994 to prevent plant closings. UNITE, however, says that while it agreed to the partnership as a job-saving measure, the current plant closings are a different issue.
>
> "We don't think that it has anything to do with the partnership," said UNITE spokesperson Jo-Ann Mort. When the partnership started, she said, the union "knew that business decisions would have to be made."
>
> But the union is saying little beyond that. In [the] statement issued when the layoffs were announced, UNITE highlighted Levi Strauss' "commitment to a high road of management" and compared the company favorably to its competitors in its treatment of workers.[26]

Fuerza Unida continues to serve as an information and counseling center for injured and laid-off workers from Texas to Tennessee, including workers in the remaining San Antonio Levi's plant, as well as El Paso workers who successfully sued Levi's for forcing them into a job re-entry program that exposed them to ridicule, humiliation and harassment from managers and other factory workers.[27] Sharing their experiences as "early victims of NAFTA" Fuerza Unida co-coordinators Petra Mata and Viola Casares joined protesters in the tear gas filled streets of Quebec, Canada in April 2001 for the Summit of the Americas. The Summit's goal, the Free Trade Area of the Americas agreement (FTAA), would extend the North American Free Trade Agreement (NAFTA) to the entire hemisphere.[28]

Like other organizations spearheading intense campaigns against the bosses, Fuerza Unida struggled to balance their anti-corporate campaign work with the distinct membership and organizational development necessary for the group's long-term sustainability as an organization rooted among the women of San Antonio's working-class barrios. This Mexicana *mutualista* "multi-tasked" as an independent union, a displaced and injured workers' organization, an education and leadership training center, a cooperative, and a grassroots women's support group.

Garment Workers Justice Campaign

Predating the Nike, Gap, El Monte, Kathie Lee Gifford, Guess, and other anti-sweatshop campaigns, AIWA's 1992-1996 Garment Workers Justice Campaign (GWJC) served as a watershed not only for Asian immigrant women workers, but also for the broader anti-corporate movement—especially the youth and student sectors of the movement. While Fuerza Unida's campaign targeted a runaway industry Goliath, AIWA's GWJC spotlighted the pyramid structure of the garment industry and manufacturers' responsibility for domestic sweatshop abuses in subcontracted shops. Similar to El Paso,[29] San Antonio,[30] and New York City,[31] by the early 1990s, large San Francisco-based manufacturers like Levi's, Esprit, the Gap, and Banana Republic had already sent much of their production overseas. Medium-sized companies like Jessica McClintock, Koret, Fritzi, and Byer subcontracted out to local sweatshops, and some began to send work to overseas contractors as well.[32]

AIWA launched the GWJC in support of 12 Chinese women who approached the organization after being stiffed out of their back wages. The sweatshop they worked for, the Lucky Sewing Co., closed down after the manufacturer, Jessica McClintock, pulled its contract. Prior to initiating the GWJC, AIWA had conducted a decade of base-building work among Chinese and Chinese-Vietnamese seamstresses and Korean hotel maids and electronics assemblers. Campaign opponents included the manufacturer and its various agents: the manufacturers' association, the contractor that violated the women workers' rights, and retailers that also profited from sweatshop labor. Institutions that stood between the employer and workers during the campaign and played contradictory roles included the Chinese subcontractors' association, the Department of Labor, and ILGWU. The campaign's core included the former Lucky workers; AIWA's Worker Board, membership, and staff; and the national campaign committees in several US cities composed principally of Asian labor, community, and student activists, with support from community, women's, labor, religious, and student organizations inside and outside the Asian community.

The campaign used a consumer boycott, pickets, public actions, supporter mobilization, media coverage, work with elected and government officials, and other tactics to bring the company to the negotiating table. Similar to the anti-sweatshop campaigns of other workers' centers, the GWJC evolved through several different periods reflecting the level of contention between the principal players. These stages can be delineated: from McClintock's 1992 refusal to talk to the women and the launching of the GWJC until her offer of "charitable donations" to workers if they would sign papers saying the manufacturer was not responsible; from a declaration of partial victory for the "charitable donations" until McClintock escalated attacks on the GWJC, AIWA, and KIWA; from McClintock's escalation of attacks until the manufacturer closed down the flagship San Francisco boutique; from broadening the campaign to include retailers' accountability for sweatshop conditions and pickets at Macy's until the Department of Labor blunder of including McClintock

(and Levi's) on its "Fashion Trendsetter" holiday season list of manufacturers; and from the Department of Labor's mistake to negotiations, settlement, and wrap-up of the boycott and campaign in
1996.[33]

Immigrant women workers won an undisclosed cash settlement, an education fund for garment workers to learn about their
rights, a scholarship fund for workers and their children, a bilingual
hotline for workers to report any violations of their rights in shops
contracted with McClintock, and an agreement from both sides to
work to improve conditions within the industry.[34] The campaign developed workers' leadership, broke the façade of manufacturers'
lack of responsibility for sweatshop abuses, won greater visibility
and support for immigrant workers, consolidated AIWA's base
among low-income workers, and, together with Fuerza Unida,
helped kick-start the broader anti-sweatshop movement.

The GWJC enabled AIWA to refine its educational, leadership
development, and organizing methodology and brought another
generation of Asian youth and students into community-based
struggles for corporate and governmental accountability. AIWA
transformed its youth project to one led by the children of garment
and other low-waged immigrant women workers. During the early
1990s the GWJC served as a cutting-edge nationwide campaign linking many activists and organizations within the Asian and other economic and environmental justice movements.[35] KIWA used lessons
and infrastructure built through the GWJC in its work with the El
Monte workers. Eventually the ILGWU/UNITE, the National Labor Committee, and Global Exchange used what they observed of
AIWA's campaign in their anti-corporate campaigns against Gap,
Nike, and Guess, and in organizing students through Union Summer and United Students Against Sweatshops.[36]

Retailers Accountability Campaign

Just as the Jessica McClintock campaign threw a spotlight on
the role of manufacturers in the garment industry, so did the El
Monte case on the increasingly powerful role of retailers in setting
wages and working conditions. The case marked a major turning

point in the development and visibility of immigrant sweatshop industry workers struggles, with ripple effects within the industry, government enforcement agencies, and the broader anti-sweatshop movement. In August 1995, Chanchanit "Chancee" Martorell, director of the Thai Community Development Center (Thai CDC) in Los Angeles, got a call from the State Labor Commissioner's office to accompany and translate for agents raiding a sweatshop in El Monte, California, where Thai and other immigrant workers toiled behind razor wire and locked gates. Martorell agreed on the condition that workers would not be sent to the INS. After the August 2 raid, however, the INS re-incarcerated the El Monte workers in detention centers for interrogation and possible deportation.

KIWA, which shares office space with Thai CDC and the Pilipino Workers' Center, had accumulated some guerrilla tactics and infrastructure from the AIWA's GWJC that proved very helpful to the El Monte workers. KIWA organizer Paul Lee said when the INS re-incarcerated the workers, "That's when the roller coaster started."[37] Thai CDC, KIWA, and other groups quickly cobbled together the Sweatshop Watch coalition to respond. Throughout the hectic months of the campaign, Thai CDC took on the Thai workers' survival, social service, and translation needs; Asian Pacific American Legal Center (APALC), the workers' legal issues; and KIWA, the campaign organizing for retailers' accountability.

According to Lee, the enormity of the case came to light five days after the raid when the government made public the major brand name manufacturers and retailers who had contracted with the shop over the previous five years. KIWA launched the Retailers Accountability Campaign (RAC) after retailers denied responsibility for the abuses. KIWA organized holiday shopping season actions against targeted retailers such as Sears, Robinson's May, Bullocks/Macy's, Nordstrom, Neiman Marcus, Target/Dayton Hudson, and Montgomery Ward, pressuring some to the negotiating table.[38]

Twenty-four Latina/o workers approached KIWA in December 1995, describing how they had also been exploited by the same owners. KIWA ultimately represented 55 Latina/os in a lawsuit against the retailers that employed the sweatshop subcontractor, while APALC filed the lawsuit for the Thai workers. Thai CDC, KIWA, and APALC organized monthly general meetings of the Thai and Latino workers to exchange information, analyze developments, map out strategies, and plan actions.[39]

The El Monte campaign demonstrates how solidarity between different ethnic workers can be built and how community organizations with *relatively* more developed infrastructures (like the 1.5 generation Korean-American organizers in KIWA) can help support newer emergent communities (like the Thai). KIWA runs a Summer Activist Training program for young Asians of diverse national origins and works in partnership with Central American and Mexican immigrant worker organizers of the Coalition for Humane Immigrant Rights of Los Angeles. In January 2001, various Asian, Chicano, and ethnically mixed groups jointly opened the Garment Workers Center in the heart of LA's fashion district.

In July 1999, nearly four years after the government raid on the El Monte sweatshop, the workers won over $4 million from major companies—including Montgomery Ward, Mervyn's, Miller's Outpost, B.U.M. Equipment, and Tomato, Inc.—all of whom initially denied responsibility for the sweatshop conditions of their subcontractor.[40] The campaigns of the Thai and Latina/o workers in Los Angeles and the Chinese workers in Oakland spurred passage of a California state legislative bill, AB 633, which imposed a "wage guarantee" in the garment industry so that manufacturers and retailers who manufacture their own private label clothing must pay workers their minimum wage and overtime compensation when the contractors they use fail to do so, as well as other measures.[41]

National Mobilization to End Sweatshops and the "Ain't I a Woman?!" Campaign

While organizing Jing Fong restaurant workers and garment workers in different shops in 1995, CSWA experienced a big influx of Chinese high school and college students. Many stayed on to work in CSWA's Youth Group and in a number of other capacities in the organization, creating a process of fusion between generations and the launching of the National Mobilization Against Sweat-shops (NMASS) in 1996. As CSWA's positive assertion of how to build a mass anti-sweatshop movement from the bottom up, NMASS seeks to build a "new civil rights movement" among all those who are hit by the spread of sweatshop-like conditions. NMASS calls for class, race, and gender solidarity between all those oppressed by the corporate system, instead of asking for consumers' sympathy for sweatshop victims. NMASS campaigns have increas-ingly attracted immigrant workers from the Caribbean and Eastern Europe in other industries seeking support in disputes with employ-ers and government agencies.[42]

NMASS took on the defense of Chinese and Latina garment workers at a Donna Karan subcontracted, unionized shop and launched the "Ain't I a Woman?!" Campaign in 1999. That organiz-ing effort propelled workers from other shops to step forward and led to a class action lawsuit against the manufacturer filed by the Asian American Legal Defense and Education Fund on behalf of all Donna Karan garment workers in New York City. Since 1992 the DKNY workers had toiled 70- to 80-hour work weeks and were never paid overtime wages; some did not even earn minimum wage.[43] The women's campaign has also drawn endorsements and solidarity from workers' groups in Asia and Mexico, regions where DKNY's goods have been outsourced and marketed, and from where the immigrant women workers who toil in her shops have mi-grated.[44] Through this campaign, the workers are pressuring Donna Karan to correct the problem of sweatshop labor *inside* New York City rather than simply shutting down, dumping workers, and run-ning away to other domestic and overseas sweatshops as manufac-turers have done many times in the past.

Innovator Impacts on Anti-Corporate Movements

These workers' centers influenced the development of the broader anti-sweatshop and anti-corporate movements. Globaliza-tion of the sweatshop pyramid spurred anti-corporate campaigns that stressed corporate abuses of immigrant women workers in Asia, Latin America, and the Caribbean. Small, innovative, guerrilla, workers' centers helped play a spark-plug role by reviving the anti-corporate campaign and boycott as a tool to broaden consciousness and support for the struggles of immigrant women workers against deindustrialization and the spread of sweatshops in US inner city stations of the global assembly line. Workers' center campaigns served multiple functions: making sweatshop industry workers inside the United States visible to the public, including within their own communities; opening up the base for workers' support among other sectors, especially young people; training workers and their organizations and supporters; winning key concessions from employers and spurring greater consciousness and organizing among the growing numbers of people grossed out by corporate greed.

The giant protests that followed—against the World Trade Organization in 1999, the World Bank and IMF in Washington, DC, the national Democratic and Republican conventions in LA and Philadelphia in 2000, and the FTAA in Quebec City in 2001—signaled mounting opposition among youth, workers, environmentalists, and other diverse sectors to global corporate capital and its international financial institutions. Such political moments provided new opportunities for building cross-class, cross-sector, multi-racial fronts, and episodes of fusion between youth, intellectuals, and professionals with those sections of the labor movement most critical of free trade and the brutalization of workers, communities, and the planet. At the same time, the anti-corporate movement has remained highly segregated along class, race, and national lines.

Far too often white, middle-class, and First World organizations have demonstrated little accountability to the workers and communities hardest hit by global economic restructuring and corporate greed.[45] Anti-corporate groups that insert themselves into the sweatshop pyramid structure as middle men in order to negotiate with corporations, governments, and international financial institutions—without respecting the self-determination of grassroots people on the bottom of the pyramid—invariably replicate the top-down approaches of the very institutions they seek to change.

To be effective, anti-corporate campaigns must be linked to worker and grassroots community organizing.[46] Regarding the strategy of boycotts, Sweatshop Watch, a coalition of legal advocates, workers centers, unions, and anti-sweatshop groups in California, has declared that it:

> only supports boycotts that are led by workers themselves. Boycotts that are not well organized may harm workers by creating less demand for products, thus forcing workers out of jobs…We believe that boycotts are effective when it is the workers who have decided that that is what they need in order to have their voices heard.[47]

Taking the lead from those on the bottom of the power pyramid upholds the finest traditions of solidarity. The international anti-apartheid movement helped reduce the South African regime to pariah status at the behest of a liberation movement that declared its willingness to weather a global boycott and sanctions in order to force its jailers to sit down at the negotiating table. The sober challenge staring the labor and anti-corporate movements in the face is the protracted, painful struggle of organizing workers and grassroots people "glocally" (globally *and* locally) to force their oppressors to change their ways, to build people and earth-centered alternatives, and to develop cooperative relations of mutual respect and solidarity.

In sum, ethnic-based organizing among sweatshop industry workers provided an early warning signal both of the deleterious effects of global economic restructuring on the most vulnerable workers and the means through which these women could organize to defend themselves. The workers' centers are breathing new life into labor and community organizing. Their guerrilla tactics are tailored to the specific gender, ethnic, cultural, workplace, national, and local characteristics of the workers they are organizing. They help workers navigate new territory and negotiate the borders where the different languages, cultures, and institutions of women's home and adopted countries meet. They promote a strong sense of class, ethnic, and gender consciousness among women workers by using a variety of methods to develop their leadership and organizing capacities. As the women have begun to rock the industries and communities where they live and work, their struggles have rippled out and raised waves—and hopes—in the broader labor, anti-sweat-shop, and anti-corporate movements.

Jay Mendoza of the Pilipino Workers Center; Paul Lee, KIWA; Rojana "Na" Cheunchujit, El Monte workers struggle; and Chancee Martorell of the Thai Community Development Center at their joint offices.
Photo by Miriam Ching Yoon Louie (1997)

Rojana "Na" Cheunchujit

Former garment worker in El Monte, California
Veteran Leader

The Thai workers got help from the Thai CDC, which was launched in 1993 in the wake of two major events: the 1992 Los Angeles civil unrest in which Thai shops mistaken for Korean businesses were destroyed and the earthquake in Northridge, California that left many Thai immigrants homeless. According to Thai CDC's Chancee Martorell, some 50,000 Thai immigrants living in Los Angeles came in three waves. The first wave came in the late 1950s and early 1960s as students and professionals to get education and training to bring back to Thailand. The second wave came after the 1965 immigration reforms and included entrepreneurs and students funded by the Thai government. The third and largest wave has come from the 1970s to the present. Like the El Monte slave-shop workers, many migrated from rural parts of north and northeast Thailand due to industrial and golf course displacement of subsistence farmers. While some found jobs working in factories in Bangkok, others migrated to the Middle East, Malaysia, Hong Kong, Taiwan, and the United States.

Thai CDC estimates that some 50 percent of the immigrants are undocumented, with many working in indentured servitude to employers who paid "horses" to arrange their passage and placement. Chinese and Vietnamese crime rings also operate brothels of sex trafficked and prostituted women from Thailand and mainland China. Thai CDC offers a number of programs to help newcomers gain survival language skills; access to legal, immigration, housing, job support, community economic development, and family services; and workers' rights training and defense.[48] Thai CDC shares office space with KIWA and Pilipino Workers Center, which organizes Filipino workers in the health industry and in solidarity with labor, migrant, and national liberation struggles in the Philippines and the Filipina/o diaspora.[49]

I was born January 26, 1970, in Thailand in the village of Petchaboon. My parents worked in the rice fields when I was growing up. I have one brother and two sisters and I am the oldest. I have two children; my daughter is six years old now and my son is five.

I went to school in Thailand, but only for nine years, and finished middle school. I sewed eight or nine years in Thailand, starting when I was 15 but sometimes would do other things. A village elder introduced me and my husband. I didn't want to get married, [laughs] but I didn't want my parents to worry about me so I got married when I was 19. My husband got a job working as an electrician and got paid pretty good wages.

After I got married sometimes I continued to help my parents work on the farm, but I [also] got sewing jobs to support them. I worked in a big factory in Bangkok, and in many sewing factories before coming to the US. But one place was kind of big and special. My friends told me about the job there. During the two years at work right before coming to the US the pay was pretty good, it was better than my other jobs. Before that, the pay and working conditions were pretty bad.

I came to the US in 1994. When I was still in Thailand this person came to the village to recruit people to work at the shop in El Monte. He told me that the pay was very good. He said that if I wanted to come to the US, he would be able to arrange it for me for 125,000 baht [US$5,000] which I paid him.

I came to the US with my friends, not with my family. I thought I would stay and work in the US for three years. What happened to me after I came? [laughs] Well, that's a long story! I was locked up in the sewing shop by the owners. They fed us poorly. Then the government put me in a second jail. As soon as I arrived in this country, they took me directly to El Monte [where] they basically told me I would have to work continually, non-stop and only have a day off from time to time. This was completely the opposite of what I had been told in Thailand before coming here. In Thailand they told us that we would work from 8am to 6pm every day, five days a week, and that we would have two days off every week. After they told us the situation in El Monte, I realized I had been duped.

Before arriving here they said we could come and go as we pleased, go shopping for our own groceries, and do things with the money we made. But of course when we got here we weren't allowed to go in and out of the factory at all; we were imprisoned.

There were over 70 Thai workers at the shop. We worked 20 hours a day for the whole one year and four months I was there

—until the day I was liberated. I cooked for myself. We ordered food from the owners, but they charged us really high prices, at least twice the amount.

After paying the $5,000 to get here, they told me I had to pay an additional $4,800. They said they would keep me as long as it took to pay off the $4,800 debt. It didn't matter to them how long they kept you; no specific amount of time was calculated.

The family that owned the business ran different places, and two of the family members supervised us. The factory was a set of duplex apartments, lettered from A to G. The units are basically on one side and on the other side was the driveway and a little grass area. Each unit had two stories. Some of the owners' family members lived in Unit A and Unit F, on both ends, while we workers were spread out between Units B and D.

The owners threatened to set the homes of our families on fire if we dared to escape because they knew where all of us were from, about our villages back in Thailand. Some people actually got punished. One person tried to escape but was unsuccessful; they beat him up pretty badly. They took a picture of him and showed it to all the other workers, to tell us what would happen if we tried to escape. It was unbearable to look at the worker who was beaten; they really messed him up completely. After the beating you couldn't even recognize him at all. They did this to intimidate us.

The day the government raided the factory, we heard knocking on the door; they went to each unit and banged real hard. The banging woke us up and we were so scared that we didn't know what to do. We had been told by the owners never to open the door so we felt really unsure. We didn't know if we were finally going to be set free or if we were going to get in more trouble. So no one dared to open the door. The doors were locked from the outside to keep us in. If there had ever been a fire there was no way that we could have gotten out; we would have been trapped.

One of the policemen broke down the door and shoved it in. In fact he hit one of the workers on the forehead—my friend Kanit. Her head got swollen where she was hit [causing] a huge knot [to swell up] on her forehead. [shakes her head] We were all told to come out, sit down in the driveway, and just wait. Then later they sent the INS bus to take us away to the detention center.

Oh, my God! We were all so confused. We were interviewed by everyone, by the Department of Labor, by the INS, by lots and lots of people [including the US Attorney's office, State Labor Commissioner's office, and Employment Development Department]. Then about two or three days after we had been in detention, we met the folks from the Thai CDC and KIWA. But that was after the Thai Counsel General had already come and spoken with us.

When the Consul General came to see us, he told us to go back home to Thailand, that there was no need for us to be here. He said we were here illegally and what we did was wrong. He said it was our fault that we put ourselves in this situation. He said that we were just fighting against a brick wall by staying here, and we were being a burden on the US government!

Everybody was confused. We didn't know what to do. Me too, I was confused. But I got one idea after I met Chancee [Thai CDC Director], Julie [Asian Pacific American Legal Center attorney], and Paul [KIWA organizer]. I thought, "Okay I need these people." So I signed up with them.

The INS agent who was in charge of our case was very confusing. It was hard to know what his real intentions were. Although he was nice and friendly to us, he was not against the idea of deporting us. This became clear when the INS tricked us. Chancee, Julie, and Paul had come to see us at the INS Terminal Island Detention Center where we were kept to eat and sleep. But when the INS found out they were coming [again] at *seven* in the morning, the INS took us to the downtown detention center at *five*. When Chancee, Julie, and Paul showed up, we weren't there. That's when I began to doubt the INS' intentions towards us and whether they were really trying to help us.

Julie, Paul, and Chancee gave us their phone numbers the first time they came to see us. A lot of us decided to give them our A numbers [alien registration number that INS assigns to every detainee] so that they would be allowed to meet with us. The INS asked each of us who we had called and a lot of people were afraid to say anything so they didn't. When they took us down to the downtown office while Julie, Chancee, and Paul were waiting for us at the Terminal Island Detention Center, I realized that we were in the wrong place. They put us in a cell at the downtown center. Then I kept pounding on the door and telling the INS to take us all back to Terminal Island because that was where Chancee, Julie, and Paul were waiting to meet us. I told this all to the Thai interpreter working for the INS and asked them to tell the INS to bring us back.

It turns out that at the same time, Chancee, Julie, and Paul had called the INS. Steve Nutter from the garment workers union also called and threatened to call the press to see how the INS would answer their questions. They finally took us back to Terminal Island. When we saw Chancee, Paul, and Julie waiting for us there, we got so happy. My gosh! They kept us on Terminal Island for nine, almost ten days before they let us out. We kept going back and forth to the downtown center to be processed.

When we finally got out, Oh! Oh! [laughs] It was like being a group of tourists with Chancee as our guide. We could see so many new things. Wow! We got a big smile. They took us to a place to look at the stars, to the park for a barbecue, to the beach, and to Disneyland. We got free tickets to Disneyland. We went there in three buses all given for free. It was a lot of fun.

After we got out, Chancee, Julie, and Paul found us three different shelters to live in for over a month and a half. They had asked the Thai temples to take us in, but they had all refused. That's another bad story. The day that we were liberated from the detention center, some people from the Thai community invited us to a reception at a Thai temple to celebrate our freedom, but it turned into a media disaster. They had promised us they would not invite the media to the reception at the temple. But when our bus arrived the whole place was filled with press people from everywhere with their cameras. We couldn't get into the temple to worship and pay respects to Buddha at the shrine; we couldn't eat. The reporters kept pulling us to speak to the TV cameras and pushing their microphones into our faces.

It was really terrible! We asked Thai CDC to take us back to the shelters. Then we could eat and rest. Aiiii! At that time we were afraid the owners would punish us and our families. In fact when my mother saw my face on TV in Thailand, she fainted. She did not come out of it and recover for two days because she was sick and worried.

The Thai press did us an injustice. After the big disaster at the Thai temple, we left on the school bus that took us back and forth from the shelter. Because the Thai press did not know where the bus was taking us, they reported in the Thai papers, which also reached Thailand, that we had disappeared and that no one knew where we went after we boarded the school bus. So they scared everyone [including] all our family members back home.

A little over a week after being liberated from El Monte, the telephone company donated phone cards to so we could call our families back home; we each got three minutes. After that we made collect calls. My mother was really sick after hearing the news, and she couldn't stop crying. I told her what had happened to me, everything, everything.

Now my mother is watching my children at home in Thailand. How long will I stay here? Wow! I'll stay until I am no longer afraid of being punished when I return home, as long as the safety of my family and me can be assured.

Because we had only been locked up in the factory, we didn't know anything or where anything was. I didn't know how to do this thing or that thing. [laughs] We had to learn how to shop for food, find housing, get work, everything. Chancee, Julie, and Paul took us to job interviews and helped us look for work.

The first [garment] shop I worked for after I got out was a Thai shop close to here. Now I'm working for another Thai shop with Mexican workers. The shops are small. At my first job there were about 12 or 15 people. Now it's almost 20 people where I work. It's a different shop and better than the first place. It's clean. I think the salary is okay, it's much better. At the first place I worked ten hours a day and got paid about $180 a week after taxes. Now I work about eight or nine hours a day, sometimes half day on Saturday until about one or two o'clock. Sometimes its half and half Thai and Mexican and sometimes there are more Latino workers than Thais. The labels we sewed in the El Monte shop were Clio, BUM, Tomato, and others. Paul has the whole list. I haven't come across any of the same labels I sewed in El Monte since I've been out.

Because of the oppression I went through I can now be very direct and assertive. It kind of forced me to express myself more, and be less tolerant of wrongs. [laughs] What I've learned from this whole experience and ordeal is a lesson that will stay with me for the rest of my life. Sometimes it hurts so much that I get numb and lose all feeling. Of course, after meeting so many caring people like the folks involved in this case, like Chancee, Julie, Paul, and the people at Thai CDC and KIWA, it really helped us to overcome the terrible things we went through. We felt like we were part of a larger family of people who really cared for us, people who loved us whom we could trust.

For example, all of them were very sensitive to our needs, fears, and concerns. They would always ask us first and never forced us to do anything. They let us make our own decisions. I believe I got stronger. In the very beginning, throughout the first year and a half every time questions like this came up from reporters or anyone else, talking about what happened always touched us emotionally and made us break down. We were always crying. We've cried so much. The fact that we're able to sit through this and not cry and have to break down kind of shows that we have become stronger. Yes, it's very rare to sit through this without crying. [laughs] Chancee would translate for eight or nine of us, like Kanit and all of our friends. First one person would start to cry, then all of us would start to cry and everybody would end up crying! Chancee and Julie would be crying too. We still see each other and some of the people live together. Chancee keeps a list of our addresses and numbers, but everyone is always moving around.

I like the Retailers Accountability Campaign [initiated by KIWA and Sweatshop Watch] because it's like an act of resistance that shows we are not willing to tolerate and accept these poor working conditions. It makes the workers' voices heard and known. It goes beyond laws that might not really have much of an impact, because people can hear directly from the workers.

We have picketed, leafleted, and visited different department stores. We try to go into the department store, meet with the management, and educate the consumers to support the boycott for accountability. We get promises from consumers not to shop at the department store again unless they change their policy. After meeting us some consumers told us they felt bad about what happened to us and promised they wouldn't go back and shop there anymore.

The garment factory owners threaten to go to Mexico to get the work done. But when they do, they have problems. When the clothes are delivered back here, there's repair work that needs to be done. They expect the local factories here to do the repair work because it wastes too much time sending it back down to Mexico. So this is just a threat.

Participating in the campaign was not scary, not after what we'd been through! Maybe others think that I am a troublemaker out to cause problems. But really, all of the workers being part of this campaign makes us feel like we are helping develop a better understanding among the general public about who we are and about working conditions in the garment industry. We are finally letting the people know about what happens to the money they spend on a piece of clothing, where that clothing came from, who made it, and how little they got paid. This campaign might help redistribute the wealth; it might help people understand that workers are not getting their fair share. We want people to know that the clothes they wear are being produced by the same kind of people as us, the workers who were slaves in El Monte.

—Los Angeles, California, March 25, 1997

1   From amended complaint in US District Court Central District of California case number 95-5958-ABC (BQRx), October 25, 1995:19, cited in Liebhold and Rubenstein, 1999:63.

2   The task force, the Apparel Industry Partnership, included UNITE, the National Consumers League, the Retail, Wholesale Department Store Union, the Interfaith Center on Corporate Responsibility, and the Lawyers Committee for Human Rights, as well as representatives from large manufacturers, like Liz Claiborne, Nike, Reebok, and L.L. Bean. See Ross, 1997:293. For a critique of the task force and UNITE's role within it, see Kwong, Peter, 1997:194-196.

3   Interview with Rojana "Na" Cheunchujit, March 25, 1997.

4   See Parker and Slaughter, 1994.

5   This was the Black Panther Party's rough translation of North Korea's "*juche*" ideology of self-reliance. See Cumings, 1997:394-433 for more on *juche*.

6   For example, Charles J. Kim, executive director of the Korean American Coalition in Los Angeles says that the stance some Korean restaurant owners have taken towards KIWA's organizing is "*nuh juk-ko, na juk-ja*" (You die and I die)." See Kang, Connie, 1998c:A26.

7   Thus, CSWA exposes how employer appeals for Chinese ethnic unity against "*lofan* [outsiders] who really don't understand us" is often nothing but a fig leaf for shafting workers. At the same time the group does not let the manufacturers and retailers who benefit from the whole set up laugh themselves all the way to the bank while "Asians fight Asians" in the enclave. Similarly, the clashes between Koreatown bosses and workers have unfolded "Korean style," i.e., "in your face," "up close and personal," with both sides issuing strong moral appeals and using whatever leverage they could to bolster their positions. The emergence of first-generation immigrant workers as an organized force, supported by "20- and 30-something" Korean-American organizers with ties to outside labor and grassroots movements in other racial communities, is shaking up the class, gender, age, and racial status quo and knocking open a space for workers voices in Koreatown. See also Chinese Staff and Workers Association, 1999:5; Chinese Staff and Workers Association, 1997; Interview with JoAnn Lum, March 1, 2000; Kang, 1998c; Interview with Paul Lee, March 21, 1997; and Korean Immigrant Workers Advocates, 1999:4.

8   See API Force, 1997; Center for Political Education, 1999; Korean American Coalition to End Domestic Abuse, 1999; and the Labor Institute, 1994.

9   Committee for Asian Women, 1991; and Martens, Margaret Hosmer and Swasti Mitter (ed.), 1994.

10 For example, in addition to launching its innovative Justice for Janitors drive, SEIU also played the lead role in initiating the Campaign for Justice, a multi-union offensive targeting janitors, low-waged subcontracted manufacturing jobs, and service jobs in Silicon Valley, San Jose, California. The effort was spearheaded by SEIU Local 1877, and joined by HERE, Communication Workers of America, ACTWU, and the Teamsters. The

short-lived campaign provided the inspiration for the formation of the Los Angeles Manufacturing Action Project (LAMAP), a multi-union, multi-employer, industry-wide, community-based organizing project that sought to organize workers in the Alameda Corridor in Los Angeles. According to immigrant labor sociologist Héctor L. Delgado, this project ran aground because "Few unions were prepared to put aside self-interest, pool resources, and act in concert with one another to develop deeper and broader ties with workers in the communities where they lived and worked." For an excellent summation of LAMAP, see Delgado, 2000: 237.

11 See for example, Morey, 2001; Bacon, 2000; Moody, 1996; Milkman, 2000; Acuña, 1996; and *Labor Notes*, 1998.

12 Martínez, Anne and Edwin García, 2001.

13 According to state librarian Kevin Starr, "The Hispanic nature of California has been there all along, and it was temporarily swamped between the 1880's and the 1960's, but that was an aberration. This is a reassertion of the intrinsic demographic D.N.A. of the longer pattern, which is part of the California-Mexico continuum." (Purdum, 2001.)

14 Greenhouse, 2001b.

15 For example, ILGWU, ACTWU, and later UNITE observed the organizing work of the centers and replicated what the union saw as their most successful organizing tactics. Lifting from the CSWA, La Mujer Obrera, Fuerza Unida, and AIWA models, ILGWU opened its own immigrant garment workers' centers and experimented with offering English classes and associate membership in New York, San Francisco, and Los Angeles. ILGWU, ACTWU, and eventually UNITE, also utilized AIWA, Fuerza Unida, and KIWA's successful anti-corporate campaigns, national boycotts, and organizing among a newly awakened generation of students and youth.

The rub, however, comes when UNITE prioritizes working with the manufacturers over fighting for the rights of its members. (See the chapter on Chinese garment workers.) UNITE's stance as a business union shapes its relationship with the workers centers. The union has borrowed from the workers centers where expedient, but taken a hostile stance toward them when it feels like the workers' disputes will jeopardize its relationship with the employers. As labor historian Peter Kwong has shown, in New York's Chinatown this problem stems from the top-down manner in which the union works in partnership manufacturers to get jurisdiction over subcontractors and the workers. Kwong says that this top-down method does not require that workers also be organized from the bottom-up, it gives the union divided loyalties, and the highly centralized union "does not appreciate activism from its members." See Kwong, 1987:149-150; and Center for Economic and Social Rights, 1999:3. For coverage of UNITE's controversial use of "liquidated damages" see Henriques, 1998:B3, 1999 and 2000; and Fitch, 1998a, 1998b, 1998c & 2000. When some manufacturers pull work from union shops to send production overseas, they pay the union penalties called "liquidated damages."

16 For example, the immigrant workers centers in California built mutual solidarity with SEIU and HERE locals during organizing campaigns among homecare, hotel, garment, healthcare, janitorial, and restaurant workers. Additionally, other union and labor movement affiliated institutions that

specifically organize low-waged women and Asian, Pacific Islander, and Latino workers have shared cooperative relations with some of the workers' centers. 9 to 5, the National Association of Working Women, has been very supportive of a number of the women workers' centers. 9 to 5 is the nation's largest non-profit membership organization of working women which has organized low-waged workers in sex-segregated jobs to end sexual harassment and discrimination, and to win better wages, working conditions, and family-friendly policies. Some of the centers have also received solidarity from the AFL-CIO women's department, the Asian Pacific American Labor Alliance, and the Labor Council for Latin American Advancement. Additionally a number of the workers' centers belong to the Southwest Environmental and Economic Justice Network together with workers' centers and independent unions from the northern Mexico border region.

17 "Presentación de los Centros de Trabajadores en Chicago" provided by María Carmen Domínguez, February 24, 1997.

18 See Scharlin and Villanueva, 1994; Acuña, 1988:324-330; Martínez, Elizabeth, 1998:91-99; Rose, Margaret, 1990 and 1995.

19 Levi's CEO Bob Haas, who is the great-great-grandnephew of the company's founder, started out life with an inheritance of some $10 million. Haas emerged as the company's chief executive in 1984, presiding over the closure of Levi's plants across the United States, outsourcing of production overseas, and massive layoffs, including in San Antonio where workers were dumped just as the company scored record-making profits. During Haas' tenure stock prices rose from $2.53 to $265 a share, a 105-fold increase, by 1995. In 1996, after a leveraged buyout of $4.3 billion, the company added $3.3 billion to the corporate debt, for which the Levi's workers paid dearly, despite record sales that year of $7.1 billion. With the buyout, Haas transferred and further concentrated control and wealth to a 4-man voting trust: himself, his uncle Peter Haas, Sr., cousin Peter Haas Jr., and a distant relative, Warren Hellman, who is a partner in Hellmann & Friedman, a San Francisco investment banking firm. Haas family members owned 95 percent of the company stock and Bob Haas' personal stake in the company was estimated to be worth more than $900 million in 1997, the year that the company began once again to downsize thousands of its U.S. workers. See Sherman, 1997 and Stehle, 1998.

20 Johnston, 1997.

21 Baca, 1997.

22 18,500 jobs were lost at 28 US and one Canadian plant. The company also closed one French and three Belgian plants. Emert, 1999; Colliver, 2000; Schoenberger, 2000; Associated Press, 1998b; Frost, 1998.

23 Zoll, 1998.

24 Interviews with Ruben Sólis, April 5, 2000 and Pamela Chiang, April 14, 2001. Union members were pressured to break off support for Fuerza Unida in 1994, but they re-joined the women in protesting Levi's firings of workers during the 1997-1999 layoffs.

25 *San Francisco Examiner,* 1994.

26   *Labor Notes,* 1998:2.
27   Tanaka, 1997a and 1997b; King, 1998; Associated Press, 1998a.
28   Interview with Viola Casares, May 3, 2001. Sweatshop Watch, 2001.
29   La Mujer Obrera, 1990, 1991, 1996b; and Márquez, 1995.
30   Kever, 1990.
31   Blumenberg and Ong, 1994:313-316.
32   Testimony of Domingo González, Texas Center for Policy Studies, in Asian
     Immigrant Women Advocates, 1995a:18-19.
33   Louie, Miriam, 1996.
34   US Department of Labor, 1996: 96-108.
35   See Delloro, 2000.
36   See note 15 above.
37   Interview with Paul Lee, March 21, 1997.
38   Sweatshop Watch and Korean Immigrant Worker Advocates, 1996.
39   Interviews with Paul Lee, March 21, 1997, Rojana "Na" Cheunchujit, March
     25, 1997, and Chanchanit Martorell, March 25, 1997. See also Su, 1997.
40   See Sweatshop Watch, 1999:2; Su, 1997; Liebhold and Rubenstein, 1999.
41   See Sweatshop Watch, 1999:1-2.
42   National Mobilization Against Sweatshops, 1999. Interview with Nancy Eng,
     April 13, 2001.
43   Interview with Nancy Eng, April 13, 2001.
44   Although some 60 percent of its annual revenues are earned through sales in
     the United States, Donna Karan contracted close to 60 percent of its
     production to Asian facilities, 20 percent to European, and about 20 to 22
     percent to US contractors, using between 440 to 500 contractors worldwide.
     See Donna Karan International, *Annual Reports,* 1997-1998, cited in Center
     for Economic and Social Rights, 1999:11.
45   For more on the race and class blinders within sections of the anti-corporate
     movement see Elizabeth Martínez's much-read and discussed piece, "Where
     Was the Color in Seattle? Looking for reasons why the Great Battle was so
     white." 2000. See also how a large proportion of company layoffs takes place
     overseas, Leonhardt, 2001. For critical views from movements in the global
     South about proposals from those in the North, see Raghavan, no date; and
     Khor, 2000. For a critique of corporate codes of conduct by workers'
     organizations in Asia and Latin America, see Shepherd, no date; and Jeffcott
     and Yanz, 1998.
46   For examples of worker- and community-based codes of accountability see
     the principles developed at the First National People of Color
     Environmental Leadership Summit, 1991; Working Group Meeting on
     Trade and Globalization, 1996.
47   See Sweatshop Watch, "Frequently Asked Questions."
48   Interview with Chanchanit Martorell, March 25, 1997; Martorell, 1994.
49   Interview with Jay Mendoza, March 27, 1997.

Conclusion

Returning to the Source

Korea designates those musicians, dancers, dramatists, and artists who carry within their bodies, minds, hearts, souls, and memories the collective heritage of the Korean people to be *inkan munhwa jae* [Living Cultural Treasures]. The pieces that they create are recognized as *muhyo'ng munhwa jae* [Intangible Cultural Assets], a kind of shared intellectual and spiritual property of the Korean people. These living treasures drink from, then pass along, the cup of what they have learned from the oppression and resilience of their people—to rejuvenate the community, young and old. As Ku Hee-Seo has noted, many have struggled not to be crushed by bitter hardship, but to maintain their self-respect and dignity. They celebrate the zest of life, the human spirit, earth, sky, wind, waves, and all that lies between and beyond.

The women who weather the transformation from sweatshop industry workers to sweatshop warriors could be designated the Living Cultural Treasures of our communities, and their campaigns and creations, Intangible Cultural Assets. In fighting to maintain their sense of dignity and self worth, they are learning and teaching the fine art of how the people can win justice and release their pent-up human suffering and potential. In the heart of this book—the stories of Chinese, Mexican, Korean, (and Thai) immigrant workers—the women shared so many precious, hard-learned lessons. They told us both how they had suffered at the hands of the sweatshop industries, *and* how they are building a successful movement to change those industries and develop new ways of working, thinking, and living. Let's examine a few of the nuggets that these women unearthed.

First, many of the women's defensive battles shot straight through the heart of the US sweatshop system and its multiple violations of workers' most basic, legally guaranteed rights. For example, "Lisa" and the other Streetbeat garment workers incurred the bosses' wrath when they protested that their bodies and spirits could no longer tolerate the killing 100-hour work weeks. Getting cheated out of their hard-earned back pay was the last straw that drove women like Wu Wan Mei and Bo Yee to stand up and fight for what Jenny Chen called "our sweat and blood money." María del Carmen Domínguez of La Mujer Obrera went around for a long time angry that she had not known about the law and what women workers could do to defend their rights. Lee Jung Hee was shocked when she first learned about her rights during a labor law seminar offered by KIWA at her job site, then later sought out the organization when she suffered injuries. Kim Chong Ok and her co-workers got so frustrated and miserable when their boss cheated and berated them about the law that they went to KIWA to find out what the law actually said about workers' rights. Kim Seung Min cried when she went to KIWA for help and saw the picture of Chun Tae Il, the young garment worker martyr who had self-immolated holding a copy of the Korean labor code book in his hand.

The women in the sweatshop segments of the US workforce are fighting defensive battles just to get the most basic rights that workers in more protected sectors of the working class often take for granted. The laws codify a set of workers' rights won through pitched battles against bosses in previous periods of US history: the right to a minimum wage, a 40-hour week, overtime pay, no blocked exits, and other basic standards. Labor laws reflect the ground rules for the current stage of contention and balance of power between the owning and working classes. They fall far short of guaranteeing workers living wages, humane hours, and safe working environments. The sweatshop industries' violation of the women's minimally guaranteed rights is not an aberration, but business as usual, as manufacturers and retailers are fully aware. But the law is of little use to workers unless they know their rights and organize to force employers to comply and respect them as human beings. The women stood up to fight when they could no longer tolerate bosses' abuses. As they fought and learned more about what their rights were from their organizations, they got even more angry and energized to fight and win.

Second, in the course of fighting for their most basic rights, the women also began to challenge the fundamental premises of the sweatshop pyramid. For example, Bo Yee and the Lucky Sewing Company workers started out fighting for their back wages, but after learning about the sweatshop industry pyramid and the minuscule cut that went to their wages, they quickly went beyond demanding their legally guaranteed rights. Asserting a higher standard of ethics in capitalist relations, the women demanded that manufacturers take responsibility for violations of workers' rights inside subcontracted shops. Annie Lai both challenged her immediate boss for unjustly firing her *and* demanded accountability from DKNY, thus opening the door for other women working for DKNY subcontractors to come forward with evidence of violations of their rights.

The women of La Mujer Obrera and Fuerza Unida organized against irresponsible employers who ran away with their jobs, often encouraged to do so by US government free trade policies at taxpayers expense, leaving behind a trail of injuries and tears. María Antonia Flores joined her *compañeras* in civil disobedience on an international bridge on the border to interrupt the trafficking of workers' jobs through NAFTA and demand government accountability to the displaced. Petra Mata argued that the relationship between companies and workers needed to be 50/50, instead of the bosses hogging 100 percent of the power and profits. Kyung Park, Lee Jung Hee, and Kim Chong Ok warned that the bosses had to change their "employer mindset" and start treating workers with respect. Han Hee Jin declared that Korean restaurant workers would no longer tolerate hate crimes by the bosses, as when they would call women, "you waitress bitch." Pathbreakers like Paek Young Hee and Chu Mi Hee stood up for their rights despite industry blacklisting, community censorship, and family members' fears.

These poor yet tenacious sweatshop industry workers called into question some of the central lynchpins of the "new economy." Through their campaigns, the women started to bump up against the limits of their legally guaranteed rights and scale the walls that shield manufacturers and retailers from responsibility for sweatshop abuses and for the injury and dumping of hundreds of thousands of workers in the United States and abroad. The women demanded that some of the famous name darlings in the industries and ethnic enclaves where they worked and the ambitious politicians who foisted their pet policies on their backs, start to remember who had made them rich and powerful and upon whose lives and communities they were trampling.

The women's campaigns revealed the need to put caps on corporate greed and institute a more equitable redistribution of wealth within industry pyramids. They demanded that bosses start to modify their behavior, change their master-class ways, and become better human beings—by first respecting the human rights of the workers. And when they talked back to their bosses, the women challenged old patterns of control, domination, censorship, fear, and internalized oppression within their industries, communities, and families.

Third, as they carried out their battles the women started to define not only what they were fighting *against*, but also what they were fighting *for*. For example, María Antonia Flores talked about the crisis engulfing El Paso workers, even as her organization laid down the building blocks for workers to independently secure their basic rights to dignified work, housing, nutrition, health, and freedom of expression and affiliation. The former Levi's Docker workers created their own sewing and food coops, and surrounded by newly sewn bedding and bags, they dreamed of once again making pants. The Koreatown restaurant workers began fashioning their own health, check-cashing, and child-care systems, as they organized around the marriage of labor and community needs. María del Carmen Domínguez reveled in all the skills she had learned, feats she had accomplished, and great friends she had made through joining the movement. Lee Jung Hee, Lin Cai Fen, Kyung Park, and

Rojana "Na" Cheunchujit struggled to learn English, declare their own victories, and aspire to be fuller human beings beyond the stifling confines of their jobs. Carmen Ibarra, María del Carmen Domínguez, Yu Sau Kwan, Kyung Park, and others testified in word and deed about how their transformation included a revolution in gender relations within their families and in who their daughters and sons have grown up to be.

Even as they continued to fight in defense of their rights within the sweatshop pyramid, the women began to switch to the offense, experimenting with and creating their own independent alternative visions and programs. Outside the crushing environment of the sweatshop, the women started to envision the basic rights and needs to which every human being should be entitled. As they visualized these rights, they began brainstorming how they could help their co-workers, neighbors, and family members get access to such simple pleasures as creative labor, a full stomach, education for their kids, a warm place to sleep, freedom to express oneself without fear, and the company of one's friends. They started using the skills they had learned through a lifetime of labor to hatch their projects, programs, and mutual support systems. They learned to build a new world through trial and error. Sometimes they stopped to laugh and console themselves that they couldn't do any worse than the bosses and politicians had done in running their communities. Every now and then they stood back in amazement and admired the fine workswomanship of what they created, the skills they learned, the new consciousness and energy that coursed through their veins, the sister spirits they befriended, the communities they harvested.

Fourth, as the women conducted their defensive and offensive battles, as they dreamed and experimented with their alternative visions and structures, they began to fashion a collective, sharing, bottom-up, group-oriented methodology that enabled them to magnify their consciousness, wisdom, and strength. For example, Bo Yee condensed volumes of lifetime experience and years of grassroots organizing methodology into two deceptively simple sentences: "Let the people talk about their broad experiences. Let them pinpoint where the problems are, and from there how to organize themselves to solve these problems." When recounting the fight for back wages and against factory closure thrust upon workers at a sub-contracted shop producing for Kathy Lee Gifford, Jaclyn Smith and Tracy Evans, Lee Yin Wah declared with obvious pride, "The workers were so smart." She talked about how "we stress that problems can't just be solved by oneself," and how immigrant women have to deal with disempowering messages from both their home and adopted lands. Jenny Chu, Annie Lai, and Bo Yee insisted that they were tough enough to stand up for their rights—if they could get translation help in carrying out their battles. Wu Wan Mei and Kim Seung Min described the struggle for women's autonomy from repressive family and work systems. Annie Lai talked about the mutual interdependence between the development of each woman's capacity to fight and that of her organization to back and link her to the broader workers' movement.

Fuerza Unida members spoke of retraining themselves to work cooperatively, breaking the competitive patterns they had learned at Levi's and helping working-class women cross the deep valley of depression to get to the other side. Carmen Ibarra and Viola Casares reflected on how their faith in God steadied their participation in the movement, while the Korean women survivors of domestic abuse drew on shared cultural and spiritual sources to release their suffering and build sisterhood.

Through their trust and belief in the wisdom of women workers, these sweatshop warriors are calling on the power of the people to share and analyze their life experiences and map the road ahead. They are reaching out to each other and linking arms to break through the walls of silence and censorship that isolate them, no matter who erected these barriers. Especially as poor women on the bottom of multiple pyramids of oppression, they recognize that their strength depends on working together and pooling their knowledge and resources. They are fine-tuning the tension between the music they make and risks they take as individuals with that of the combined harmonies of their many hued, ethnically diverse *comadres* when they sing, dance, picket, and perform together as fusion artists to rejuvenate their communities. They are struggling hard to overcome the individualism, competition, and narrow self-interest they learned from their bosses and the sweatshop system through identifying with and taking responsibility for their grassroots sisters locally and globally. These Living Cultural Treasures are both channeling and enriching the collective wisdom, culture, and spirit of the people.

Through the pages of this book, you, Dear Reader, have participated in a kind of written word "workers' exchange" and "study tour" that poor peoples' groups have organized across the decades for their friends in labor, women's, church, student, community, and human rights movements. You have accompanied the workers during their peripatetic wanderings—from the villages and sprawling cities of their homelands to the factories, sweatshops, restaurants, hospitals, hotels, and inner-city barrios of their adopted country. The women who clothe, feed, and care for us, who take risks and lead resistance on our behalf, have shared their stories with us so we can better understand their movements and join them in their struggles. And they are not alone. They are joined by workers of other industries, races, cultures, communities, and nations. And they have you and me.

Listening to the women speak cannot be an act of consumerism. Seeing them fight for their rights cannot be an act of voyeurism. Listening to the women means returning to the source, to the heart of what today's struggles for justice and dignity are all about. Just as the women have stepped forward, pushed themselves harder, and struggled to take on new challenges with oh-so-scarce resources, so each of us is called upon to do the same, wherever we may work and live, with whomever we consider our sisters and brothers, co-workers, and community. We must ask ourselves individually and collectively what we are doing to challenge the pyramids of oppression we face. Turning down the volume of the elite's chatter, we must train our ears to listen harder to hear the vibrant voices and lyrical leadership of grassroots folk on the bottom, the foundation rock of mass movements. As we embrace our labors of urgency and love, let us always remember to make the time to walk those picket lines, send in those protest letters, mail in those labels, organize those actions, and extend our unstinting solidarity to grassroots women everywhere.

Sewing Sisterhood

In sewing fastening trimming final threads of this book
Colors textures woof weave of women's stories
Come humming back
Viola Casares confides to her comadre Petra Mata
Levi's treats us like we're stupid
Like only thing we're good enough to do is sew for them
Ad nauseum *big shot corporate execs media moguls policy wonks*
Devalue disrespect immigrants women workers
But when we ask listen learn cry belly-laugh with women
We can slice chop cleaver clean through such simplistic stereotypes
Yes, you'd better believe these hard working women are "good for sewing"
They are lightning speed sewers cutters knitters weavers assemblers solderers
Cookers cleaners cultivators caretakers healers harvesters agronomists
     miracle workers
Whose work spins this world 'round
Kyung Park declares they go deep down inside mines
Sweat breathe black dust into their lungs
Know how it really feels to work at pit bottom
To tell the story right strike the pay load rich
Wu Wan Mei insists they make up half the world hold up half the sky
Do double triple shift duty birthing babies families communities movements.

Corporate elites are dead wrong treating women
As "stupid" "only good enough" to sew service slave
These dear women—our very own grandmothers
Mothers sisters cousins girlfriends wives lovers—
Are smart savvy strong survivors "good" for so much and more
Like leading movements to liberate us all
From sins of runaway corporate greed/globalization gone amuck
Women who shelter gently cradled in palms of golden brown hands
Tough tender tiny seeds shoots roots bulbs buds
Of homegrown healing herbs remedies treatments solutions
To stop corporate trampling on lives workers communities
Our Pacha Mama/*Mother Earth*/Uri Tang/Huang Tudi
Women are not powerless victims to be pitied

Used for some fly-by-night sweatshop exposé
Trod upon like "this bridge called my back"
In hot panting pursuit of profits positioning careers
Nor are they superwomen to be placed on pedestal
Sky high above pain pimples of rest of us—
We who have been known to suddenly burp fart sob bleed
Break out break down fall flat on our faces
Sometimes step-by-step
Sometimes flying by the seat of their
Double knit stretch pantalones/ba-ji/cheuhngfu
Women learn on-the-job through school-of-hard-knocks
How to organize grassroots people
To weave own webs networks demands visions
Na Cheunchujit says women are finally letting people know
What happens to money they spend on clothing
Who made that clothing
How little workers got paid
How women's kick-butt campaigns
Might just help redistribute the wealth.

But witnessing these mighty piñata-busters
Swinging away at sweatshop system
Must not be mere spectator sport
Women's well-aimed blows must kindle ignite activism solidarity
From extended families sister communities
In increasingly multi-colored sweatshop nation/plantation/reservation
Women's family tree roots/branches reach ancestors/descendants
Of indigenous mestizo *mulatto peoples of Americas*
Of coolie/*bitter strength* nodongja-nongmin/*worker-peasants of Asia*
African survivors of Middle Passage
Migrants refugees workers of all colors
Eager to free ourselves
From shackles of our colonizers
Like the women, we each bring our own
Experiences interests strengths weaknesses talents challenges
Like the women, we must struggle individually collectively
To recognize confront conquer our oppression
To decide to focus principally on immediate family survival
Or shoulder added responsibility for community movement society planet

To determine how high a price we are willing to pay for speaking out
Or for our silence
To toil and sweat together with people inside outside
Our own race gender generation sexual orientation class community
*To both give and receive energy/*ánimo/chi/ki *to our sistahs and bruddahs in*
    struggle
To let our spirits sing shout chant graffiti-tag drum beat create
New corridos/minyo/mahngo/*songs of labor love life*
For this movement to survive succeed
Grassroots women must be at its core—
Our very heartbeat head hands breath soul
Let us join our sister sweatshop warriors design trace cut stitch hem press weave
Wrap each other in rainbow banner of our liberation.

Thai garment workers from the El Monte "slaveshop" attending and performing in the National Coalition for Redress and Reparations Annual Fundraiser at the Japanese Community and Cultural Center, Little Tokyo, Los Angeles.
Photo courtesy of Thai Community Development Center.

Bibliography

Abate, Tom. 1993. "Heavy Load for Silicon Valley Workers." *San Francisco Chronicle*, May 23, p. E-1.

Abeles, Schwartz, Haeckel, Silverblatt, Inc. 1983. *The Chinatown Garment Industry Study*. New York: ILGWU Local 23-25 and New York Skirt & Sportswear Association.

Abelmann, Nancy. 1996. *Echoes of the Past, Epics of Dissent: A South Korean Social Movement*. Los Angeles: UC Press.

Abelmann, Nancy and John Lie. 1995. *Blue Dreams: Korean Americans and the Los Angeles Riots*. Cambridge, MA: Harvard UP.

Acuña, Rodolfo F. 1988. *Occupied America: A History of Chicanos*. New York: Harper & Row.

—1996. *Anything But Mexican: Chicanos in Contemporary Los Angeles*. London: Verso.

Alvarado, Sylvia. 1997-98. "Closing down plants, closing down lives." *La Voz de Esperanza* 10:10 (Dec.-Jan.), p. 9. San Antonio: Esperanza Peace & Justice Center.

Amott, Teresa and Julie Matthaei. 1996. *Race, Gender, and Work: A Multicultural Economic History of Women in the United States*. Boston: South End.

Anderson, Sarah, John Cavanagh, Chuck Collins, Chris Hartman, and Felice Yeskel. 2000. *Executive Excess 2000: Seventh Annual CEO Compensation Survey*, pp. 3-4. Boston: United for a Fair Economy and Washington, D.C.: Institute for Policy Studies.

Angwin, Julia. 1996. "Garment Industry Blues: Price wars unraveling local clothing makers." *San Francisco Chronicle*, Mar. 20, p. C1.

APEC Labour Rights Monitor (ALARM). 1996. "Workers' Primer on APEC." *ALARM Update* 4 & 5 (July and Aug.). Hong Kong: ALARM.

API Force. 1997. "An Open Letter to Progressive Activists." Statement on sexism and sexual harassment endorsed by different organizations, June, www.api-force.org.

Arizpe, Lourdes. 1981. "The Comparative Advantage of Women's Disadvantages." *Signs* 7:2 (Winter), pp. 453-473.

Arnold, Cindy. 1995. "PRRAC Researchers Report: NAFTA's Impact on El Paso Garment Workers." *Poverty & Race* 4:1 (Jan./Feb.), pp. 17-20.

Arteaga, Mathilde. (no date) "Las siete plagas del TLC en México." *Tema Central,* pp. 5-6.

Asian American Legal Defense and Education Fund. 2000. "Factory Workers in NYC's Fashion District File Class Action Lawsuit Against Donna Karan." Media Release. June 7. New York: ALDEF.

Asia Monitor Resource Center. 1996. *Proceedings of the International Conference for Toy Workers' Health and Safety,* Jan. Hong Kong: AMRC.

—1996-1997. "Striking Back." *Asian Labour Update* 23 (Nov.-Mar.).

—1998a. *We In The Zone: Women Workers in Asia's Export Processing Zones.* Hong Kong: AMRC.

—1998b. "The Asian Miracle Mess." *Asian Labour Update* 27 (Feb.-May), pp. 1-4.

Asian Immigrant Women Advocates. 1993. *Environmental Safety and Health Proposal.* Oakland: AIWA.

—1995a. *Immigrant Women Speak Out On Garment Industry Abuse: Testimony and Recommendations.* Oakland: AIWA.

—1995b. "Immigrant Convalescent Care Worker Wins Order on Back Wages." *AIWA News* 11 (Winter), p. 1.

—1996. "Justice, Solidarity." May 5 event program. Oakland: AIWA.

—1998. *Building On Our Past, Rising Up in Unity Toward Our Future: Celebrating Asian Immigrant Women Workers.* Oakland: AIWA.

—1999. "Helen Wong: Portrait of a Community Activist." *AIWA News* 15 (Aug.) p. 1.

—2000. "AIWA Breaks New Ground: California's First Women Workers' Clinic." *AIWA News* 16, p. 2.

Asian Immigrant Women Advocates and INTERCEDE: Toronto Organization for Domestic Workers. 1995. "Round Table of Migrant & Women Workers' Centers & Initiatives: Fight for Women Workers' Rights in the Global Economy." Workshop at UN 4th World Conference on Women, NGO Forum, Aug. 31, Huairou, China.

Asian Migrant Centre. 1995. *Living and Working with Migrants in Asia: Report on the Conference on Migrant Labour Issues, Hsinchu, Taiwan, 15-19 May, 1994.* Hong Kong: AMC.

—1996a. *People on the Move in China: Report of a Study Tour to China, 22-30 May, 1995.* Hong Kong: AMC.

—1996b. "The Globalization of Asian Migrants." *Asian Migrant Forum* Special Issue 11 (Nov.). Hong Kong: AMC.

—1998. *Asian Migrant Yearbook 1998: Migration Facts, Analysis and Issues in 1997.* Hong Kong: AMC

Associated Press. 1998a. "Levi settles retaliation cases out of court." *Laredo Morning Times,* July 17, p. 5A.

—1998b. "2,000 in Belgium Protest Levi Plant Closings." Oct. 5.

—1999. "G.I.'s Tell of a US Massacre in Korean War." *New York Times,* Sept. 30.

—2000. "N. Korea Accuses US of Atrocities." Mar. 22.

Atzlan. 1993. "Las Obreras: The Politics of Work and Family." 20:1 & 2. Los Angeles: Chicano Studies Research Center Publications.

Baca, Aaron. 1997. "Severance Package Earns Praise for Levi Strauss." *Albuquerque Journal,* Nov. 11.

Bacon, David. 2000. "Labor's Push for New Amnesty for Immigrants." *Pacific New Service,* June 21.

Barmé, Geremie and John Minford (ed). 1989. *Seeds of Fire: Chinese Voices of Conscience.* New York: Noonday Press.

Barnes, Edward. 1998. "Slaves of New York." *Time Magazine,* Nov. 2.

Barrett, Wayne and Tracie McMillan. 1998. "Geraldine Ferraro: Sweatshop Landlord." *Village Voice,* Mar. 3.

Battistella, Graziano (ed). 1993. *Human Rights of Migrant Workers: Agenda for NGOs.* Quezon City: Scalabrini Migration Center.

Battistella, Graziano and Anthony Paganoni (ed). 1996. *Asian Women in Migration.* Quezon City: Scalabrini Migration Center.

Beal, Frances M. 1970. "Double Jeopardy." In Morgan, *Sisterhood Is Powerful.*

Bell, Brenda, John Gaventa, and John Peters (ed). 1990. *Myles Horton and Paulo Freire, We Make the Road by Walking: Conversations on Education and Social Change.* Philadelphia: Temple UP.

Bello, Walden. 1998. "The End of the Asian Miracle." *APC Focus* 11 & 12, pp. 1 & 7-8. Washington, DC: Asian Pacific Center for Justice & Peace.

Bello, Walden and Stephanie Rosenfeld. 1990. *Dragons in Distress: Asia's Miracle Economies in Crisis.* San Francisco: Institute for Food and Development Policy.

Benería, Lourdes. 1994. "La Globalización de la Economía y El Trabajo de las Mujeres." In Bustos and Palacio, *El Trabajo Feminino en America Latina*.

Benería, Lourdes and Martha Roldán. 1987. *Crossroads of Class & Gender: Industrial Homework, Subcontracting, and Household Dynamics in Mexico City*. Chicago: Univ. of Chicago Press.

Berry, Jon. 1990. "Levi's to Cut 1,100 in Texas." *San Francisco Chronicle*, Jan. 18, pp. C1 & 10.

Bhattacharjee, Anannya. 1997. "A Slippery Path: Organizing Resistance to Violence Against Women." In Shah, *Dragon Ladies*.

Blackwelder, Julia Kirk. 1984. *Women of the Depression: Caste and Culture in San Antonio, 1929-1939*. College Station: Texas A&M UP.

—1997. *Now Hiring: The Feminization of Work in the United States, 1900-1995*. College Station: Texas A&M UP.

Bluestone, Barry and Bennett Harrison. 1982. *The Deindustrialization of America*. New York: Basic.

Blumenberg, Evelyn and Paul Ong. 1994. "Labor Squeeze and Ethnic/Racial Recomposition of the U.S. Apparel Industry." In Bonacich, et al., *Global Production*.

Bonacich, Edna. 1992. "Alienation among Asian and Latino Immigrants in the Los Angeles Garment Industry: The Need for New Forms of Class Struggle in the Late Twentieth Century." In Felix Geyer and Walter R. Heinz (ed.), *Alienation, Society, and the Individual*. New Brunswick: Transaction.

Bonacich, Edna and Richard Appelbaum. 2000. *Behind the Label: Inequality in the Los Angeles Apparel Industry*. Berkeley: UC Press.

Bonacich, Edna, Lucie Cheng, Norma Chinchilla, Nora Hamilton, and Paul Ong (ed). 1994. *Global Production: The Apparel Industry in the Pacific Rim*. Philadelphia: Temple UP.

Bonacich, Edna and David V. Walker. 1994. "The Role of US Apparel Manufacturers in the Globalization of the Industry in the Pacific Rim." In Bonacich, et al., *Global Production*.

Borchard, Dagmar. 1995. "Holding Up Half the Sky: The Legal Position of Women in China." In Feminist Press Travel Series, *China for Women*.

Boris, Eileen and Elisabeth Prügl (ed). 1996. *Homeworkers in Global Perspective: Invisible No More*. New York: Routledge.

Boserup, Ester. 1970. *Woman's Role in Economic Development*. New York: St. Martin's.

Branch, Taylor. 1989. *Parting the Waters: America in the King Years, 1954-63*. New York: Simon & Schuster.

—1998. *Pillar of Fire: America in the King Years, 1963-65*. New York: Simon & Schuster.

Browning, Harley and Roldolfo O. de la Garza (ed). 1986. *Mexican Immigrants and Mexican Americans: An Evolving Relation*. Austin: Center for Mexican American Studies Publications, University of Texas.

Burchett, Wilfred G. 1968. *Again Korea*. International Publishers: New York.

Burciaga, José Antonio. 1993. "Piñatas," in *Drink Cultura: Chicanismo*. Santa Barbara: Joshua Odell Editions.

Burnham, Linda. 1989. "Struggling to Make the Turn: Black Women in the Post-industrial Economy." Paper delivered at the Schomberg Center for Research and Black Culture. New York.

—1997. "African-American Women and Homelessness at Century's End." Ph.D. dissertation, California State Hayward University.

—2001. "The Wellspring of Black Feminism." *Southern University Law Review*, forthcoming.

Burnham, Linda and Kaaryn Gustafson. 2000. *Working Hard, Staying Poor: Women and Children in the Wake of Welfare "Reform."* Berkeley: Women of Color Resource Center.

Bustamente, Jorge A. 1975. "Espaldas mojadas: Materia prima para el expansión del capital norteamericano." *Cuadernos del Centro de Estudios Sociológicos* 9. México, D.F.: El Colegio de México.

Bustos, Beatriz and Ferman Palacio (ed). 1994. *El Trabajo Feminino en America Latina: Los Debates en la Década de Los Noventa*. Guadalajara: Universidad de Guadalajara y Instituto Latinoamericano de Servicios Legales Alternativos.

Calderón, Roberto R. and Emilio Zamora. 1990. "Manuela Solis Sager & Emma Tenayuca: A Tribute," In Córdova, et al., *Chicana Voices*.

Canadian Tribune. 1991. "Mexican-American Women Fight Levi-Strauss," Nov. 4.

Carson, Clayborne. 1981. *In Struggle: SNCC and the Black Awakening of the 1960s*. Cambridge, MA: Harvard UP.

Castañeda, Antonia I. 1997. "Language and Other Lethal Weapons: Cultural Politics & the Rites of Children As Translators of Culture." *La Voz de Esperanza*, June, pp. 3-6.

Castells, Manuel and Alejandro Portes. 1989. "World Underneath: The Origins, Dynamics, and Effects of the Informal Economy." In Portes, et al., *The Informal Economy*.

Center for Economic and Social Rights. 1999. *"Treated Like Slaves": Donna Karan, Inc. Violates Women Workers' Human Rights*. New York: CESR.

Center for Political Education. 1999. "Combating Sexism in the Movement: A Roundtable Discussion." Held Dec. 1, San Francisco.

Center for Women's Global Leadership. 1995. Compiled by Mallika Dutt, Susana T. Fried and Deevy Holcomb. *From Vienna to Beijing: the Copenhagen Hearing on Economic Justice and Women's Human Rights at the United Nations World Summit on Social Development, Copenhagen, March 1995.* New Brunswick, NJ: CWGL.

Centro de Trabajadores and La Mujer Obrera. 1993. *Escuela Popular Para Trabajadores Curriculum.* El Paso: CT & LMO.

Cervantes-Gautschi, Peter. 1998. "Low Wage Organizing: A Concept Paper." Unpublished.

Chai, Alice Yun. 1988. "Women's History in Public: 'Picture Brides' of Hawaii." *Women's Studies Quarterly* 1 & 2, pp. 51-63.

Chiang, Pamela. 1994. "501 Blues: Boycott Levi's." *Breakthrough* 18:2 (Fall), pp. 2-7. San Francisco: John Brown Education Fund.

Chan, Marcia Jean and Candice Cynda Chan (ed). 1973. *Going Back.* Hong Kong: self-published.

Chan, Ying. 1993. "Horrors or a Kidnap Victim." *New York Daily News*, Oct. 10, p. 20.

Chang, Edward T. and Russell C. Leong (ed). 1994. *Los Angeles—Struggles toward Multiethnic Community: Asian American, African American, & Latino Perspectives.* Seattle: UW Press.

Chang, Grace. 2000. *Disposable Domestics: Immigrant Women in the Global Economy.* Boston: South End.

Chang, Pil-wha. 1986. "Women and Work: A Case Study of a Small Town in Korea." In Chung, Sei-wha, *Challenges for Women.*

Chansanchai, Athima. 1997. "maid in the usa." *Village Voice*, Oct. 7, p. 49.

Chant, Sylvia. 1991. *Women and Survival in Mexican Cities: Perspectives on Gender, Labour Markets and Low-Income Households.* Manchester: Manchester UP.

Cheng, Lucie and Edna Bonacich (ed). 1984. *Labor Immigration Under Capitalism: Asian Workers in the United States before World War II.* Los Angeles: UC Press.

Chicago Religious Task Force on Central America. 1990. "Challenge to the Central America Movement: Confronting Racism." *¡Basta!* (Dec.) Chicago: CRTFCA.

Chin, Steven A. 1989. "Boom feeds on refugees." *San Francisco Examiner*, Feb. 13, p. A10.

China Labour Bulletin/Zhongguo Laugong Tonxun. 1995. "Feature: Fourth UN Women Conference." *China Labour Bulletin* 19 & 20 (Dec.), pp. 1-4. Hong Kong: CLB.

China Labour Education and Information Centre. 1995. *The UNofficial Report: Women Workers in China.* Hong Kong: CLEIC.

China Rights Forum. 1994. "Workers Rights " Special Issue, Fall. New York: CRF.

—1995. "Women's Rights = Human Rights" Special Issue, Fall. New York: CRF.

—1999. "Objects of protection...Or subjects of rights?" Spring. New York: CRF.

Chinese Staff and Workers Association. 1997, "Will Slave Labor End at Jing Fong?" *CSWA News,* 5:2 (Fall), p. 4. New York: CSWA.

—1998. "CSWA Celebrates the Lives and Struggles of Chinese Working Women." Calendar. New York: CSWA.

—1999a. "CSWA's First 20 Years: Workers Fighting Sweatshops Here." *CSWA News* 7:1 (Summer), pp. 1-10. New York: CSWA.

—1999b. "Student Diary: 16 year old me & my garment worker mom." *CSWA News* 7:1 (Summer), p. 10.

—2000. "After Two-Year-Effort 446 Garment Workers Win Major Settlement," press advisory, Jan. 13.

Cho, Hyuong. 1986. "Labor Force Participation of Women in Korea." In Chung, Sei-wha, *Challenges for Women.*

Choi, Sang Rim. 1999. "Let's stand firm with the pride of five million women workers!" *Working Women,* 20:11, pp. 7-11. Seoul: Korean Women Workers Association.

Chung, Hyung Back. 1991. "Women in Korea." Presentation on opening panel of Korea Reunification Symposium Committee co-sponsored with the Department of Asian American Studies, Mar. 14, University of California, Berkeley.

Chung, Sei-wha (ed.) and Shin Chang-hyun (trans.). 1986. *Challenges for Women: Women's Studies in Korea.* Seoul: Ewha Women's UP.

Churchill, Thomas. 1995. *Triumph over Marcos.* Seattle: Open Hand.

Coalición en Los Angeles para los Derechos Humanos del Inmigrante, "Dignidad para Domésticas" Proyecto. 1997. *Super Doméstica en: El Caso de Las Trabajadoras Explotadas.* Comic book. Los Angeles: CHIRLA.

Cockburn, Alexander. 1992. "Like Carter, but worse?" *New Statesman & Society,* Oct. 30.

Cohen, Lizabeth. 1990. *Making a New Deal: Industrial Workers in Chicago, 1919-1939*. New York: Cambridge UP.

Colliver, Victoria. 2000. "Levi Strauss looking blue." *San Francisco Examiner*, May 5, p. B1.

Combahee River Collective. 1977. "A Black Feminist Statement." In Barbara Smith (ed.), *Home Girls: A Black Feminist Anthology*. Piscataway, NJ: Rutgers UP.

Committee for Asian Women. 1991. *Many Paths, One Goal: Organizing Women Workers in Asia*. Hong Kong: CAW.

—1995a. *Silk and Steel: Asian Women Workers Confront Challenges of Industrial Restructuring*. Hong Kong: CAW.

—1995b. "Impact of Industrial Restructuring on Women Workers in Asia." Workshop at UN 4th World Conference on Women, NGO Forum, Sept. 2, Huairou, China.

—1995c. "Platform for Change: Beijing and After." *Asian Women Workers Newsletter* 14:4 (Oct.), pp. 2-5.

Committee for Asian Women and Korean Women Workers Association. 1992. *When the hen crows...Korean Women Workers Educational Programs*. Hong Kong: CAW.

Conover, Ted. 1997. "The Last Nanny: The Last Best Friends Money Can Buy." *New York Times Magazine*, Nov. 30, pp. 124-132.

Córdova, Teresa, Norma Cantú, Gilberto Cardenas, Juan García and Christina M. Sierra (ed.) for National Association for Chicano Studies. 1990. *Chicana Voices: Intersections of Class, Race & Gender*. Albuquerque: UNM Press.

Cordtz, Richard W. 1995. "Worker-friendly Jeans." *Union* (Mar./Apr.), p. 19.

Cornelius, Wayne A. 1976. "Outmigration from Rural Mexican Communities." In *The Dynamics of Migration: International Migration. Interdisciplinary Communications Program, Occasional Monograph Series 2:5*. Washington, DC: Smithsonian Institute.

—1988. "Los Migrantes de la Crisis: The Changing Profile of Mexican Labor Migration to California in the 1980s." Paper presented at the conference, "Population and Work in Regional Settings." El Colegio de Michoacán, Zamora, Michoacán, Mexico, Nov. 28-30.

Cornelius, Wayne A., Philip L. Martin and James F. Hollifield (ed). 1994. *Controlling Immigration: A Global Perspective*. Stanford: Stanford UP.

Corporate Watch. 1997. "Corporate Watch Interview with Lora Jo Foo." www.corpwatch.org/trac/feature/foo.html

Coyle, Laurie, Gail Hershatter and Emily Honig. 1980. "Women at Farah: An Unfinished Story." In Mora and Del Castillo, *Mexican Women in the United States.*

Cumings, Bruce. 1981 and 1990. *Origins of the Korean War. Volume 1: Liberation and the Emergence of Separate Regimes, 1945-1947. Volume 2: The Roaring of the Cataract, 1947-1950.* Princeton: Princeton UP.

—1997. *Korea's Place in the Sun: A Modern History.* New York: Norton.

Danini, Carmina. 1993. "Protesters keep vigil during meeting." *San Antonio Express-News,* Jan. 9.

Davis, Mike. 1996. "Kajima's Throne of Blood." *The Nation,* Feb. 12, pp. 18-20.

Davis, Mike, Steven Hiatt, Marie Kennedy, Susan Ruddick and Michael Sprinker. 1990. *Fire in the Hearth: The Radical Politics of Place in America.* London: Verso.

De la O, María Eugenia and María José González. 1994. "Perspectivas de la fuerza de trabajo feminina frente a la globalización económica. De la experiencia de la Unión Europea al Tratado de Libre Comercio." *Frontera Norte* 6:12 (Julio-Diciembre). Tijuana: El Colegio de la Frontera Norte.

Delgado, Héctor L. 2000. "The Los Angeles Manufacturing Action Project: An Opportunity Squandered?" In Milkman, *Organizing Immigrants.*

Delloro, John. 2000. "Personal is Still Political: Reflections on Student Power." In Ho, *Legacy to Liberation.*

Dr. Loco's Rockin' Jalapeño Band. 1992. "El Picket Sign." Traditional music with lyrics adapted by José B. Cuéllar, arrangement by Dr. Loco's RJB. *Movimiento Music* CD. San Francisco: Jaguar & Flying Fish Records.

Dollars and Sense. 1995. "Women in the World Economy." 202 (Nov.-Dec.).

Douglass, Frederick. 1962. *Life and Times of Frederick Douglass: His Early Life As a Slave, His Escape From Bondage, and His Complete History.* Reprinted from the revised edition of 1892. London: Collier-MacMillan Ltd.

DuBois, W.E.B., 1903. "The Talented Tenth." In *The Negro Problem.* New York: James Pott and Company.

Durán, Lisa, Bill Gallegos, Eric Mann, and Glenn Omatsu (ed). 1994. *Immigrant Rights and Wrongs.* Los Angeles: Labor/Community Strategy Center.

Durand, María F. 1996. "Union dishes out hope: Cafeteria workers unite in SASD." *San Antonio Express-News,* May 6, p. A8.

Dutt, Mallika, Leni Marin, and Helen Zia (ed). 1997. *Migrant Women's Human Rights in G-7 Countries: Organizing Strategies.* San Francisco & New York: Family Violence Prevention Fund and Center for Women's Global Leadership.

Dwyer, Augusta. 1994. *On the Line: Life on the US-Mexican Border.* London: Latin America Bureau.

Economic Intelligence Unit. 1994. *Mexico: Country Report, 1st Quarter 1994.* New York: EIU.

Economic Research Associates. 1987. *The Economic and Employment Impacts of Visitors to San Francisco.* San Francisco: San Francisco Planning and Urban Research Association.

Egan, Timothy. 1997. "Teamsters and Ex-Rival Go After Apple Industry: All Out Drive to Expand Low-End Ranks." *New York Times*, Aug. 19, p. A10.

Elbaum, Max. 2001. *Revolution in the Air.* London: Verso.

Emert, Carol. 1998. "Levi's Expanding in China." *San Francisco Chronicle*, Apr. 9, pp. D1 & 4.

—1999. "Levi's to Slash US Plants: Competitors' foreign-made jeans blamed." *San Francisco Chronicle*, Feb. 23, pp. A1 & 12.

Enloe, Cynthia. 1989. *Bananas, Beaches & Bases: Making Senses of International Politics.* Los Angeles: UC Press.

Espinosa Solís, Suzanne. 1994. "Ex-Workers Take On Levi Strauss." *San Francisco Chronicle*, July 18, pp. A1 & 6.

Espíritu, Yen Le. 1997. *Asian American Women and Men: Labor, Laws, and Love.* Thousand Oaks, London, New Delhi: Sage Publications.

Ewell, Miranda and K. Oanh Ha. 1999a. "High Tech's Hidden Labor: Outside the eyes of the law, Silicon Valley companies pay Asian immigrants by the piece to assemble parts at home." *San Jose Mercury News*, June 27.

—1999b. "Why piecework won't go away: The practice helped fuel growth at Solectron, and others imitated it." *San Jose Mercury News*, June 28.

Faison, Seth. 1995. "Changle Journal: With Eye on Dollar, Chinese Are Blind to Danger." *New York Times*, Oct. 21, p. 2.

Falk, Pamela S. 2001. "Easing Up at the Border." *New York Times*, Feb. 15, opinion page.

Featherstone, Liza and Doug Henwood. 2001. "Clothes Encounters: Activists and Economics Clash Over Sweatshops." *Lingua Franca*, 11:2 (March).

Feminist Press Travel Series. 1995. *China for Women: Travel and Culture.* New York: Feminist Press.

Fernández-Kelly, María Patricia. 1983. *For We Are Sold, I and My People: Women and Industry in Mexico's Frontier.* Albany: SUNY Press.

—1993. "Labor Force Recomposition and Industrial Restructuring in Electronics: Implications for Free Trade." *Hostra Labor Law Journal* 10:2, pp. 623-717.

—1994. "Making Sense of Gender in the World Economy: Focus on Latin America." *Sage* 1:2, pp. 249-275.

Fernández-Kelly, M. Patricia and Anna M. García. 1989a. "Hispanic Women and Homework: Women in the Informal Economy in Miami and Los Angeles." In Boris and Daniels, *Homework.*

—1989b. "Informalization at the Core: Hispanic Women, Homework, and the Advanced Capitalist State." In Portes, et al., *The Informal Economy.*

—1992. "Power Surrendered, Power Restored: The Politics of Work and Family among Hispanic Garment Workers in California and Florida." In Tilly and Gurin, *Women, Politics, and Change.*

Fernández-Kelly, M. Patricia and Saskia Sassen. 1991. *A Collaborative Study of Hispanic Women in Garment and Electronics Industries: Executive Summary.* New York: Center for Latin American and Caribbean Studies.

Fernández-Kelly, María Patricia and Richard Schauffler. 1994. "Divided Fates: Immigrant Children in a Restructured US Economy." *International Migration Review* 28:4, pp. 662-689.

Fisk, Catherine L., Daniel J. B. Mitchell, and Christopher L. Erickson. 2000. "Union Representation of Immigrant Janitors in Southern California: Economic and Legal Challenges." In Milkman, *Organizing Immigrants.*

First National People of Color Environmental Leadership Summit. 1991. *Principles of Environmental Justice,* Oct. 27, Washington, DC. Distributed by Southwest Network for Environmental and Economic Justice, Albuquerque.

Fitch, Robert. 1998a. "The Union From Hell: How It Fails To Protect Garment Workers." *Village Voice,* Jan. 20, p. 32.

—1998b. "UNITE: Still Fighting for Lower Wages." Testimony to US Congress House Committee on Education and the Workforce. Hon. Peter Hoekstra, Chairman, Mar. 31.

—1998c. "Workers Betrayed: How the garment union helped Liz Claiborne screw 600 employees." *Village Voice,* Apr. 14, pp. 36-40.

—2000. "Union Reformation." *Tikkun* 15:2 (Mar.-Apr.), pp. 21-56.

Fix, Michael and Jeffrey S. Passel. 1994. *Immigration and Immigrants: Setting the Record Straight.* Washington, DC: Urban Institute.

Fong, Timothy P. 1994. *The First Suburban Chinatown: The Remaking of Monterey Park.* Philadelphia: Temple UP.

Foo, Lora Jo. 1994. "The Vulnerable and Exploitable Immigrant Workforce and the Need for Strengthening Worker Protective Legislation." *Yale Law Journal* 103:8 (June), pp. 2179-2212.

——1999. Presentation at "Sweatshop Labor on the US Marianas Island" Forum sponsored by Sweatshop Watch, Global Exchange, and UNITE. Feb. 3, UNITE office, San Francisco.

Freire, Paulo. 1990. *Pedagogy of the Oppressed.* New York: Continuum.

Friedlander, Eva (ed). 1996. *Look at the World Through Women's Eyes: Plenary Speeches from the NGO Forum on Women, Beijing '95.* New York: Women, Ink.

Friendlander, Peter. 1975. *The Emergence of a UAW Local, 1936-1939.* Pittsburgh: UP Press.

Friedman, Arthur. 1996. "Continued Slide in Jobs Clouds Union's Future on UNITE's Birthday," *Women's Wear Daily,* Aug. 27, p. 6.

Froebel, Folker, Jürgen Heinrichs, and Otto Kreye. 1980. *The New International Division of Labor: Structural Unemployment in Industrialised Countries and Industrialisation in Developing Countries.* Cambridge: Cambridge UP.

Frost, Greg. 1998. "Human rights groups assail Levi Strauss over China." *Reuters,* Apr. 10.

Fuentes, Annette and Barbara Ehrenreich. 1984. *Women in the Global Factory.* Boston: South End.

Fuerza Unida. 1992. "Fuerza Unida Presents Tribunal #1, Sept. 19." Program. San Antonio: FU.

——1998. *Hilo de La Justicia/Thread of Justice* 1:1 (Spring).

Galarza, Ernesto. 1964. *Merchants of Labor: The Mexican Bracero Story.* Santa Barbara: McNally & Loftin.

Gamio, Manuel. 1971. *Mexican Immigration to the United States: A Study of Human Migration and Adjustment.* New York: Dover.

García, Arnoldo. 1993. "La Fuerza Unida." Traditional Mexican Guadalupana song adapted by the Chicano Movement, new version by Arnoldo García, performed at Levi's Plaza, San Francisco.

——1996. "NAFTA and Neoliberalism: The Deepening Mexican Crisis." *Network News,* Summer, pp. 6-7 & 14. Oakland: National Network for Immigrant and Refugee Rights.

García, Juan R. and Thomas Gelisnon (ed). 1995. "Mexican American Women Changing Images" Special Issue. *Perspectives in Mexican American Studies 5.* Tucson: Mexican American Studies & Research Center, University of Arizona.

García, Mario T. 1981. *Desert Immigrants: The Mexicans of El Paso, 1880-1920.* New Haven: Yale UP.

—1994. *Memories of Chicano History: The Life and Times of Bert Corona.* Los Angeles: UC Press.

García, Robert. 1990. "Riots & Rebellion: Civil Rights, Police Reform and the Rodney King Beating." www.ldfla.org/cyber.html

Gee, Emma (ed). 1976. *Counterpoint: Perspectives on Asian America*, Los Angeles: UCLA Asian American Studies Center.

Gereffi, Gary and Miguel Korzeniewicz (ed). 1994. *Commodity Chains and Global Capitalism.* Westport, CT: Greenwood.

Gerlin, Andrea. 1994. "Spread of Illegal Home Sewing Is Fueled by Immigrants." *Wall Street Journal,* Mar. 15, p. B1.

Ginsberg, Steve. 1998. "Coming Apart at the Seams. Ripped Levi's: Blunders, Bad Luck Take Toll." *San Francisco Business Times,* December 11.

Gómez-Quiñones, Juan. 1994. *Mexican American Labor, 1790-1990.* Albuquerque: UNM Press.

Gómez-Quiñones, Juan and David R. Maciel. 1998. "'What Goes Around, Comes Around': Political Practice and Cultural Response in the Internationalization of Mexican Labor, 1890-1997." In Maciel and Herrera-Sobek, *Culture Across Borders.*

Gordon, Jennifer. 2000. "Immigrants Fight the Power: Workers Centers Are One Path to Labor Organizing and Political Participation." *The Nation,* Jan. 3, pp. 16-20.

Gorham, John. 1998. "The World's Working Rich." *Forbes Magazine,* July 6.

Grant, Joanne. 1998. *Ella Baker: Freedom Bound.* New York: John Wiley.

Greater Texas Workers Committee. 1997. Appeal, Nov. 11, care of La Mujer Obrera, El Paso.

—1997. "Greater Texas Workers Committee Needs Your Help!" El Paso.

Green, Nancy L. 1997. *Ready-To-Wear and Ready-To-Work: A Century of Industry and Immigrants in Paris and New York.* Durham: Duke UP.

Greenhouse, Steven. 2000. "Lawsuit Accuses Fashion House of Running Sweatshops," *New York Times,* June 8.

—2001a. "Beatings and Other Abuses Cited at Samoan Apparel Plant That Supplied US Retailers," *New York Times,* Feb. 6, p. A14.

—2001b. "Los Angeles Warms to Labor Unions as Immigrants Look to Escape Poverty." *New York Times,* April 9.

Guerin-Gonzales, Camille and Carl Strikwerda (ed). 1993. *The Politics of Immigrant Workers: Labor Activism and Migration in the World Economy since 1830.* New York: Holmes & Meier.

Guerra, Luz. 1990. "Witness for Peace and Comprehensive Inclusion: A Microcosm of Struggle within the Central America Movement." In Chicago Religious Task Force on Central America, "Challenge to the Central America Movement."

—1997. "Las Nuevas Revolucionarias." *AFSC-Texas-Arkansas-Oklahoma* 10:3, pp. 1-2. Austin: American Friends Service Committee.

—1999. *Technical Assistance & Progressive Organizations for Social Change in Communities of Color.* New York: Funding Exchange.

Gutiérrez, José Angel. 1998. *The Making of a Chicano Militant: Lessons from Cristal.* Madison: UW Press.

Gust, Kelly and Carolyn Newberg. 1991. "Threadbare Dreams: Abuses abound in Oakland sweatshops." *Oakland Tribune,* July 28, pp. A1, 8 & 9.

Ha, Julie. 1998. "Labor Activists Seek to Clean Up Korean Restaurants." *Rafu Shimpo,* Feb. 23, pp. 1 & 4.

Habal, Stella, 2000. "How I Became a Revolutionary." In Ho, *Legacy to Liberation.*

Hahuri, Tono. 1985. "Military occupation and prostitution tourism." In *Female sexual slavery and economic exploitation: Making local and global connections.* UN Non-Governmental Liaison Service Consolidation held in San Francisco, Oct. 25, 1984.

Hall, Christine. 1997. *Daughters of the Dragon: Women's Lives in Contemporary China.* London: Scarlet Press.

Hamamoto, Darrell. 1994. *Monitored Peril: Asian Americans and the Politics of TV Representation.* Minneapolis: UM Press.

Hamamoto, Darrell Y. and Rodolfo D. Torres (ed). 1997. *New American Destinies: A Reader in Contemporary Asian and Latino Immigration.* New York: Routledge.

Hansen, Niles. 1981. *The Border Economy: Regional Development in the Southwest.* Austin: UT Press.

Haq, Farhan. 1998. "Labour-US: Chinese Garment Workers Fight for Lost Wages." *Interpress Third World News Agency,* Apr. 10.

—1998. "Labour-US: Garment Union Under Attack From All Sides." *Interpress Third World New Agency,* June 2.

Hathaway, Dale. 1996. *The FAT and the Workers' Center of Juárez.* Pittsburgh, PA & Juárez: United Electrical, Radio & Machine Workers of America & Frente Auténtico del Trabajo.

—2000. *Allies across the Border: Mexico's "Authentic Labor Front" and Global Solidarity.* Cambridge, MA: South End.

Hays, Constance L. 1989. "Waiters Win $760,000 in Union Case." *New York Times*, Feb. 2.

Hazen, Don (ed). 1992. *Inside the L.A. Riots*. New York: Institute for Alternative Journalism.

Headden, Susan. 1993. "Made in the USA." *US News & World Report*, Nov. 22, pp. 48-55.

Henriques, Diana B. 1998. "Apparel Maker Sues Liz Claiborne and Union." *New York Times*, May 9, p. B3.

—1999. "Suit in Liz Claiborne Dispute Is Given Class-Action Status." *New York Times*, Jan. 5.

—2000. "US Court Rejects Appeal by Brooklyn Garment Workers." *New York Times*, May 25.

Henry, Sarah. 1993. "Labor and Lace: Can An Upstart Women's Group Press a New Wrinkle into the Rag Trade Wars?" *Los Angeles Times Magazine*, Aug. 1, pp. 20-38.

Hernández Palacios, Luís, and Juan Manuel Sandoval (ed). 1989. *Frontera Norte: Chicanos, Pachucos y Cholos*. México: Universidad Autónoma de Zacatecas y Universidad Autónoma Metropolitana.

Heyzer, Noeleen. 1988. *Daughters in Industry: Work, Skills and Consciousness of Women Workers in Asia*. Kuala Lumpur: Asian and Pacific Development Centre.

Heyzer, Noeleen and Tan Boon Kean. 1988. "Work, Skills and Consciousness of Women Workers in Asia." In Heyzer, *Daughters in Industry*.

Hing, Bill Ong. 1993. *Making and Remaking Asian America Through Immigration Policy 1850-1990*. Stanford: Stanford UP.

Ho, Fred (ed). 2000. *Legacy to Liberation: politics and culture of revolutionary asian pacific america*. San Francisco: AK Press & Big Red Media.

Ho, Laura, Catherine Powell and Leti Volpp. 1996. "(Dis)assembling Rights of Women Workers along the Global Assemblyline: Human Rights and the Garment Industry." *Harvard Civil Rights-Civil Liberties Law Review* 31:2, pp. 383-414.

Hodge, Warren. 2000. "Bodies of 58 Asians in Dover: An 'Evil Trade in People.'" *New York Times*, June 20, pp. A1 & A20.

Hom, Sharon K. 1992a. "Law, Ideology, and Patriarchy in China: Feminist Observations of an 'Ethnic Spectator.'" *International Review of Comparative Public Policy* 4, pp. 173-191.

—1992b. "Female Infanticide in China: The Human Rights Specter and Thoughts towards (An)other Vision." *Columbia Human Rights Law Review* 23:2 (Summer), pp. 249-314.

Hondagneu-Sotelo, Pierrette. 1994. *Gender Transitions: Mexican Experiences of Immigration.* Los Angeles: UC Press.

Hondagneu-Sotelo, Pierrette and Cristina Riegos. 1997. "Sin Organización, No Hay Solución: Latina Domestic Workers and Non-traditional Labor Strategies." *Latino Studies Journal* 8:3 (Fall); pp. 54-81.

Hong Kong Women Workers Association. 1996. *Annual Report 1994/95.* Hong Kong: HKWWA.

——1998. *Annual Report 1996/1997.* Hong Kong: HKWWA.

Honig, Emily. 1996. "Women at Farah revisited: political mobilization and its aftermath among Chicana workers in El Paso, Texas, 1972-1992." *Feminist Studies* 22:2 (Summer), pp. 425-453.

Honig, Emily and Gail Hershatter. 1988. *Personal Voices: Chinese Women in the 1980's.* Stanford: Stanford UP.

Hook, Brian (ed). 1996a. *Guangdong: China's Promised Land.* New York: Oxford UP.

——1996b. *Fujian: Gateway to Taiwan.* New York: Oxford UP.

Horn, Robert. 1996. "Thailand forms crossroads of people-smuggling business." *Eastern Express,* Jan. 12.

Hosmer, Ellen. 1990. "Bread and Politics: Organizing El Paso's Garment Workers." *Texas Observer,* Oct. 12, pp. 8-9.

Hossfeld, Karen J. 1988. "Division of Labor, Divisions of Lives: Immigrant Women Workers in Silicon Valley." Ph.D. dissertation, Department of Sociology, University of California, Santa Cruz.

Houston Chronicle Service. 1994. "Feds turn up heat on Asian immigrants' home sweatshops." *San Antonio Express-News,* Aug. 7, p. 23A.

Howard, Keith and The Korean Council for Women Drafted for Military Sexual Slavery by Japan (ed). 1995. *True Stories of the Korean Comfort Women.* London: Cassell.

Hsiao, Andrew. 2000. "Color Blind: Activists of Color Bring the Economic War Home, But Is the Movement Missing the Message." *Village Voice,* July 19-25.

Huang, Fung-Yea. 1997. *Asian and Hispanic Immigrant Women in the Work Force: Implications of the United States Immigration Policies Since 1965.* New York: Garland.

Huang, Vivian and Tom Robbins. 1995. "Chinatown wage war: Target restaurants." *Daily News,* Apr. 20.

Hull, Jennifer Bingham. 1996. "Cecilia Rodríguez: Zapatista, Feminista." *Ms. Magazine* (Nov.-Dec.), pp. 28-31.

Human Rights in China. 1995a. *Caught Between Tradition and the State: Violations of the Human Rights of Chinese Women.* New York: HRIC

—1995b. *Fighting for Their Rights: Chinese Women's Experiences Under Political Persecution.* New York: HRIC

Human Rights Watch Women's Rights Project. 1996. "Mexico/No Guarantees: Sex Discrimination in Mexico's Maquiladora Sector." *Human Rights Watch* 8:6 (Aug.).

Hune, Shirley. 1991. "Migrant Women in the Context of the International Convention on the Protection of the Rights of All Migrant Workers and Members of Their Families." *International Migration Review* 25:4, pp. 800-817.

Hurh, Won Moo. 1998. *The Korean Americans.* Westport, CT: Greenwood.

Hurh, Won Moo and Kwang Chung Kim. 1984. *Korean Immigrants in America: A Structural Analysis of Ethnic Confinement and Adhesive Adaptation.* London: Associated University Presses.

Ijima, Chris and Nobuko Miyamoto. 1970. "We Are the Children," issued on *A Grain of Sand* album (1973) by Chris Kando Iijima, Nobuko Miyamoto, "Charlie" Chin. New York: Paredon Records.

Ishi, Tomoji. 1988. "International Linkage and National Class Conflict: The Migration of Korean Nurses to the United States." *Amerasia Journal* 14, pp. 23-50.

Isis International and Committee for Asian Women. 1985. "Industrial Women Workers in Asia." *Isis International Women's Journal* 4 (Sept.).

I Wor Kuen. 1973. *Chinese-American Workers: Past and Present—an Anthology of Getting Together.* San Francisco: IWK.

James, Ian. 1995. "Freed Thai Workers File Lawsuit." *Los Angeles Times,* Sept. 6.

Jaschok, Maria and Suzanne Miers (ed). 1994. *Women and Chinese Patriarchy: Submission, Servitude and Escape.* Hong Kong UP. London: Zed.

Jeffcott, Bob and Lynda Yanz, 1998. "Code breaking." *New Internationalist* 302 (June), pp. 23-24.

Jiménez-Tan, Marion and Agnes Khoo (ed). 1998. *A Resourcebook for Training and Organizing Work Among Asian Women Workers.* Hong Kong: Committee for Asian Women.

Johnston, David Cay. 1997. "At Levi Strauss, A Big Cutback, With Largess." *New York Times,* Nov. 4, Business section, pp. 1 & 26.

Kadesky, Elizabeth. 1993a. "Clean Rooms, Dirty Secrets." *San Jose Metro,* Mar. 25-31, pp. 12-15.

—1993b. "High-Tech's Dirty Little Secret." *The Nation,* Apr. 19, pp. 517-520.

Kahn, Joseph. 2000. "Vietnam and the US Sign 'Historic' Trade Agreement." *New York Times*, July 14, p. A3.

Kamel, Rachel. 1990. *The Global Factory: Analysis and Action for a New Economic Era*. Philadelphia: American Friends Services Committee.

Kang, K. Connie. 1998a. "Ex-Workers' Suit Seeks Back Wages." *Los Angeles Times*, Aug. 5, pp. B1 & 8.

———1998b. "41 Restaurants Violated Labor Laws." *Los Angeles Times*, Aug. 22, pp. B1 & 3.

———1998c. "Activism Opens Generational Rift in Koreatown Workplaces." *Los Angeles Times*, Sept. 6, pp. A1, 24 & 26.

———1998d. "Koreatown Workers Speak Out so That Others May Benefit." *Los Angeles Times*, Nov. 15, p. B3.

Kaufman, Leslie and David Gonzalez. 2001. "Labor Standards Clash With Global Reality." *New York Times*, April 24, A1 and A10.

Kelley, Robin D. G. 1990. *Hammer and Hoe: Alabama Communists during the Great Depression*. Chapel Hill: UNC Press.

——— 1994. *Race Rebels: Culture, Politics, and the Black Working Class*. New York: Free Press.

Kempadoo, Kamala and Jo Doezema (ed). 1998. *Global Sex Workers: Rights, Resistance, and Redefinition*. New York: Routledge.

Kever, Jeannie. 1990. "A Thousand Lives," *San Antonio Light*, Special Series, Nov. 11-15.

Khor, Martin. 2000. "The Situation at the WTO A Year Since Seattle." Third World Network, www.twnside.org.sg/title/situation.htm.

Kim, Bok-Lim C. 1981. *Women in shadows: a handbook for service providers working with Asian wives of US military personnel*. LaJolla: National Committee Concerned with Asian Wives of US Servicemen.

Kim, Elaine H. and Eui-Young Yu. 1996. *East to America: Korean American Life Stories*. New York: New Press.

Kim, El-Hannah. 1998. "The Social Reality of Korean American Women: Toward Crashing with the Confucian Ideology." In Song and Moon, *Korean American Women*.

Kim, Hyung-chan. 1974. *The Korean Diaspora*. Santa Barbara: ABC-Clio Press.

Kim, Ilsoo. 1981. *New Urban Immigrants: The Korean Community in New York*. Princeton, NJ: Princeton UP.

Kim, Joungwon (ed.) 1997. *Korean Cultural Heritage, Volume III, Performing Arts*. Seoul: Korea Foundation.

Kim, Luke I. 1991. "Korean Ethos: Concept of Jeong and Haan." Paper presented at the Scientific Meeting of Pacific Rim College of Psychiatrists, Los Angeles.

——1998. "The Mental Health of Korean American Women." In Song and Moon, *Korean American Women*.

Kim, Seung-Kyung. 1997. *Class Struggle or Family Struggle?: The Lives of Women Factory Workers in South Korea*. New York: Cambridge UP.

Kim, Yung-Chung (ed). 1976. *Women of Korea: A History from Ancient Times to 1945*. Seoul: Ewha Women's UP.

Kim, Warren Y. 1971. *Koreans in America*. Seoul: Po Chin Chai Printing Co.

Kim-Goh, Mikyong. 1998. "Korean Women's Hwa-Byung: Clinical Issues and Implications for Treatment." In Song and Moon, *Korean American Women*.

King, Ralph. 1997. "Its Share Shrinking, Levi Strauss Lays Off 6,395." *Wall Street Journal*, Nov. 4.

——1998. "Levi's Factory Workers Are Assigned to Teams, And Morale Takes a Hit" and "Injured Workers Sue Levi's Over 'Re-Entry Program.'" *Wall Street Journal*, May 20, p. A1 & 6.

Kirk, Gwyn and Margo Okazawa-Rey. 1998. *Women's Lives: Multicultural Perspectives*. Mountain View, CA: Mayfield.

Koo, Hagen. 1987. "Women Factory Workers in Korea." In Yu and Philips, *Korean Women in Transition*.

Korea Times Chicago. 1994. "The Return Migration Update." Jan. 12, p. 6.

Korean American Coalition to End Domestic Abuse. 1999. *Peaceful Homes, Healthy Relationships*. San Francisco: Asian Women's Shelter.

Korean Immigrant Workers Advocates. 1996a. "Workers Win Job Security in Largest Restaurant in K-Town." *KIWA News* 5 (Spring), pp. 1 & 8.

——1996b. "KIWA Programs." *KIWA News* 6 (Summer), pp. 5-7.

——1997a. "National Korean American Studies Conference On the Fifth Anniversary of L.A. Civil Unrest." *KIWA News* 5 (Spring), pp. 3 & 15.

——1997b. "Industry-wide Organizing in Koreatown Restaurants." *KIWA News* 5 (Spring), pp. 7-9.

——1998a. "Voices of Restaurant Workers: Restaurant Owners, does it have to be this way?" *KIWA News* 6 (Summer), pp. 2 & 13.

——1998b. "Worker Testimonies." Community Town Hall Meeting, Nov. 14. Los Angeles: KIWA.

——1999. "KIWA Proposal." Los Angeles: KIWA.

Korean Sexual Violence Relief Center. 1991. *Korea Sexual Violence Relief Center*. Pamphlet. Seoul: KSVRC.

Korean Women Workers Associations United and Korean Women's Trade Union. 2000. *The Herstory of Korean Women Workers Movement in the 20th Century.* Video. Seoul: Halmikkot Productions.

Korean Women Workers Associations United and The Promotion Committee for the Korean Women Workers' Trade Union. 1999. *Unorganized Women Workers in Korea: Current Conditions and Future Tasks.* Seoul: KWWA.

Krasnowski, Matt. 1998. "Exploitation in Koreatown: Restaurant workers cite tiny wages." *San Diego Union-Tribune,* July 5, p. A3.

Krupat, Kitty 1997. "From War Zone to Free Trade Zone: A History of the National Labor Committee." In Ross, *No Sweat.*

Ku, Hee-Seo. 1997. "Masters of Traditional Dance." In Kim, Joungwon, *Korean Cultural Heritage.*

Kuruvila, Matthai. 2001. "Asian-Americans lead county population gain." *San Jose Mercury News,* March 30, pp. 1B & 7B.

Kwak, Tae-Hwan and Seong Hyong Lee. 1991. *The Korean-American Community: Present and Future.* Seoul: Kyungnam UP.

Kwan, Shek Ping and Trini Leung. 1998. "Export Processing Zones in China." In Asia Monitor Resource Center, *We In The Zone.*

Kwong, Amy. 1998. "Working with AIWA for Social Justice." *AIWA News* 14:2 (Sept.), p. 6.

Kwong, Peter. 1979. *Chinatown, N.Y.: Labor & Politics, 1930-1950.* New York: Monthly Review.

—1987. *The New Chinatown.* New York: Noonday Press.

—1992. "The First Multicultural Riots." In Hazen, *Inside the L.A. Riots.*

—1994a. "The Wages of Fear: Undocumented and Unwanted, Fuzhounese Immigrants Are Changing the Face of Chinatown." *Village Voice,* Apr. 26, pp. 25-29.

—1994b. "China's Human Traffickers." *The Nation,* Oct. 17, pp. 442-425.

—1997. *Forbidden Workers: Illegal Chinese Immigrants & American Labor.* New York: New Press.

Kwong, Peter and JoAnn Lum. 1988. "How the Other Half Lives Now." *The Nation,* June 18, pp. 858-860.

La Botz, Dan. 1998. "Women: The New Leaders in Mexican Society." *Mexican Labor News and Analysis* 3 (Mar.), pp. 6-11.

Labor Institute, The. 1994. *Sexual Harassment at Work: A Training Workbook for Working People.* New York: Labor Institute.

Labor Notes. 1998. "Fuerza Unida Renews Call for Solidarity Against Levi's." 226 (Jan.), p. 2.

La Mujer Obrera. 1990. "A Crisis de La Industria de La Costura..." *Unidad y Fuerza* 1:1, pp. 1-2.

—1991. "The Strike for a Just Future Continues" and "Chronology of the Strike." *Unidad y Fuerza* 1:5 (July), pp. 1 & 7.

—1996a. *XV Aniversario Mujer Obrera: ¡Felicidades!* El Paso: LMO

—1996b. "Join the Association of Border Workers" and "Camp Dignity: The Workers' Struggle for Respect Continues." *Unidad y Fuerza (Aug.-Sept.), pp. 1-4.*

—1996c. *Testimonies of workers displaced by Nafta.* El Paso: LMO.

—1996d. "Organization's History and Accomplishments." El Paso: LMO.

—2000. "Desastre causado por NAFTA-caused Disaster." El Paso: LMO.

— 2001. "The Opening of Café Mayapan," *Voz de Mujer* (Feb.), p. 4.

Lai, Him Mark. 1972. "A Historical Survey of Organizations of the Left Among the Chinese in America." *Journal of Concerned Asian Scholars* 4:3 (Fall), pp. 10-20.

Lai, Him Mark, Genny Lim and Judy Yung. 1980. *Island: Poetry and History of Chinese Immigrants on Angel Island, 1910-1940.* Seattle and London.

Lam, Dean. 1976. "Chinatown Sweatshops." In Emma Gee (ed.), *Counterpoint: Perspectives on Asian America,* Los Angeles: UCLA Asian American Studies Center.

Lam, Wing.1990. "Can unions transform their members?" New York: Chinese Staff & Workers' Association.

Landler, Mark. 1998. "Reversing Course, Levi Strauss Will Expand Its Output in China." *New York Times,* Apr. 9, Business section, pp. 1 & 5.

—2000. "Making Nike Shoes in Vietnam." *New York Times,* Apr. 28, C1 & 20.

—2001. "Hi, I'm in Bangalore (but I Dare Not Tell)." *New York Times,* March 21.

Lee, Ching Kwan. 1998. *Gender and the South China Miracle: Two Worlds of Factory Women.* Los Angeles: UC Press.

Lee, Daniel. 1991. "Transculturally Married Korean Women in the US: Their Contributions and Sufferings." In Kwak and Lee, *The Korean-American Community.*

Lee, Jai-eui. 1999. *Kwangju Diary: Beyond Death, Beyond the Darkness of the Age.* Los Angeles: UCLA Asian Pacific Monograph Series. Originally published in Korean under the name of Hwang, Sog-yong. 1985. *Chugum ul nomo sidae ui odum ul nomo : Kwangju 5-wol minjung hangjaeng ui kirok /* Chonnam Sahoe Undong Hyobuihoe pyon. Seoul City: Pulpit.

Lee, Jai Yun. 1998. "Thoughts on the Causes of the Korean Economic Crisis and Its Impact on Workers." *Asian Labour Update* 27 (Feb.-May), pp. 17-19. Hong Kong: Asia Monitor Resource Center.

Lee, Mary Paik, with introduction by Sucheng Chan. 1990. *Quiet Odyssey: A Pioneer Korean Woman in America*. Seattle: UW Press.

Lee, Paul. 1995. "Retailers Must Share Responsibility for El Monte 'Slave Shop.'" *AIWA News* 11 (Nov.), pp. 1 & 3.

Lee, Sharon M. 1996. "Issues in Research on Women, International Migration and Labor." In Battistella and Paganoni, *Asian Women in Migration*.

Leeming, Frank. 1977. *Street studies in Hong Kong: Localities in a Chinese City*. Hong Kong & New York: Oxford UP.

Leeper Buss, Fran (ed). 1993. *Forged Under the Sun/Forjada Bajo el Sol: The Life of Maria Elena Lucas*. Ann Arbor: UM Press.

Leonhard, David. 2001. "Behind Layoffs, Reality Is Often Less Severe in US," *New York Times*, Feb. 19, p. A1 & A17.

Lewin, Tamar. 1997. "Hospitals Serving the Poor Struggle to Retain Patients." *New York Times*, Sept. 3, p. A16.

Lie, John. 1991. *From kisaeng to maech'un: The transformation of sexual work in Twentieth-Century Korea*. Unpublished manuscript.

—1994. *The State as Pimp: Prostitution and the Patriarchal State in 1940s Japan*. Paper presented at 1992 annual meeting of the American Sociological Association, Pittsburgh, PA, May.

—1995. "The Transformation of Sexual Work in 20th-Century Korea." *Gender & Society* 9:3 (June), pp. 310-327.

Liebhold, Peter and Harry R. Rubenstein (ed). 1999. *Between a Rock and Hard Place: A History of American Sweatshops, 1820- Present*. Los Angeles: UCLA Asian American Studies Center & Simon Wiesenthal Museum of Tolerance.

Liem, Deann Borshay (producer/director/writer). 2000. *First Person Plural*. Film, USA.

Liem, Ramsay and Jinsoo Kim. 1992. "Pico Korea Worker Struggle, Korean Americans, and the Lessons of Solidarity." *Amerasia Journal* 18:1, pp. 49-68.

Light, Ivan and Edna Bonacich. 1988. *Immigrant Entrepreneurs: Koreans in Los Angeles, 1965-1982*. Los Angeles: UC Press.

Lim, Linda Y. C. 1983. "Capitalism, Imperialism, and Patriarchy: The Dilemma of Third-World Women Workers in Multinational Factories." In Nash and Fernández-Kelly, *Women, Men, and the International Division of Labor*.

Limón, José E. 1986. "Language, Mexican Immigration, and the 'Human Connection': A Perspective from the Ethnography of Communication." In Browning and de la Garza, *Mexican Immigrants and Mexican Americans.*

Liu, Lisa, as told to David Bacon. 2000. "The Story of a Garment Worker." *Dollars and Sense* (Sept./Oct.).

Loo, Chalsa M. 1991. *Chinatown: Most Time, Hard Time.* New York, Westport,: Praeger.

Logan, Paul. 1990. "Closed Texas Plant Sparks Levi's Boycott." *Albuquerque Journal,* Sept. 29, p. B1.

López-Garza, Marta. 1989. "Immigration and Economic Restructuring: The Metamorphosis of Southern California (Introduction). *California Sociologist* 12:2 (Summer), pp. 93-110.

López-Stafford, Gloria. 1996. *A Place in El Paso: A Mexican American Childhood.* Albuquerque: UNM Press.

Louie, Miriam Ching. 1989. "Third world prostitutes." *off our backs* 6:10 (Nov.), pp. 14-15.

—1990. "First International Exchange of Women Unionists." *off our backs* 7:3 (Mar.), pp. 18-19.

—1992. "Immigrant Asian Women in Bay Area Garment Sweatshops: 'After sewing, laundry, cleaning and cooking, I have no breath left to sing.'" *Amerasia Journal* 18:1 (Winter), pp. 1-27.

—1993. "It's A Respect Thing: Organizing Immigrant Women." *Equal Means* 2:1 (Fall), pp. 21-23.

—1995a. "Minjung Feminism: Korean Women's Movement for Gender and Class Liberation." *Women's Studies International Forum* 18:4, pp. 417-430.

—1995b. "In the World of Free Trade Sweatshops Thrive." Letter to the Editor, *New York Times,* Feb. 13, p. A14.

—1996. "Garment Workers Justice Campaign: Reflections." Unpublished working paper, Oakland.

—1997a. "Economic Globalization Exploits Migrant Women Workers." *Response* 29:7 (July-Aug.), pp. 9-11. Cincinnati: United Methodist Women.

—1997b. "Breaking the Cycle: Women Workers Confront Corporate Greed Globally." In Shah, *Dragon Ladies.*

— 1998. "Life on the line." *New Internationalist* 302 (June), pp. 20-22.

Louie, Miriam Ching and Cathi Tactaquin. 1996. "In the Shadow of NAFTA: The Conditions of US Migrants and the Challenges." *Asian Migrant Forum* 11.

Louie, Miriam Ching and Linda Burnham. 2000. *Women's Education in the Global Economy: A Workbook.* Berkeley: Women of Color Resource Center.

Louie, Steve, Glenn Omatsu, and Mary Uyematsu Kao (ed), 2001 (forthcoming), *Asian Americans: The Movement and the Moment.* Los Angeles: UCLA Asian American Studies Center Press.

Lusane, Clarence. 1997. *Race in the Global Era: African Americans at the Millennium.* Boston: South End.

Ma, Xia and Wang Weizhi. 1993. *Migration and Urbanization in China.* Beijing: New World.

Mar, Don. 1991. "Another Look at the Enclave Economy Thesis: Chinese Immigrants in the Ethnic Labor Market." *Amerasia Journal* 17:3, pp. 5-21.

Maciel, David R. and María Herrera-Sobek (ed). 1998. *Cultural Across Borders: Mexican Immigration & Popular Culture.* Tuscon: Univ. of Arizona Press.

Maril, Robert Lee. 1989. *Poorest of Americans: The Mexican Americans of the Lower Rio Grande Valley of Texas.* Notre Dame: Univ. of Notre Dame Press.

Márquez, Benjamin. 1995. "Organizing Mexican-American Women in the Garment Industry: La Mujer Obrera." *Women & Politics* 15:1, pp. 65-87.

Marrero, María del Pilar. 1996. "Trabajadores de la costura reclaman dos millones en salarios atrasados: 39 obreros latinos exigen pago." *La Opinión,* Apr. 5, pp. A3-4.

Martens, Margaret Hosmer and Swasti Mitter (ed). 1994. *Women in Trade Unions: Organizing the Unorganized.* Geneva: International Labour Office.

Martínez, Anne and Edwin García. 2001. "Latinos, Asians Lead Statewide Boom." *San Jose Mercury News,* pp. 1C-20A.

Martínez, Elizabeth (ed). 1991. *500 Años del Pueblo Chicano: 500 Years of Chicano History in Pictures.* Albuquerque: SouthWest Organizing Project.

—1998. *De Colores Means All of Us: Latina Views for a Multi-Colored Century.* Boston: South End.

—2000. "Where Was the Color in Seattle? Looking for reasons why the Great Battle was so white." *ColorLines* 3:1 (Spring), pp. 11-12 & www.colorlines.com (expanded version).

Martínez, Elizabeth and Arnoldo García. 1997. "What is 'Neo-Liberalism'?" *Network News,* Winter, p. 4. Oakland: National Network for Immigrant and Refugee Rights.

Martorell, Chanchanit. 1994. "Thai Community Profile." Working Paper, Los Angeles.

Massey, Douglas S., Rafael Alarcón, Jorge Durand & Humberto González. 1987. *Return to Aztlan: The Social Process of International Migration from Western Mexico.* Los Angeles: UC Press.

Mata, Petra. 1997. "A Spiritual Place." *AFSC-Texas-Arkansas-Oklahoma* 10:3, pp. 1-2. Austin: American Friends Service Committee.

Mattielli, Sandra (ed). 1977. *Virtues in conflict: Tradition and the Korean woman today.* Seoul: Royal Asiatic Society.

Mau Dicker, Laverne. 1979. *The Chinese in San Francisco: A Pictorial History.* New York: Dover.

McDonnel, Patrick J. 1996a. "Hotel Boycott Is a High-Stakes Battle for Union." *Los Angeles Times*, Feb. 3, pp. B1 & 3.

—1996b. "Retailers Assailed in Sweatshop Protest." *Los Angeles Times*, Feb. 24.

—1999. "US Votes Could Sway Mexico's Next Elections." *Los Angeles Times*, Feb. 15, p. A17.

McMillen D.H. and S.W. Man (ed). 1994. *The Other Hong Kong Report.* Hong Kong: Chinese University of Hong Kong.

McWilliams, Carey. 1971. *Factories in the Field: The Story of Migratory Farm Labor in California.* Santa Barbara & Salt Lake City: Peregrine Publishers.

Mei, June. 1984. "Socioeconomic Origins of Emigration: Guangdong to California, 1850 to 1882." In Cheng and Bonacich, *Labor Immigration Under Capitalism.*

Menard, Valerie. 1991. "Fuerza Unida fasts for justice." *La Prensa* 6:47, Nov. 29, Austin.

Milkman, Ruth (ed). 2000. *Organizing Immigrants: The Challenge for Unions in Contemporary California.* Ithaca: ILR Press and Cornell UP.

Min, Pyong Gap. (no date). "Immigrant Enterpreneurship and Wife's Overwork: Koreans in New York City." Unpublished paper, Queens College of the City University of New York, p. 5.

—1996. *Caught in the Middle: Korean Merchants in America's Multiethnic Cities.* Los Angeles: UC Press.

—1998a. "The Burden of Labor on Korean American Wives in and outside the Family." In Song and Moon, *Korean American Women.*

—1998b. *Changes and Conflicts: Korean Immigrant Families.* Boston: Allyn & Bacon.

Min, Pyong Gap and Young I. Song. 1998. "Demographic Characteristics and trends of Post-1965 Korean Immigrant Women and Men." In Song and Moon, *Korean American Women.*

Mitter, Swasti. 1986. *Common Fate, Common Bond: Women in the Global Economy.* London: Pluto.

Moberg, David. 2001. "Labor's Critical Condition." *In These Times,* 25:07, Mar. 5.

Monto, Alexander. 1994. *The Roots of Mexican Labor Migration.* Westport: Praeger.

Moody, Kim. 1996. "New Voice for US Workers?" *CrossRoads* 60 (Apr.-May), pp. 22-24.

Moon, Ailee. 1998. "Attitudes Toward Ethnic Identity, Marriage, and Familial Life among Women of Korean Descent in the United States, Japan, and Korea." In Song and Moon, *Korean American Women.*

Moore, Michael. 1996. *Downsize This.* New York: Crown.

Mora, Magdalena. 1981. "The Tolteca Strike: Mexican Women and the Struggle for Union Representation." In Ríos-Bustamante, *Mexican Immigrant Workers in the US.*

Mora, Magdalena and Adelaida R. Del Castillo. 1980. *Mexican Women in the United States: Struggles Past and Present.* Occasional Paper No. 2. Los Angeles: Chicano Studies Research Center Publications, University of California.

Moraga Cherríe and Gloria Anzaldúa (ed). 1981. *This bridge called my back: writings by radical women of color.* Berkeley, CA: Third Woman Press (Third Edition, 2001, forthcoming).

Morgan, Robin (ed.) 1970. *Sisterhood Is Powerful: An Anthology of Writing from the Women's Liberation Movement,* pp. 340-353. New York: Random House.

Mother Jones. 1992. "Heroes: Wing Lam." Jan.-Feb.

Munk, Nina. 1999. "How Levi's Trashed a Great American Brand." *Fortune,* Apr. 12, pp. 83-90.

Nash, June and María Patricia Fernández-Kelly (ed). 1983. *Women, Men, and the International Division of Labor.* Albany: SUNY Press.

Nash, June and Helen Safa (ed). 1985. *Women and Change in Latin America.* South Hadley, Massachusetts: Bergin & Garvey.

Nathan, Debbie. 1991. *Women and Other Aliens: Essays from the US-Mexico Border.* El Paso: Cinco Puntos.

—1991. "Garment Workers: The Long, Last Strike." *Ms. Magazine* 2:1 (July-Aug.), pp. 100-101.

National Commission for Democracy in Mexico. 1997a. *Celebrating the Struggles of Women!* El Paso: NCDM.

—1997b. *The Zapatista Struggle.* El Paso: NCDM.

National Council for Research on Women. 1995. "Immigration: Women and Girls, Where Do they Land?" *Issues Quarterly* Special Issue 1:3. New York: NCRW.

National Mobilization Against Sweatshops. 1999a. "Ain't I a Woman?!: A Campaign of the National Mobilization Against Sweatshops." Brochure. New York: NMASS.

—1999b. "Groundbreaking Victory: Multi-Million-Dollar Manufacturer Streetbeat Sportswear Held Accountable for 137-Hour Work Weeks," press release and timeline, June 21.

—2000. "NMASS: Our First Three Years." *Sweatshop Nation* 1 (Spring). 9 to 5. 2000. "Making Dollars and Sense: Publicize Equal Pay Day." *Newsline* 19:2 (Mar.-Apr.).

National Network for Immigrant and Refugee Rights. 1998. *Portrait of Injustice: The Impact of Immigration Raids on Families, Workers, and Communities*, Oct. Oakland: NNIRR.

—2000. *Hands that Shape the World: Report on the Conditions of Immigrant Women in the US Five Years after the Beijing Conference*. Oakland: NNIRR.

Navarro, Armando. 1994. "The South Central Los Angeles Eruption: A Latin Perspective." In Chang and Leong, *Los Angeles—Struggles toward Multiethnic Community*.

New York Times. 1995. "Healthy Korean Economy Draws Immigrants Home." Aug. 22, pp. A1 & A12.

Nguyen, Tram. 2001. "Showdown in K-Town." *ColorLines* (Spring), pp. 26-29.

Noble, Kenneth B. 1995. "Thai Workers Held Captive, Officials Say." *New York Times*, Aug. 4, p. A1.

Ogle, George E. 1990. *South Korea: Dissent within the Economic Miracle*. London: Zed.

Okazawa-Rey, Margo. 2000. Presentation at Plenary Session, afternoon, Apr. 29. "Color of Violence: Violence Against Women of Color, A National Conference." Apr. 28-29, Women of Color Research Cluster, University of California, Santa Cruz.

Omatsu, Glenn. 1999. "Defying a Thousand Pointing Fingers and Serving the Children: Re-envisioning the Mission of Asian American Studies in Our Communities." Essay presented at a colloquium at UC Berkeley on Oct. 29-30 marking the 30th anniversary of Asian American Studies.

Ong, Paul, Eda Bonacich and Lucie Cheng. 1994. *The Asian Immigration in Los Angeles and Global Restructuring*. Philadelphia: Temple UP.

Orozco, Cynthia E. 1995. "Beyond Machismo, La Familia, and Ladies Auxiliaries: A Historiography of Mexican-Origin Women's Participation in Voluntary Associations and Politics in the United States, 1870-1990." In García and Gelisnon, *Perspectives in Mexican American Studies.*

Paik, Sook Ja. 1991. "Korean-American Women's Underemployment and Dual Labor Burden." In Kwak and Lee, *The Korean-American Community.*

Palafox, José. 1996. "Militarizing the Border." *Covert Action Quarterly* 56 (Spring), pp. 14-19.

Palmer, Louise. 1991. "Stand-off in the Sweatshops." *The Progressive* (May), pp. 12-13.

Pardo, Mary. 1990. "Mexican American Women Grassroots Community Activists: 'Mothers of East Los Angeles.'" *Frontiers,* 11:1, pp. 1-7.

—1998. *Mexican American Women Activists: Identity and Resistance in Two Los Angeles Communities.* Philadelphia: Temple UP.

Park, Edward Jang-Woo. 1992. "Asian Americans in Silicon Valley: Race and Ethnicity in the Postindustrial Economy." Ph.D. dissertation, University of California, Berkeley.

—1996. "Our L.A.? Korean Americans in Los Angeles After the Civil Unrest." In Michael J. Dear, H. Eric Schockman, and Greg Hise, *Rethinking Los Angeles,* pp. 153-168. Thousand Oaks, CA: Sage.

—1998. "Competing Visions: Political Formation of Korean Americans in Los Angeles, 1992-1997." *Amerasia Journal* 24:1, pp. 41-57.

Park, Kyeyoung. 1997. *The Korean American Dream: Immigrants & Small Business in New York City.* Ithaca: Cornell UP.

Parker, Mike and Jane Slaughter. 1994. *Working Smart: A Union Guide to Participation Programs and Reengineering.* Detroit: Labor Notes.

Pastor, Manuel. 1993. *Latinos and the Los Angeles Uprising: The Economic Context,* Claremont, California: Tomas Rivera Center.

Peña, Devon. 1990. "Between the Lines: A New Perspective on the Industrial Sociology of Women Workers in Transnational Labor Processes." In Córdova, et al, *Chicana Voices.*

Perez, Ramón "Tianguis." Translated by Dick J. Reavis. 1991. *Diary of an Undocumented Immigrant.* Houston: Arte Publico Press.

Portes, Alejandro (ed). 1995. *The Economic Sociology of Immigration: Essays on Networks, Ethnicity, and Entrepreneurship.* New York: Russell Sage Foundation.

Portes, Alejandro, Manuel Castells, and Lauren A. Benton (ed). 1989. *The Informal Economy: Studies in Advanced and Less Developed Countries*. Baltimore: Johns Hopkins UP.

Portes, Alejandro and John Walton. 1981. *Labor, Class and the International System*. New York: Academic Press.

Puente, Teresa. 2000. "WWII victims find courage to paint story." *Chicago Tribune*, Sept. 28. Section 2, pp. 1-2.

Purdum, Todd S. 2001. "California Census Confirms Whites Are in Minority." *New York Times*, March 30, pp. A1 & 16.

Raghavan, Chakravarthi. 2001. "Barking Up the Wrong Tree: Trade and Social Clause Links." Third World Network, www.twnside.org.sg/title/situation.htm.

Raphaelidis, Leia. 1997. "Sewing discontent in Nicaragua: the harsh regime of Asian garment companies in Nicaragua." *Multinational Monitor* 18:9 (Sept.), pp. 24-27.

Reavis, Dick J. 1993. "Sewing Discontent: Cut-rate Wages in the Dallas Apparel Underground." *Texas Observer*, May 7, pp. 14-19.

Reimers, David M. 1983. "An unintended reform: the 1965 Immigration Act and Third World Immigration to the U.S." *Journal of American Ethnic History* 3 (Fall), pp. 9-28.

Reyna, Juanita. 1997. "Let There Be Change." *AFSC-Texas-Arkansas-Oklahoma* 10:3, pp. 1-2. Austin: American Friends Service Committee.

Rhie, Maria Chol Soon. 1996-1997. " 'Globalisation' and the Flexibilisation of Labour in South Korea." *Asian Labour Update*, Nov.-Mar., pp. 17-19. Hong Kong: Asia Monitor Resource Center.

Ríos-Bustamante, Antonio (ed). 1981. *Mexican Immigrant Workers in the US Anthology No. 2*. Los Angeles: Chicano Studies Research Center Publications, University of California.

Rivera, Marcia. 1996. "The impact of economic globalization on women." In Friedlander, *Look at the World Through Women's Eyes*.

Resendiz, Julian. 1997. "Taking the next step: Legal immigrants have incentives to seek citizenship." *El Paso Herald-Post*, Feb. 8, A1 & 3.

Robles Ortega, Elizabeth. (no date). "Confrontar el Modelo de la Industria Maquiladora de Exportación: Una Necesidad Común." México: Servicio, Desarrollo y Paz. A.C.

Rodríguez, Cecilia. 1990. "Community Organizing: What It Means for Women of Color." Working Paper. El Paso: La Mujer Obrera.

—1994. "I ask a piece of your heart be Zapatista..." Speech to Native Forest Network, Nov. 11, Missoula, Montana.

—1996. "¡La voz de La Mujer Obrera!: voz de lucha de muchos trabajadores." In La Mujer Obrera, *XV Aniversario Mujer Obrera: ¡Felicidades!*

Rodríguez, Roberto and Patrisia Gonzáles. 1997. "As American as Chile and Apple Pie." *Chronicle Features*, Sept. 26.

Rofel, Lisa. 1999. *Other Modernities: Gendered Yearnings in China after Socialism.* Los Angeles: UC Press.

Roig de Leuchsenring, Emilio. 1967. *Martí: Anti-Imperialist.* Havana: Book Institute.

Romero, Mary. 1992. *Maid in the USA.* New York: Routledge.

Romero, Mary, Pierrette Hondagneu-Sotelo and Vilma Ortiz (ed). 1997. *Challenging Fronteras: Structuring Latina and Latino Lives in the US* New York: Routledge.

Romero, Rolando. 1990. "Muchos siguen sufriendo por el cierre de Levi's." *La Prensa*, Feb. 21, Austin & San Marcos, pp. 3 & 10.

Rose, Kalima. 1991. "Women Are Stirring the Pot." *Equal Means* (Winter), pp. 5-8.

—1992. *Where Women Are Leaders: The SEWA Movement in India.* London: Zed.

Rose, Margaret. 1990. "From the Fields to the Picket Line: Huelga Women and the Boycott, 1965-1975." *Labor History* 3 (Summer).

—1995. " 'Woman Power Will Stop Those Grapes': Chicana Organizers and Middle-Class Female Supporters in the Farm Workers' Grape Boycott in Philadelphia, 1969-1970." *Journal of Women's History* 7:4 (Winter), pp. 6-35.

Ross, Andrew. 1997. *No Sweat: fashion, free trade, and the rights of garment workers.* London: Verso.

Ross, John. 1995. *Rebellion from the Roots: Indian Uprising in Chiapas.* Monroe, ME: Common Courage.

Rowbothan, Sheila and Swasti Mitter (ed). 1994. *Dignity and Daily Bread: New Forms of Economic Organizing Among Poor Women in the Third World and the First.* New York: Routledge.

Ruíz, Vicki L. 1987. *Cannery Women/ Cannery Lives: Mexican Women, Unionization, and the California Food Processing Industry, 1930-1950.* Albuquerque: UNM Press.

—1998. *From Out of the Shadows: Mexican Women in Twentieth-Century America.* New York & Oxford: Oxford UP.

Ruíz, Vicki L. and Susan Tiano (ed). 1987. *Women on the US-Mexico Border: Responses to Change.* Boulder: Westview.

Safa, Helen, I. 1979. "Multinationals and the Employment of Women in Developing Areas: The Case of the Caribbean." Mimeographed. Graduate Department of Antrhopology, Rutgers University.

Salaff, Janet W. 1995. *Working daughters of Hong Kong: Filial Piety or Power in the Family?* New York: Columbia UP.

San Francisco Chronicle. 2000. "Slave Trade Endures In the 21st Century." July 2, p. 8.

San Francisco Examiner. 1994. "Levi, union announce partnership." Oct. 14.

Saracevic, Alan. 1997. "Levi Strauss loses worker lawsuit." *San Francisco Examiner*, Sept. 9.

Sassen, Saskia. 1988. *The Mobility of Labor and Capital: A Study in International Investment and Labor Flow.* Cambridge: Cambridge UP.

—1991. *The Global City: New York, London, Tokyo.* Princeton, NJ: Princeton UP.

—1995. "Immigration and Local Labor Markets." In Portes, *The Economic Sociology of Immigration.*

—1996. "New employment regimes in cities: the impact on immigrant workers." *New Community* 22:4, pp. 579-594.

—1998. *Globalization and Its Discontents.* New York: New Press.

Saxton, Alexander. 1971. *The Indispensable Enemy: Labor and the Anti-Chinese Movement in California.* Los Angeles: UC Press.

Schädler, Monica. 1995. "Economic Reforms and Rural Women," in Feminist Press Travel Series, *China for Women: Travel and Culture.* New York: Feminist Press.

Scharlin, Craig and Lilia V. Villanueva. 1994. *Philip Vera Cruz: A Personal History of Filipino Immigrants and the Farmworkers Movement.* Los Angeles: UCLA Labor Center, Institute of Industrial Relations and UCLA Asian American Studies Center.

Schell, Orville and David Shambaugh. 1999. *The China Reader: The Reform Era.* New York: Vintage Books.

Schey, Peter. 1993. "Human Rights Violations of Migrant Farmworkers in the US." In Battistella, *Human Rights of Migrant Workers.*

Schmetzer, Uli. 1995. "Light finally shining on China legacy of sex abuse: Government tries to clean up act before women's conference." *San Francisco Examiner*, Jan. 7, p. A3.

Schoenberger, Karl. 2000. "S.F. jeans maker retools." *San Francisco Examiner*, June 25, pp. C1 & 8-9.

Segura, Denise A. 1990. "Chicanas & Triple Oppression in the Labor Force." In Córdova, et al., *Chicana Voices.*

Sen, Rinku. 1995. *We Are The Ones We Are Waiting For: Women of Color Organizing for Transformation.* Durham: US Urban-Rural Mission of the World Council of Churches.

Servicio, Desarrollo y Paz, A. C. 1996. "SEDEPAC, 1983-1996, 13 Years: Supporting popular movements." Newsletter '96. Frontera, Coahuila: SEDEPAC.

Shah, Sonia (ed). *Dragon Ladies: Asian American Feminists Breathe Fire.* Boston: South End.

Shepherd, Ed. 2001. "Credibility Gap Between Codes & Conduct—A Smokescreen for Poor Labour Standards." Asian Labour Update, www.amrc.org.hk/alu.htm.

Sherman, Stratford. 1997. "Levi's: As Ye Sew, So Shall Ye Reap." *Fortune,* May 12.

Shimtuh, Korean Domestic Violence Program, a collaborative project of the Asian Women's Shelter, the Korean Community Center of the East Bay, and the Korean American Coalition to End Domestic Abuse. 2000. "Korean American Community of the Bay Area Domestic Violence Needs Assessment Report," Oct. 21, p. 6. Oakland: Shimtuh.

Shin, Young Hai. 1995. "Young Hai Shin" (interviewed by Miriam Ching Louie). In Sen, Rinku (ed.), *We Are The Ones We Are Waiting For: Women of Color Organizing for Transformation,* pp. 48-50. Durham: US Urban-Rural Mission of the World Council of Churches.

—1997. "Build Your Own Base." Guest editorial, *Third Force* 5:3 (July-Aug.). Oakland: Center for Third World Organizing.

Shorrock, Tim. 1996. "Debacle in Kwangju." *The Nation*, Dec. 9, p. 19-22.

Sim, Inbo. 2000. "5.18 and Korean American Movements." Paper delivered at "Kwangju After Two Decades" Conference, April 20-22, University of Southern California and University of California Los Angeles.

60 Minutes. 1994. "Behind the Seams." First aired Dec. 11. New York: CBS.

Sivananda, A. and Ellen Meiksen Wood. 1997. "Capitalism, Globalization, and Epochal Shifts: An Exchange." *Monthly Review* (Feb.).

Skinner, G. William (ed). 1977. *The City in Late Imperial China.* Stanford: Stanford UP.

Smedley, Agnes. 1995. "Silk Workers." In Feminist Press Travel Series, *China for Women.*

Smith. Barbara (ed.) 1983. *Home Girls: A Black Feminist Anthology.* Piscataway, NJ: Rutgers UP.

Smith, Greg B. 1990. "New York's Chinatown is booming: Immigrants prefer Gotham to S.F. for jobs, opportunity." *San Francisco Sunday Examiner & Chronicle*, June 17, p. A6.

Smith, Mark. 1994. "Home-sewn trouble: Textile workers exploited in spite of labor laws." *Houston Chronicle* 93:298, Aug. 7, pp. A1 & 20.

Soldatenko, María Angelina. 1993. "Organizing Latina Garment Workers in Los Angeles." *Atzlan* 20:1 & 2, "Las Obreras: The Politics of Work and Family."

Solinger, Dorothy J. 1999. *Contesting Citizenship in Urban China: Peasant Migrants, the State, and the Logic of the Market.* Los Angeles: UC Press.

Sommer, Constance. 1995. "L.A.'s cutthroat fashion industry." *San Francisco Examiner*, Sept. 24, pp. C1 & 9.

Song, Young I. and Ailee Moon (ed). 1998a. *Korean American Women: From Tradition to Modern Feminism.* Westport: Praeger.

———1998b. "The Domestic Violence against Women in Korean Immigrant Families: Cultural Psychological, and Socioeconomic Perspectives." In Song and Moon, *Korean American Women.*

Southeast Asia Chronicle and Pacific Studies Center. 1978 & 1979. "Changing Role of S.E. Asian Women: The Global Assembly Line and the social manipulation of women on the job." Special Joint Issue *SAC* 66 and *PSC* 9:5-6. Berkeley and Mountain View, CA.

Southwest Network for Environmental & Economic Justice, California Rural Legal Assistance Foundation and Earth Island Institute. 1996. "The Border." *Race, Poverty & the Environment* 6:4 and 7:1 (Summer & Fall).

SouthWest Organizing Project. 1995. *Intel Inside New Mexico: A Case Study of Environmental and Economic Injustice.* Albuquerque: SouthWest Organizing Project.

Sparr, Pamela (ed). 1994. *Mortgaging Women's Lives: Feminist Critiques of Structural Adjustment.* London: Zed.

Spence, Jonathan D. 1990. *The Search for Modern China.* New York: Norton.

Spich, Robert S. 1995. "Globalization folklore: problems of myth and ideology in the discourse on globalization." *Journal of Organizational Change Management* 8:4, pp. 6-29.

Stalker, Peter. 1994. *The Work of Strangers: A Survey of International Migration.* Geneva: International Labour Office.

Stephen, Lynn. 1997. *Women and Social Movements in Latin America: Power from Below.* Austin: UT Press.

Stehle, Vince. 1998. "Philanthropy Is in the Family Genes." *The Chronicle of Philanthropy*, May 21, pp. 1-16.

Sterngold, James. 1995. "Agency Missteps Put Illegal Aliens at Mercy of Sweatshops." *New York Times,* Sept. 21, p. A9.

Stoddard, Ellwyn R., Richard L. Nostrand, and Jonathan P. West. 1983. *Borderlands Source Book: A Guide to the Literature on Northern Mexico and the American Southwest.* Norman: Univ. of Oklahoma Press.

Stone, I. F. 1988. *The Hidden History of the Korean War, 1950-1951.* Boston: Little, Brown.

Strand, P.J. and W. Jones, Jr. 1985. *Indochinese Refugees in America: Problems of Adaptation and Assimilation.* Durham: Duke UP.

Sturdevant, Saundra Pollock and Brenda Stoltzfus. 1992. *Let the Good Times Roll: Prostitution and The US Military in Asia.* New York: New Press.

Su, Julie. 1997. "El Monte Thai garment workers: slave sweatshops." In Ross, *No Sweat.*

Suárez Aguilar, Estela. 1996. "The impact of regional integration on women: The case of Mexico." In Friedlander, *Look at the World Through Women's Eyes.*

Sweatshop Watch. 1996. "Sweatshop Watch Launches Accountability Campaign." *Sweatshop Watch* 1:2 (Winter), pp. 1-2.

—1997. "What is a Sweatshop?" www.sweatshopwatch.org/swatch/industry.

—1998. "Sweatshop Labor—Made in the USA." *Sweatshop Watch* 4:1 (Spring), pp. 1-2.

—1999. "California Adopts Toughest Sweatshop Law of its Kind in the Country." *Sweatshop Watch* 5:2 (Fall), pp. 1-2.

—2000. "The Globalization of Sweatshops." *Sweatshop Watch* 6:2 (Summer); pp. 1-3.

—2001. "Resist the FTAA—The Latest 'Race to the Bottom.'" *Sweatshop Watch* 7:1 (Spring), pp. 1 & 5.

—"Frequently Asked Questions." (no date). www.sweatshopwatch.org/swatch/questions.html.

Sweatshop Watch and Korean Immigrant Worker Advocates. 1996. "Thai & Latino Garment Workers Demand Justice: The Retailer Accountability Campaign." Los Angeles: KIWA.

Swoboda, Frank. 1994. "US Targets Clothing Retailers." *Washington Post,* Sept. 9, p. A23.

Tactaquin, Cathi. 1995. "An International Perspective on Migration." *Poverty & Race* 4:2 (Mar.-Apr.), pp. 1-6. D.C.: Poverty & Race Research Action Council.

Tanaka, Wendy. 1997a. "Levi's sued over re-entry program: Injured workers say they're underpaid, ridiculed, harassed." *San Francisco Examiner*, Sept. 5.

—1997b. "Punitive fine against Levi: $10 million." *San Francisco Examiner*, Sept. 9, 1997, p. B1.

Tanner, Mika. 1998. "Korean American Group Puts Heat on Restaurants." *Asian Week*, Aug. 20, p. 8.

Taran, Patrick and Catherine Kelly. 1991. *Proclaiming Migrants Rights: The New International Convention on the Protection of the Rights of All Migrant Workers and Members of Their Families.* Geneva: Churches' Committee for Migrants in Europe and World Council of Churches Migration Secretariat.

Thompson, Ginger. 1999. "Mexico City Journal; Tortilla Rises: Must Belts Tighten? *New York Times*, Jan. 4.

—2001. "Chasing Mexico's Dream Into Squalor." *New York Times*, February 11, pp. 1A & 6A.

Thornburg, Gina. 1998. "Koreatown's workers find a voice." *Progressive* 62:7 (July), p. 12.

Tieszen, Helen Rose. 1977. "Korean proverbs about women." In Mattielli, *Virtues in conflict.*

Tilly, Louise A. and Patricia Gurin (ed). 1992. *Women, Politics, and Change*, pp. 130-149. New York: Russell Sage Foundation Press.

Timmons, W. H. 1990. *El Paso: A Borderlands History.* El Paso: Univ. of Texas, Texas Western Press.

Toribio, Helen. 2000. "Dare to Struggle: The KDP and Filpino American Politics," In Ho, *Legacy to Liberation.*

Tsang, S.K. 1994. "The Economy." In McMillen and Man, *The Other Hong Kong Report.*

Tsukiyama, Gail. 1991. *Women of the Silk: A Novel.* New York: Saint Martin's Press.

Udesky, Laurie. 1994a. "Sweatshops Behind the Labels." *The Nation*, May 16.

—1994b. "Exchange: Which Side Are You On?" *The Nation*, Aug. 8-15, pp. 146-7.

Um, Shin Ja. 1996. *Korean immigrant women in the Dallas-area apparel industry: looking for feminist threads in patriarchal cloth.* Lanham, Md: University Press of America.

United Nations. 1995. *International Migration Policies and the Status of Female Migrants.* Proceedings of the Expert Group Meeting on International Migration Policies and the Status of Female Migrants, San Miniato, Italy, 28-31 Mar. 1990. New York: United Nations.

US Department of Labor, Women's Bureau. 1997. "Women of Hispanic Origin in the Labor Force." *Facts on Working Women.* www2.dol.gov/dol/wb/public/wb_pubs/hisp97.htm.

US Department of Labor, Office of Public Affairs. 1996. "Secretary Reich Announces Signed Agreement between Jessica McClintock, Inc. and Asian Immigrant Women Advocates," March 18. USDL:96-108, Washington, DC.

US Government Accounting Office. 1988. *Sweatshops in the US.* Washington, DC: GAO.

Valadez, Carmen and Jaime Cota. 1996. "New Ways of Organizing for Women Workers in the Maquilas." In Southwest Network for Environmental & Economic Justice, et al., *Race, Poverty & the Environment.*

Van Derbeken, Jaxon, Debra Levi Holtz and Chuck Squatriglia. 2000. "Son Sought in Berkeley Sex Case, Police want to question him about alleged plot to smuggle girls from India." *San Francisco Chronicle,* January 22, p. A1.

Vargas, Zaragosa. 1997. "Tejana radical: Emma Tenayuca and the San Antonio labor movement during the Great Depression." *Pacific Historical Review* 66:4 (Nov.), pp. 553-580.

Varona, Rex. 1998. "The Impact of the Asian Crisis on Migrant Workers." *Asian Labour Update* 27 (Feb.-May), pp. 9-11. Hong Kong: Asia Monitor Resource Center.

Vega, Bernardo. 1984. *Memoirs of Bernardo Vega: a contribution to the history of the Puerto Rican community in New York.* Cesar Andreu (ed). New York: Monthly Review.

Verhovek, Sam Howe. 1998. "Benefits of Free-Trade Bypass Texas Border Towns." *New York Times,* June 23.

—2000. "Deadly Choice of Stowaways: Ship Containers." *New York Times,* Jan. 12, p. 1.

Vickers, Jeanne, 1991. *Women and the World Economic Crisis.* London: Zed.

Villalba, May-an. 1996. "Globalisation: its Impact and Challenges to Labor Migration." Paper presented to the consultation on "Migrant Workers Challenging Global Structures" sponsored by Asian Migrant Centre, Migrant Forum in Asia and the Joint Committee on Migrants in Korea, Aug. 28 to Sept. 1, Seoul.

Waldinger, Roger D. 1986. *Through the Eye of the Needle: Immigrants and Enterprise in New York's Garment Trades*. New York: New York UP.

Walker, Dick and The Bay Area Study Group. 1990. "The Playground of US Capitalism? The Political Economy of the San Francisco Bay Area in the 1980s." In Davis, et al, *Fire in the Hearth*.

Ward, Kathryn (ed). 1990. *Women Workers and Global Restructuring*. Ithaca: ILR Press.

Wells, Miriam J. 2000. "Immigration and Unionization in the San Francisco Hotel Industry." In Milkman, *Organizing Immigrants*.

Wheat, Andrew. 1994. "Workers Rights Unravelled." *Multinational Monitor* 15:3 (Mar.), pp. 7-8.

White, George. 1995. "Workers Held in Near-Slavery, Officials Say." *Los Angeles Times*, Aug. 3, pp. A1 & 20.

White Polk, Wendy. 2000. "¡Que Mujer Obrera!: María Antonia Flores: La Mujer in Charge." *El Paso Inc.*, 6:14 (December 10-16).

Women of Color Resource Center (ed). 2001 (forthcoming). An alternative report on the status of US women of color to the 2001 UN World Conference Against Racism, Durban, South Africa. Berkeley: WCRC.

Wong, Edward. 1999. "A Seamstress Sues Donna Karan, Claiming Retaliation for a Lawsuit." *New York Times*, Dec. 26.

Workers Awaaz. 2000. Brochure. New York: Workers Awaaz.

Working Group Meeting on Trade and Globalization. 1996. "Jémez Principles for Democratic Organizing." Jémez, New Mexico, Dec. 8. Distributed by the Southwest Network for Environmental and Economic Justice, Albuquerque.

Wypijewski, JoAnn. 1994. "Profits of Pain" *The Nation*, Apr. 11, pp. 471-472.

Yang, Catherine and Christina Del Valle. 1994. "In a Sweat Over Sweatshops." *Business Week*, Apr. 4, p. 40.

Yeh, Emerald and Christine McMurry. 1996. "Sweatshop Bargains: A Shopper's Dilemma." *San Francisco Chronicle*, July 14, p. 1/Z5.

Yoneda, Karl G. 1983. *Ganbatte: Sixty-Year Struggle of a Kibei Worker*. Los Angeles: Asian American Studies Center.

Yoon, Jin-Ho. 1997. "IMF Bailout and Employment Crisis: the labour response," Dec. 11. Working paper. Seoul: Korean Confederation of Trade Unions.

Yu, Eui-Young. 1993. "The Korean-American Community." In D.N. Clark (ed.), *Korea Briefing 1993*. pp. 139-162. Boulder: Westview.

Yu, Eui-Young and Earl Philips (ed). 1987. *Korean Women in Transition: At Home and Abroad*, pp. 103-112. Los Angeles: California State University.

Yu, Renqiu. 1992. *To Save China, To Save Ourselves: The Chinese Hand Laundry Alliance of New York*. Philadelphia: Temple UP.

Yung, Judy. 1986. *Chinese Women of America: A Pictorial History*. Seattle: UW Press.

—1995. *Unbound Feet: A Social History of Chinese Women in San Francisco*. Los Angeles: UC Press.

Zachary, G. Pascal. 1994. "Levi Tries to Make Sure Contract Plants in Asia Treat Workers Well." *Wall Street Journal*, July 28.

Zamora, Rubén. 1995. "Toward a Strategy of Resistance." *NACLA Report on the Americas* 26:4 (Feb.), p. 6-21.

Zavella, Patricia. 1987. *Women's Work & Chicano Families: Cannery Workers of the Santa Clara Valley*. Ithaca: Cornell UP.

Zhou, Min. 1992. *Chinatown: The Socioeconomic Potential of an Urban Enclave*. Philadelphia: Temple UP.

Zia, Helen. 1996. "Made in the USA." *Ms. Magazine*, Jan./Feb., pp. 67-73.

—2000. *Asian American Dreams: The Emergence of an American People*. New York: Farrar, Straus & Giroux.

Zoll, Daniel. 1998. "Sweatshop blues" and "In their pocket: Levi's silences potential critics with cash." *San Francisco Bay Guardian* 32:36 (June 10-16), pp. 23, 25 & 27.

Index

About
Miriam Ching Yoon Louie

Miriam Ching Yoon Louie works with the Women of Color Resource Center and formerly served as national campaign media director of Fuerza Unida and Asian Immigrant Women Advocates. Her essays and articles on immigrant women and labor issues have been widely anthologized, and she speaks at public events internationally. She is the co-author, with Linda Burnham, of *Women's Education in the Global Economy* (Women of Color Resource Center, 2000).

Miriam Ching Yoon Louie
Photo by Belvin Louie (2000)

About South End Press

South End Press is a nonprofit, collectively run book publisher with more than 200 titles in print. Since our founding in 1977, we have tried to meet the needs of readers who are exploring, or are already committed to, the politics of radical social change. Our goal is to publish books that encourage critical thinking and constructive action on the key political, cultural, social, economic, and ecological issues shaping life in the United States and in the world. In this way, we hope to give expression to a wide diversity of democratic social movements and to provide an alternative to the products of corporate publishing.

Through the Institute for Social and Cultural Change, South End Press works with other political media projects—Alternative Radio; Speakout, a speakers' bureau; and Z Magazine—to expand access to information and critical analysis.

To order books, please send a check or money order to: South End Press, 7 Brookline Street, #1, Cambridge, MA 02139-4146. To order by credit card, call 1-800-533-8478. Please include $3.50 for postage and handling for the first book and 50 cents for each additional book.

Write or e-mail southend@southendpress.org for a free catalog, or visit our new web site at http://www.southendpress.org.

Related Titles

Disposible Domestics: Immigrant Women Workers in the Global Economy
By Grace Chang
0-89608-617-8 $18

Made in Indonesia: Indonesian Workers Since Suharto
By Dan LaBotz
0-89608-642-9 $18

Allies Across the Border: Mexico's "Authentic Labor Front" and Global Solidarity
By Dale Hathaway
0-89608-632-1 $19

Feminism is for Everybody: Passionate Politics
By bell hooks
0-89608-628-3 $12

Globalization from Below: The Power of Solidarity
By Jeremy Brecher, Tim Costello, and Brendan Smith
0-89608-626-7 $13

Dangerous Intersections: Feminist Perspectives on Population, Environment, and Development
Edited by Jael Silliman and Ynestra King
0-89608-597-X $20

De Colores Means All of Us: Latina Views for a Multi-Colored Century
By Elizabeth Martínez
0-89608-583-X $18

Dragon Ladies: Asian American Feminists Breathe Fire
Edited by Sonia Shah
0-89608-575-9 $17

Race, Gender, and Work: A Multi-Cultural Economic History of Women in the United States (Updated Edition)
By Teresa Amott and Julie Matthaei
0-89608-537-6 $21

See previous page for ordering information.

Contact information

Asian Immigrant Womens Advocates
310 8th Street, Suite 301
Oakland, CA 94607
(510) 268-0192
aiwa@igc.org

Chinese Staff and Workers Association
PO Box 130401
New York, NY 10013-0995
(212)619-7979

Fuerza Unida
710 New Laredo Highway
San Antonio, TX 78211
(210) 927-2294
fuerzaunid@aol.com

Korean Immigrant Workers Advocates
3465 West Eighth Street
Los Angeles, CA 90005
(213) 738-9050
kiwa@kiwa.org

La Mujer Obrera
2000 Texas Street
El Paso, TX 79901
(915) 533-9710
lamujer@igc.org